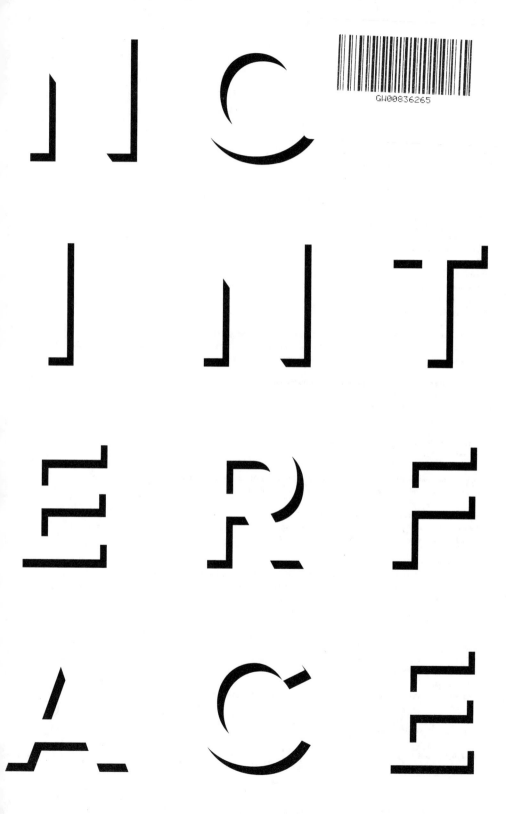

The Best Interface Is No Interface
Golden Krishna

New Riders
www.newriders.com

To report errors, please send a note to errata@peachpit.com
New Riders is an imprint of Peachpit, a division of Pearson Education.
Copyright © 2015 by Golden Krishna

Acquisitions Editor Michael Nolan
Project Editor Nancy Peterson
Development Editor Bob Lindstrom
Copyeditor Darren Meiss
Proofreader Susie Pitzen
Technical Reviewer Nils Kuehn
Indexer Valerie Haynes Perry
Production Coordinators Dennis Fitzgerald, David Van Ness
Cover, Interior Design, and Illustration Collective Material / Megan Lynch
Art Director Golden Krishna

ISBN 13: 978-0-133-89033-4
ISBN 10:   0-133-89033-3

9 8 7 6 5 4 3 2
Printed and bound in the United States of America

THE BEST INTERFACE IS
NO INTERFACE

*The Simple Path
to Brilliant Technology*

BY GOLDEN KRISHNA

Thank you for your

Kinship

Meghan Gordon
Gopal TK Krishna
Rajakumari Krishna
Alvin Krishna
Dean Krishna
Reena Krishna
Veer Krishna
Asha Krishna

Criticality

Doug LeMoine
Bob Lindstrom
Nate Clinton
Nancy Peterson
Megan Lynch
Darren Meiss
Susie Pitzen
Jakub Linowski
Timo Arnall

Air Time

Alan Cooper
Sue Cooper
Teresa Brazen
Jeff Bruss
Tim Kadlec
Meghan Sitar
Patrick McCabe
Morgan Curran
Martin Thörnkvist
Lovisa Wachtmeister
Руслан Карболсунов
Толибова Камилла
Татьяна Назарова
Григорий Коченов
Александр Богданов
Maxime Ruel
Maxine Sherrin
John Allsopp
Eric Thomas
David Allen Ibsen
Kevin Farnham
Katie Del Angel
Jeff Cram

Support

Manolo Almagro
Paul Amsbary
Marc Apon
Anmol Bahl
Thomas Barrett

Justin Basini
Jakop Berg
Amanda Bergknut
Samuel Bowden
Andreas Brændhaugen
Justin Brodeur
Harvey Brofman
Fredrik Broman
Ganesh Burle
Amber Case
Shannon Carmody
Filipe Catraia
Jackie Chang
Paul Chavez
Amit Chopra
Fionn Corcoran-Tadd
Vanessa D'Aleman
Glen Davis
Rodrigo Del Castillo
John Dial
Sherry Ding
Kasper Duhn
Peter Duyan
Sharif Ezzat
William Felker
Gustavo Ferreira
Andy Field
Tom Fletcher
Jerry Gabra
Radu Gidei
Thomas Grah
Theo Green
Ammon Haggerty
Charles Hall
Holger Hampf
Lars Holst-Lyberg
Francisco Jaimes
Tom Jay
James Jefferson
Elias Jones
Phil Jones
Jeffrey S. Jones
Ruslan Karbolsunov
Michael Kattenbeld
Patrick Keenan
Stefanie Kegel
April Kincheloe
Darren Klynsmith
Andrea Koenemann
Jon Kohrs
Prashanth Krish
Sathish Krishnan

Paul Kurchina
Katrina Lee
Erik Levitch
Jason Levy
Kate Lindeen
David Linssen
Rodny Lobos
Andrew Lunde
May Tia Ly
Alessio Macrì
Patrick McCabe
Joe Minkiewicz
Marc Minor
Andy Morris
Sjoerd Mulder
Sanjay Nayak
Cassini Nazir
Greg O'Hanlon
Roger Dean Olden
Leighton Ong
Julian Ozen
Joe Pacal
William Pate
Janne Pajulahti
Michael Pataki
Marina Pavlovic Rivas
Nicholette Piecuch
Alec Pollak
Jean-Francois Poulin
Anita Qiao
Alison Ray
Suzie Ripperton
Joel Rosado
Philipp Saile
Bryan Sieber
Baard Slaattelid
Chad Smith
Daniel Spagnolo
Mike Standish
Grayson Stebbins
Marta Strickland
Gabriel Svennerberg
Jean Tashima
Nancy Thompson
Mathew Tizard
Shaun Tollerton
Yusuf Ziya Uzun
Pau Valiente
Erik van der Meer
Job van der Zwan
Emma van Niekerk
Alex van Tienhoven

Torben Vejen
Rob Verrilli
Pavel Vilenkin
Ben Virdee-Chapman
Nina (Zhuxiaona) Wei
Lea Westort
Kiera Westphal
Lisa Wills
Alexandra Woolsey-Puffer
Oleg Yusupov
Honey Mae

Thoughtfulness

Rex Hammock
Candra Provenzano
Garrett Heath
Jesus Gil Hernandez
Matt McInerney
Nick Fogle
Kontra
Valle Hansen
Brian Lemond

Foreword

Ellis Hamburger

"**Why do phones ring?**"

Back when the telephone was first invented, ringers were used
to call our attention to important incoming messages. They
sounded like alarms, shrill electrical burps and gurgles that
duly represented the urgency. And people loved it. Much as early
travelers took pride in flying and dressed up for the occasion,
phone callers were happy to be in demand, picking up at a moment's
notice, even if it meant leaping off the toilet and tripping mid-
stride on one's underwear.

Today, ringers are just annoying. Why couldn't someone just text to
see if I'm available instead of calling and interrupting what I'm
doing? Some might even say, "Why call at all?" As our lives have
become increasingly oversaturated with screens, social networks,
and smart watches, there's less time than ever for unplanned interaction. So, the ring isn't as _useful_ as it once was. In fact,
it's downright disruptive in most scenarios, so some of the most
popular communication apps ditch the ring entirely.

As a reporter at *The Verge,* I interviewed Snapchat CEO Evan
Spiegel before the launch of the company's video chat and texting
features. Spiegel said something that really stuck out to me: "The
biggest constraint of the next 100 years of computing is the idea
of metaphors," he said. "For Snapchat, the closer we can get to 'I
want to talk to you'—that emotion of wanting to see you and then
seeing you—the better and better our product and our view of the
world will be." Instead of allowing you to ring friends for a video
chat, as with FaceTime or Skype, Snapchat forces both users to be
present inside a chat window before video can begin.

So, instead of texting someone to set up a FaceTime call, you can
simply chat them on Snapchat, and if they log on, you can start a
video chat when you're both in the same conversation. The "Hey,
want to chat?" text replaces the ring entirely.

You might have thought that Snapchat's mission was to bring "ephem-
eral," disappearing messages to the masses, when it was only one
facet of a bigger idea that Spiegel had been stewing over. He had
been thinking about digitally replicating the ways we talk in real
life—ephemerality just happened to be one means of doing so.

The point isn't to _remove_ the ring, or to make photos disappear
after they've been seen. The point is to understand how we use
communication products today, how we live today, and to embrace
those pieces of information. Thus, this example isn't as much
about altering product interfaces as it is about removing them
whenever possible.

For the tools we use every day, people are always going to take the path of least resistance and choose utility and pragmatism above all else. In other words, why swipe through TV channels by waving your hands when pushing a remote control button is so much easier? Further, why press a button at all when you can simply call out the name of the channel you want to watch? Or, instead of having to speak the channel you want, maybe your TV automatically flips to the Bears game because you watch them play every Sunday.

Getting to the root of our daily errands, conversations, and projects will yield the next age of contextual tools. The key is forgetting what we've learned about interfaces, and using our instincts (instead of hot trends like "ephemerality") as guides.

I find most Jonathan Ive quotes to be overly trite, vague, or abstract; but this one from a recent *Vanity Fair* interview resonated with me: "It's part of the human condition that if we struggle to use something, we assume that the problem resides with us," said Ive, referring to his initial frustrations with computers in the mid-'80s.

Ever since, Ive has made his mark on the world by constantly adapting to our changing needs, and admitting that tried-and-true solutions to old problems won't always become the solutions to new problems. For example, Apple has shown no reluctance to cannibalizing the success of old products and ideas (like the iPod's click wheel) when better product ideas come along.

Being able to snub our sentimentality about interfaces, old and new, will be critical. I first heard Golden Krishna speak about this very idea in his first-ever lecture—in front of an audience of over 1,500 people. When I wrote a small snippet about it on *The Verge,* it got more attention than other talks from massive companies like Google. Why? People are inherently drawn to new ideas and not old, derivative ones. People are drawn to hope for better solutions, even if they
manifest themselves in tiny, seemingly insignificant ways.

Ring, ring.

Ellis Hamburger was a reporter for the technology news and culture website The Verge *from 2012–2015. Now he's working in marketing at Snapchat.*

Welcome

The Problem

Principle One

Principle Two

Principle Three

9 *p.85*

Back Pocket Apps
This app goes perfectly
with my skinny jeans

What if instead of designing systems
to be touched and tapped, we avoided
screens, embraced typical processes,
and made apps that worked best when
our phones are in our pockets?

10 *p.111*

Lazy Rectangles
That's a great wireframe.
We nailed it. We're going to
make a billion dollars.

A great wireframe is a great design,
right? Um, no. Good experience design
isn't good screens, it's good experiences.

11 *p.127*

Computer Tantrums
Your password must be at
least 18,770 characters and
cannot repeat any of your previous 30,689 passwords

We're in the middle of an exciting
moment in technology. But despite the incredible power of a computer, technology
systems are often created to act like a two
year old. They throw unexpected tantrum
error messages, demand our attention and
ask dumb questions. They expect us to
serve them.

12 *p.135*

Machine Input
I saved your life, and I didn't
even need a password

We build technology. Why not build
technology that serves us? User input is
a hassle. Let's aim to stop asking people
for the name of their childhood best
friend, and start designing systems that
take advantage of sensors.

13 *p.147*

Analog and Digital Chores
I know, I suck at life.

We're forgetful, fragile, and busy.
Computers should do the things we don't
want to do, that we don't know we
should do, and that we aren't able to do.

14 *p.161*

Computing for One
You're spécial

You're unique. You have your own
set of preferences, desires, and interests.
But that's not how we build software.
We make software for an average. But
some data scientists have taken an
opposite approach.

15 *p.173*

Proactive Computing
In the future, I'll talk
to my computer!

If technology knows all about us, we
don't want it to be spreading gossip
to the girl we've had a crush on since
third grade.

The Challenges

Conclusion

Welcome

1. Introduction
Why Did You Buy This Book?

I don't know why you bought this book.

It's the 21st century, this is a book, and books are dead. You would think someone buying a book about technology would know that. And it's not like this is the next great American novel. This is a technology theory book. About *interfaces*. Cue your boredom and regret.

Well, maybe you purchased this book because it is expanded from one of the most shared design essays in the past decade. Maybe you saw my keynote at South by Southwest that some called the best of the year. Or maybe you just ignored comments like this on the Internet:

▉ "This guy is a clown."

That's a real Internet comment about me, and you know what? It's probably a solid point. Not only do I like polka dots, but here I am, preaching THE BEST INTERFACE IS YADA YADA, and technically, I'm not even using the word *interface* correctly.

The common use of *interface* has morphed from its dictionary definition (a way in which you interact with another thing, like a doorknob for a door) to short for a *graphical user interface* (the thing with the buttons and icons you see on a computer screen).

Literalists, lexicographers, be warned: this book will routinely substitute *interface* for *graphical user interface*. Embrace a cultural tendency to shorten.

Note that when the reputable *MIT Technology Review* published an article titled "A Tale of Two Newspaper Interfaces,"[1] it was not about the interface of folding broadsheet newspapers, but about the graphical user interface of the newspapers' websites.

Or that when the *Christian Science Monitor*, which has been in print for over one hundred years, published an article titled "Netflix Rolls Out Updated, Smarter TV Interface,"[2] it was not about the interface of a hand-held remote control, but a new graphical user interface delivered in a software update.

Or that when the *Washington Post* published "Apple TV: A Simpler Interface, Easier Access to Media Through the iCloud"[3] it was not about a new kind of hardware interface, but a new kind of graphical user interface.

There's good reason you don't see Lowe's home improvement billboards advertising their latest doorknobs as "a breakthrough in interfaces!"

Enough with the semantics. This book is about an idea. It's an urgent call to action. One of the most revered inventions of the past fifty years is leading us down a terrible path.

Another real Internet comment:

▰ "The title says it all."

I'm hardly the first to identify it. As you will soon learn, visionaries like Mark Weiser, Alan Cooper, and Don Norman saw the signs long before me.

My take on the story sparks with a tale of tragic, crazy love, a *l'amour fou*. The world lavishes adoration on the graphical user interface as it blazes its way to a potentially disturbing conflagration:

Our love for the digital interface is out of control. And our obsession with it is ruining the future of innovation.

2. Screen-based Thinking
Let's Make an App!

Somewhere, at some point in time, we fell in love.

I really don't know when. Like all relationships, it seemed to happen in the blink of an eye—from the blur of whatever we were doing before, to a passionate, unquestioning love for the modern, handsome, beautiful interface of the moment: apps.

Maybe it was these gently whispered sweet nothings from all the way back in 2009:

"What's great about the iPhone is that if you want to check snow conditions on the mountain, there's an app for that."[1]

Forget that the National Ski & Snowboard Retailers Association reported that only 2.6 percent of Americans actually downhill ski—or that they did so only about eight days a year[2] when these nothings were first whispered.[3] When we heard that siren song, nothing else mattered. Love and reason? Well, they're like oil and water.

The commercial continued. Our pulses quickened. "And if you want to check where exactly you parked the car . . ."

Don't tease me. We all know how to end that phrase. Six beautiful trademarked words that may have unintentionally fenced in this generation's limitations on technological creativity.

There's an app for that.™

Forget that 780 million[4] people in the world, give or take, don't have access to clean drinking water, or that more than half a million people[5] are homeless in the wealthy United States. We moved way past "mundane" social issues and collectively propelled the technology field—where disruption and innovation has a proven track record of changing everyday lives—to giving the world what it really needs: more mobile apps.

But not ideal, meaningful, invisible apps running quietly and efficiently on your smartphone, smartwatch, or tablet (which we will cover later in this book). Instead, shallow, skin-deep apps that seductively offer the life-affirming, itch-scratching swipes and two-finger pinches that the world needs, wants, and craves.

Love is patient. Love is kind. Love is 99 cents to download.

Name a news source. Odds are they have a recent article, column, or perhaps an entire section devoted to swooning over the latest apps. It may be because reporters want to showcase that they're hip—*yeah, we know apps*—but it's probably because they're also love drunk with touchscreen oxytocin.[6]

An app, just by being an app, doesn't guarantee that it produces anything of merit to anyone anywhere, but please—*shh!*—we must defend our loved one's honor. An app's creation is told as a gospel of wonder and miracle: we're blessed that someone wrote working code that somehow illuminated the dark, mythical path to Apple or Google's app catalog.

The *New York Times* featured an "App of the Week," and had a recurring "App Smart Extra"[7] column with heart-throbbing titles like "A Weather App That Works."[8] *It works!?* What glorious times with our love.

And during the financial crisis, the *New York Times* featured a Bloomberg app as "App of the Week"[9] because it revealed "basic stock market data." *What? Extraordinary!*

Perhaps you, too, poured a glass of Chablis and cued up Norah Jones to set the mood as you reread the touching *USA Today* piece, "5 New Apps That Will Change Your Life."[10] My heart melts at that opening line: "Apps, apps, and more apps . . . truly life changing."

Or maybe you're thinking, "Oh, I'll just turn on talking head CNN and forget about my app muse." Think again, my friend. Here are real CNN headlines.[11]

Stuck in snow?
There's an app for that.[12]

Moody?
There's an app for that.[13]

Staying safe in danger zones?
There's an app for that.[14]

Remote sex?
There's an app for that.[15]

No TP?
There's an app for that.[16]

Need to pray?
There's an app for that.[17]

Sending top secret information?
There's an app for that.[18]

Need a concierge?
There's an app for that.[19]

On a health kick?
There's an app for that.[20]

Ordination on the go?
There's an app for that.[21]

Want to know how attractive you are?
There's an app for that.[22]

Save the whales?
There's an app for that.[23]

Dead?
There's an app for that.[24]

Being arrested?
There's an app for that.[25]

Are you sick?
There's an app for that.[26]

New Year's Eve?
There's an app for that.[27]

Sting's career?
There's an app for that.[28]

Stalking?
There's an app for that.[29]

Want to be a priest?
There's an app for that.[30]

Can't sleep?
There's an app for that.[31]

Wedding plans?
There's an app for that.[32]

Passover?
There's an app for that.[33]

Heart attack?
There's an app for that.[34]

Need a college?
There's an app for that.[35]

Giving birth?
There's an app for that.[36]

Home security?
There's an app for that.[37]

Want to save cash?
There's an app for that.[38]

World Cup?
There's an app for that.[39]

Cooking dinner?
There's an app for that.[40]

Britney Spears?
There's an app for that.[41]

Whether you're out of toilet paper, trying to stalk someone, or are actually dead, well, "There's an app for that."™

Justin Bieber. One Direction. God. According to Google Trends,[42] none has been as popular a search term as "app."

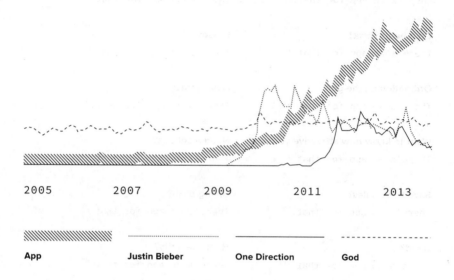

2005   2007   2009   2011   2013

App   **Justin Bieber**   **One Direction**   **God**

Not surprisingly, almost every major automotive company has been working on apps for smartphones. Who wouldn't want in on the love affair? And an industry that has been working on the same four-wheeled concept for over 120 years[43] could always use some refreshing. Some of the apps touted in press releases and blogs have the ability to unlock your car doors.

"My BMW remote app unlocks car doors, starts the AC, and more!"

This begs the question: How do you make a better car key?

Most of these automotive door-opening apps work similarly, so for the sake of demonstration, let's see how amazing it was to actually use the BMW app on an iPhone when a recent version of Apple's mobile operating system was launched. In Apple's words, this is "the world's most advanced mobile OS. In its most advanced form."

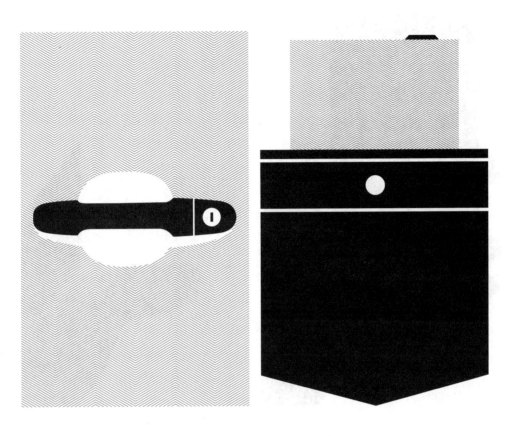

1. Walk up to my car.

I walk toward my car, and want to open my car door.

2. Pull out my smartphone.

I want to open my car door. So, I reach into my pocket and carefully pull out my smartphone because I definitely don't want to drop something made of glass and thin metal onto a cement parking lot.

3. Wake up my phone.

I want to open my car door. So, I look down at my phone and, almost unconsciously, I regrip my smartphone to "wake up" my phone by pressing and clicking in the main button.

4. Unlock my phone.

I want to open my car door. So, I look down at my phone and hit the circular Home button at the bottom of my phone for the fingerprint reader to unlock my phone.

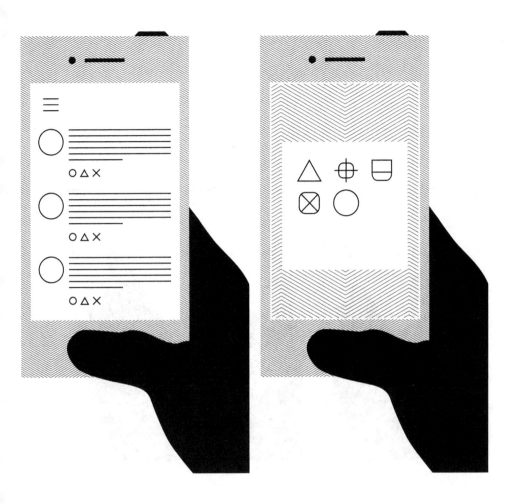

5. Exit my last opened app.

I want to open my car door. So, I look down at my phone, I see my last opened application, and I hit the Home button to exit the application. (Hopefully I don't get distracted by my Twitter stream. Speaking of, did you see the new pictures of the royal baby? He's growing up so fast! I'm sorry, what are we doing here?)

6. Exit my last opened group.

I want to open my car door. So, I look down at my phone, I see the group of applications that my last opened application was categorized under, and I press the Home button to exit the group view.

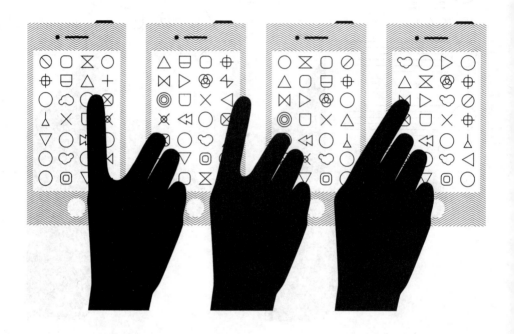

7. Swipe through a sea of icons, searching for the app.

I want to open my car door. So, I look down at my phone and see the Home screen. I swipe right-to-left across the screen through a sea of icons, scanning their logos and the tiny type underneath, trying to find the app.

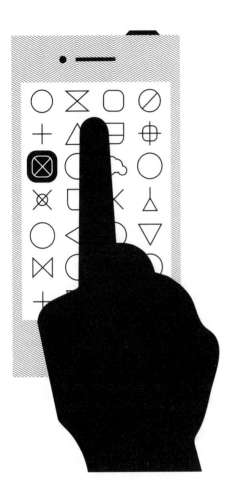

8. Tap the app icon.

I want to open my car door. So, I look down at my phone and tap the app icon to open the car app.

9. Wait for the app to load and try to find the unlock action.

I want to open my car door. So, I look down at my phone and see a beautiful map of North America.

10. Make a guess with the menu and tap Control.

I want to open my car door. So, I look down at my phone. I've got a lot of choices. I cross my fingers and tap the Control tab option at the bottom.

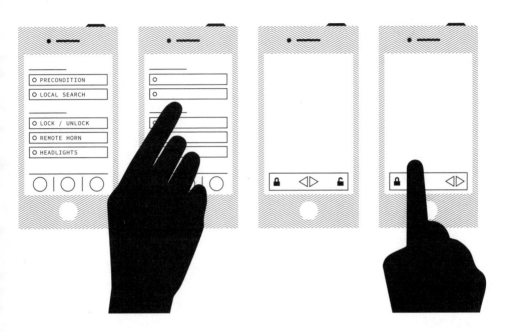

11. Tap the Unlock button.

I want to open my car door. So, I look down at my phone, and I see more choices. A button right at the top of the list says Locking/Unlocking. I tap that.

12. Slide the slider to unlock.

I want to open my car door. So, I look down at my phone, and a two-way slider pops up with a lock icon to the left and an unlock icon to the right. I slide the slider to the right because (for those not paying attention) I want to open my car door.

13. Physically open the car door.

I want to open my car door. So, I look down at my phone, and it says, "Data transfer successful." Not totally sure what that means, but I think that did it . . . *Heaven, I'm in heaven! My heart beats so that I can hardly speak . . .* [44] Yes, my doors are now unlocked, and I can open my car doors!

Wait, thirteen steps? What happened here?

There was me, walking up to my car.

And there was my goal: to open my car door.

(This isn't complicated.)

1.	**Walk up to my car.** ———————————————— **Me**
2.	Pull out my smartphone.
3.	Wake up my phone.
4.	Unlock my phone.
5.	Exit my last opened app.
6.	Exit my last opened group.
7.	Swipe through a sea of icons, searching for the app.
8.	Tap the app icon.
9.	Wait for the app to load and try to find the unlock action.
10.	Make a guess with the menu and tap Control.
11.	Tap the Unlock button.
12.	Slide the slider to unlock.
13.	**Physically open the car door.** ——————————— **My goal**

Then, there were all the steps I had to do with the app's digital interface:

1.	Walk up to my car.
2.	**Pull out my smartphone.**
3.	**Wake up my phone.**
4.	**Unlock my phone.**
5.	**Exit my last opened app.**
6.	**Exit my last opened group.**
7.	**Swipe through a sea of icons, searching for the app.**
8.	**Tap the app icon.**
9.	**Wait for the app to load and try to find the unlock action.**
10.	**Make a guess with the menu and tap Control.**
11.	**Tap the Unlock button.**
12.	**Slide the slider to unlock.**
13.	Physically open the car door.

Digital Interface

I had a goal, and to accomplish it, I had to use a screen. And thanks to the app, it only took me over a dozen steps to unlock my car doors.

Has our love deceived us? Is this app an improvement on the car key? Sit down and steel yourself. The answer, my friend, is no.

I know. It ain't easy, giving up your heart.

Say, instead, we applied the first principle of *the best interface is no interface*, entirely avoided using a screen, and embraced our typical processes. After all, as Edward Tufte once said, "Overload, clutter, and confusion are not attributes of information, they are failures of design."[45]

If we eliminate the graphical user interface, we're left with only two steps:

1. **A driver approaches her car.**
2. **She opens her car door.**

Anything beyond these two steps should be frowned upon.

Seem crazy? Well, more than a decade before that thirteen-step app was released, and before we were seduced by screen-based infatuation, the situation was solved by Siemens,[46] and first used by Mercedes-Benz.

Here's how their solution works: When you grab the car door handle (a logical part of opening a car door), the car sends out a low frequency radio signal to see if your keys are in close proximity—say, in your pocket or in your purse—and if they are, the doors unlock instantaneously, without any additional work.

An improvement on the car key? Yes.

Some people have said to me, "Come on man, this is our love. What about when we've locked our keys in the car? That's when we need the app."

Don't let your emotions blind you: The car can sense where the keys are, so the doors won't lock if your keys are inside. And the trunk? It won't even close if the keys are in the trunk. In other words, you could never lock your keys in the car.

By reframing the design context from a digital screen to our natural course of actions, Siemens created an incredibly intuitive and wonderfully elegant car entry solution for Mercedes. (If this sounds familiar and you don't own a Mercedes, that's because their solution was adopted by other automotive companies.)

Is the Siemens system an improvement on the key?

Duh. Embracing a typical process means you can do what you normally do. Avoiding a digital interface means you don't waste time learning, troubleshooting, and using a screen you don't need to be using anyway. That's good design thinking, especially when designing around common tasks.

And that's what this book is about:

The best interface is no interface.

This book is about taking a second look at today's screen-obsessed world—how we got here, why we're still here, why this awful trend is so awful, and how people are moving beyond screens and breaking off their love affair with mundane apps.

This book isn't a rant. It's filled with ideas for entrepreneurs, startups, designers, engineers, gadget-lovers, and people who are just interested in technology. It shows a new way to think about the future of tech, and how to fall in love with something more alluring than a weather app.

The topics covered here are relevant to you and society. Yes, my message may turn heady, but this isn't a textbook. It's like a bar conversation between friends about a simple path to brilliant technology.

Bottoms up.

The Problem

3. Slap an Interface on It!
Slimmer TVs! Faster computers! And an overlooked epidemic of awful.

You can't write a tech book today without giving credit to us. It truly is impressive what we've done as a society—teachers to venture capitalists—to push important technology forward.

Good job, everyone.

Let's say we filled your entire hard drive with high-definition movies. The dot below represents how many movies you could have stored on the largest hard drive you could buy in 2006:

●

About 180 movies (4GB movies on a 750GB hard drive)[1, 2]

Seven years later, on the largest hard drive available, you could store enough movies to watch them for 125 days straight.

About 1,500 movies (4GB movies on a 6,144GB hard drive)[2, 3]

Imagine the black background on this page represents
the percentage of American adults who had access to fast,
broadband Internet speeds in 2000.

15%

The black on this page is how many had access to
broadband speeds about ten years later.[4]

94%

We're not only able to store more of the things we love, we've also made it possible to get the things we want faster than ever before. Say the height of this paragraph represents how fast you could download a three-minute song on America's fastest smartphone Internet connection in 2009.

3 seconds

This is how fast it was three years later.

1 second[5]

There's really so much to celebrate in technology today. We've created materials that reduce the sun's glare. Really. We've made screens that have greater clarity than ink on paper. We've not only built a really useful Internet but made it available across almost the entire world at really fast speeds in the palm of our hands. It's kind of ridiculously amazing how awesome we are.

Our list of technological achievements is long, but an awful trend is emerging. A growing epidemic in the way experiences with technology are built.

I'm a user experience (UX) designer. That means my job is to understand your common, everyday problems and to use technology to solve them. I've worked at an innovation lab for Zappos, where I helped design and imagine the future of how a customer service company could solve customer problems. I've worked at a Samsung innovation lab, where I helped design and imagine new services and consumer electronics to solve people's problems. And I worked at Cooper, a design consultancy where we solved everyday problems for our clients' customers.

My job is to solve people's problems, but as an industry we've gotten away from solving people's problems. As an industry, we've gotten caught up in a globally evident technological impotence of me-too thinking that is taking us away from real innovation.

1. BioCon Valley, 2. Bit Valley, 3. Brazilian Silicon Valley, 4. CFK Valley, 5. Cwm Silicon, 6. Cyber District, 7. Cyberabad, 8. Dallas-Fort Worth Silicon Prairie, 9. Dubai Silicon Oasis, 10. Etna Valley, 11. Food Valley, 12. Health Valley, 13. Illinois Silicon Prairie, 14. Isar Valley, 15. Lima Valley, 16. Measurement Valley, 17. Medical Valley, 18. Mexican Silicon Valley/Silicon Valley South, 19. Midwest Silicon Prairie, 20. Philicon Valley, 21. Russian Silicon Valley, 22. Silicon Allee, 23. Silicon Alley, 24. Silicon Anchor, 25. Silicon Beach, 26. Silicon Border, 27. Silicon Bridge, 28. Silicon Canal, 29. Silicon Canal, 30. Silicon Cape, 31. Silicon Coast, 32. Silicon Corridor, 33. Silicon Desert, 34. Silicon Dock, 35. Silicon Docks, 36. Silicon Fen, 37. Silicon Forest, 38. Silicon Glen, 39. Silicon Goli, 40. Silicon Gorge, 41. Silicon Gulf, 42. Silicon Harbor, 43. Silicon Hill, 44. Silicon Hills, 45. Silicon Lagoon, 46. Silicon Lane, 47. Silicon Mall, 48. Silicon Mallee, 49. Silicon Mill, 50. Silicon Peninsula, 51. Silicon Pier, 52. Silicon Roundabout, 53. Silicon Sandbar, 54. Silicon Savannah, 55. Silicon Saxony, 56. Silicon Sentier, 57. Silicon Shipyard, 58. Silicon Shire, 59. Silicon Shore, 60. Silicon Sloboda, 61. Silicon Slopes, 62. Silicon Spa, 63. Silicon St, 64. Silicon Surf, 65. Silicon Swamp, 66. Silicon Taiga, 67. Silicon Valley, 68. Silicon Valley of China, 69. Silicon Valley of India, 70. Silicon Valley of Indonesia, 71. Silicon Valley of South Korea, 72. Silicon Valley of Taiwan, 73. Silicon Valley North, 74. Silicon Vineyard, 75. Silicon Wadi, 76. Silicon Walk, 77. Silicon Welly, 78. Silicon Woods, 79. Silicotton Valley, 80. Solar Valley, 81. Ticino Valley Area, 82. Wyoming Silicon Prairie (also called the Silicon Range)

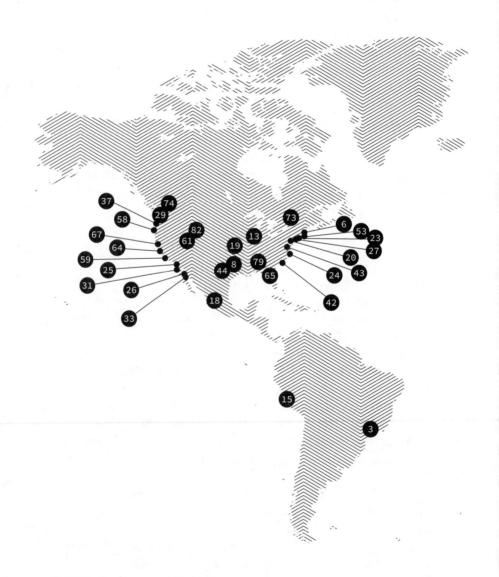

"Innovation" centers around the world.
(Sources: *Wired* magazine, *Inc.* magazine, CNBC, Wikipedia)

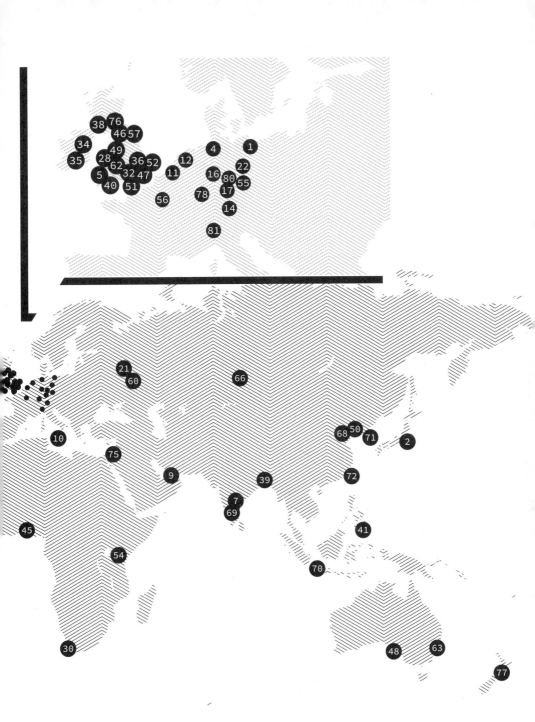

Oh, the unoriginal places you'll go.

Guy Kawasaki, formerly an advisor for Google and Apple, once gave these words of advice: "There's one more thing you need to do: Aim higher than merely trying to recreate Silicon Valley. You should try to kick our butt instead."[6]

Many brilliant thinkers, dreamers, designers, engineers, developers, and entrepreneurs have made and will continue to make great strides enriching the human experience through technology in many of these locations. But in an ultracompetitive global market where fast and lean are more valued than deep thinking or original solutions, many of us—including myself—have been caught up in reactionary rectangles, thoughtless habits, and the self-delusion that the way things have gone the past few years is the way we should keep going forever.

Put yourself in the mind of an "innovative" company, and let's play a game.

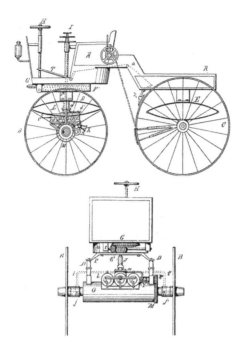

(Source: USPTO)

Q: HOW DO YOU MAKE A BETTER CAR?

Above, is one of the earliest patent drawings for an automobile. The technologists of the day solved a real problem with transportation. And as a result, the car changed the way we live. The way our cities are built. Who and what we can see, and when and where we can see them.

So today, utilizing the amazing technological progress we've made in the over one hundred years since, what technique have modern technologists used to improve the car?

A: SLAP AN INTERFACE ON IT!

Who would need to look at the road while driving? Leaning over to touch a screen is so much more fun.

Tesla is one of the most innovative companies in the world—that's why they've got a seventeen-inch touchscreen center console. Sure, there are haters. Some lost soul at *The Verge* wrote, "I don't want a web browser in my car, and more importantly, I don't want the drivers around me to have one."[7] But consider scrollbars in your center console. I know. Amazing.

Among the many wonderful options for screens in your car, there's BMW's Mini model with a screen in the middle of the speedometer that— yes, really—lets you check your Twitter and Facebook instead of focusing on how fast you're driving.[8]

Driving is about the road? Nah, it's about screens, brah.

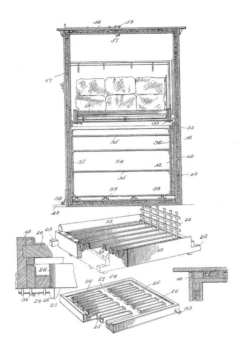

(Source: USPTO)

Q: HOW DO YOU MAKE A BETTER FRIDGE?

Above is one of the earliest patent drawings for a refrigerator. The technologists of the day solved an important problem: keeping our food fresh. And it goes without saying, the refrigerator also changed the way we live. Domestic and international food distribution has changed enormously thanks to the refrigerator, and fresher and healthier choices are now more readily available to more people thanks to innovations that came from drawings like this.

Screenfridge (Source: Electrolux)

A: SLAP AN INTERFACE ON IT!

Yes! This is where I want to look through my photo albums. Other man-ufacturers offer fantastic features like updating our Evernote when we go to get ice.[9] Or listening to Pandora from the refrigerator door. With the most wonderful refrigerator models today we can, obviously, update Facebook and Twitter above the ice dispenser.[10]

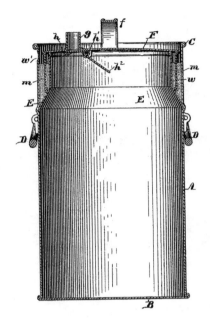

(Source: USPTO)

Q: HOW DO YOU MAKE A BETTER TRASH CAN?

Recycling bins in London (Source: Bonnie Alter / CC BY 2.0)

A: SLAP AN INTERFACE ON IT!

Hope you got this obvious one: You can make a better trash can by turning it into a $47,000 LCD recycling bin, so that you can see if it's raining outside when you're standing outside in the rain. One hundred of these incredible bins were installed in London just before the 2012 Olympic Games to help the city show off its futuristic wonders.[11] And why not? Screens are so futuristic.

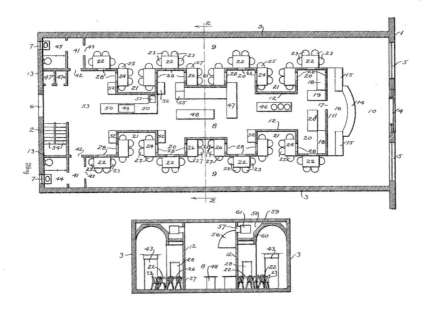

Q: HOW DO YOU MAKE A BETTER RESTAURANT?

(Source: Golden Krishna)

A: SLAP AN INTERFACE ON IT!

Finally. I'm so sick of talking to people.

Customer service saviors like Chili's and Applebee's have installed these kinds of touch-screen ordering systems in thousands of restarants across the country to replace frightening conversations with another person. A Chili's senior vice president once told the *Wall Street Journal* that the interfaces get more people to buy more stuff—like coffee and desserts that flash on the screen.[12] That's obviously a great thing for America's diet. And since I'm basically just staring at my phone the whole time while dining with my friends anyways, what's the harm of another screen on the table?

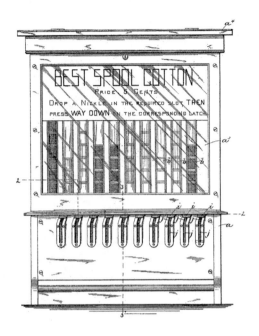

(Source: USPTO)

Q: HOW DO YOU MAKE A BETTER VENDING MACHINE?

A: SLAP AN INTERFACE ON IT!

Thank you! I hate seeing the product I'm about to buy through clear glass.

That's why companies like Coca-Cola and Pepsi are working on touch interfaces so that you can order your favorite drinks through a series of menus and error messages. As *USA Today* wrote of Coca-Cola's efforts, "This teen-targeting, touch-screen dispenser flavors self-created beverages in micro-doses. It may be Coke's best hope to keep Millennials fully engaged, socially involved and buying fizzy drinks at a time industry sales are falling faster than water down the drain."[13]

Duh. Touchscreens are totally going to help sales.

4. UX ≠ UI
I make interfaces because that's my job, bro

Yeah, we went down the wrong path, but it's not really our fault.

Look at these job listings. No, these aren't cherry-picked posts copied and pasted from generic companies and small businesses doomed for failure. They're real, recent listings from the technology elite, the perceived-to-be successful and knowledgeable that are revered from *60 Minutes* to TechCrunch:

Sr. UX/UI Designer
Amazon Corporate LLC, Seattle, WA

UI/UX Designer
Apple Inc., Cupertino, CA

Lead User Experience & UI Designer
HP, Sunnyvale, CA

UX/UI Developer
Adobe, San Jose, CA

UI/UX Designer I
Samsung Telecommunications
America, San Jose, CA

UX/UI Mobility Designer
Dell, Round Rock, TX

Senior UX/UI Designer
GoPro, Cardiff-by-the-Sea, CA

UI/UX Designer
Evernote, Austin, TX

Intern UX/UI Designer
Pebble, Palo Alto, CA

Sr. UX/UI Designer
Nook, Palo Alto, CA

eCommerce UX/UI Designer
Beats by Dre, Los Angeles, CA

Lead UX/UI Mobile Designer
Logitech, Newark, CA

UI/UX Designer
Philips Global, Foster City, CA

User Experience Designer (UX/UI)
ADP, San Dimas, CA

UI/UX Developer
AutoTrader.com, Overland Park, KS

UX/UI Designer
NewEgg, Industry, CA

UX/UI Developer
JPMorgan Chase, New York, NY

Senior Product / UX Designer
Outbrain Inc., New York, NY

UX/UI Designer
CBS Interactive, New York, NY

UI/UX Designer
Zillow, Irvine, CA

UX/UI Designer Job
American Express, New York, NY

UX/UI Information Architect
Caterpillar, Mossville, IL

Sr. UX/UI Designer
NBC Universal, Universal City, CA

UI/UX Designer
Staples, San Mateo, CA

Senior Product (UX/UI) Designer
Ancestry.com, San Francisco, CA

Lead UX/UI Designer
Glassdoor, San Francisco, CA

I know. UI and UX are just acronyms (not even good ones) for "user interface" and "user experience." And the hiring managers who listed them probably have good intentions. But blurring the two disciplines upon hiring designers has played an important role in our approach to creating technological experiences. It likely lies near the root of the commonly pervasive and disturbingly screen-obsessed approach to design. The result is that much of our lives today is dominated by digital interfaces asking us to tap, touch, swipe, click, and hover because that's what people were hired to create.

HP CEO Meg Whitman says, "We've got to continue the innovation engine."[1] Amazon CEO Jeff Bezos says, "We innovate by starting with the customer and working backwards."[2] Apple CEO Tim Cook says, "Innovation is so deeply embedded in Apple's culture."[3]

But when you specifically hire someone to generate UI, you won't get new, innovative solutions. You'll get more UI, not better UX.

This is UI:

Navigation, subnavigation, menus, drop-downs, buttons, links, windows, rounded corners, shadowing, error messages, alerts, updates, checkboxes, password fields, search fields, text inputs, radio selections, text areas, hover states, selection states, pressed states, tooltips, banner ads, embedded videos, swipe animations, scrolling, clicking, iconography, colors, lists, slideshows, alt text, badges, notifications, gradients, pop-ups, carousels, OK/Cancel, etc. etc. etc.

This is UX:

People, happiness, solving problems, understanding needs, love, efficiency, entertainment, pleasure, delight, smiles, soul, warmth, personality, joy, satisfaction, gratification, elation, exhilaration, bliss, euphoria, convenience, enchantment, magic, productivity, effectiveness, etc. etc. etc.

Somewhere along the way, we confused the two. And instead of pursuing the best, most creative, inventive, and useful ways to solve a problem, we started solving problems with screens because that was our job description. When we saw problems, we slapped an interface on it. UX stopped being about people, and started being about rounded rectangles and parallax animations.

It's gotten to the point where many of our greatest minds aren't being pushed into advancing science or taking us into space; they're working at the new screen-based megacorporations that have surpassed oil companies in profits[4] and political influence.[5] They're cranking out glorified digital billboards masked as websites and apps that are trying to monetize your eyeballs by pushing creepy ads onto all of your screens.

In the words of Jeff Hammerbacher, a former manager at Facebook and the founder of Cloudera, "The best minds of my generation are thinking about how to make people click ads. That sucks."[6]

There's a better path. There's a better way of thinking. When we separate the two roles, we can start defining new, better experiences.

Unfortunately, some of tech's most elite companies are stuck in a strange, complex trap.

5. Addiction UX
Click here to cut down
your belly fat by using
this one weird tip

1.0

STUFF YOU CARE ABOUT

2.0

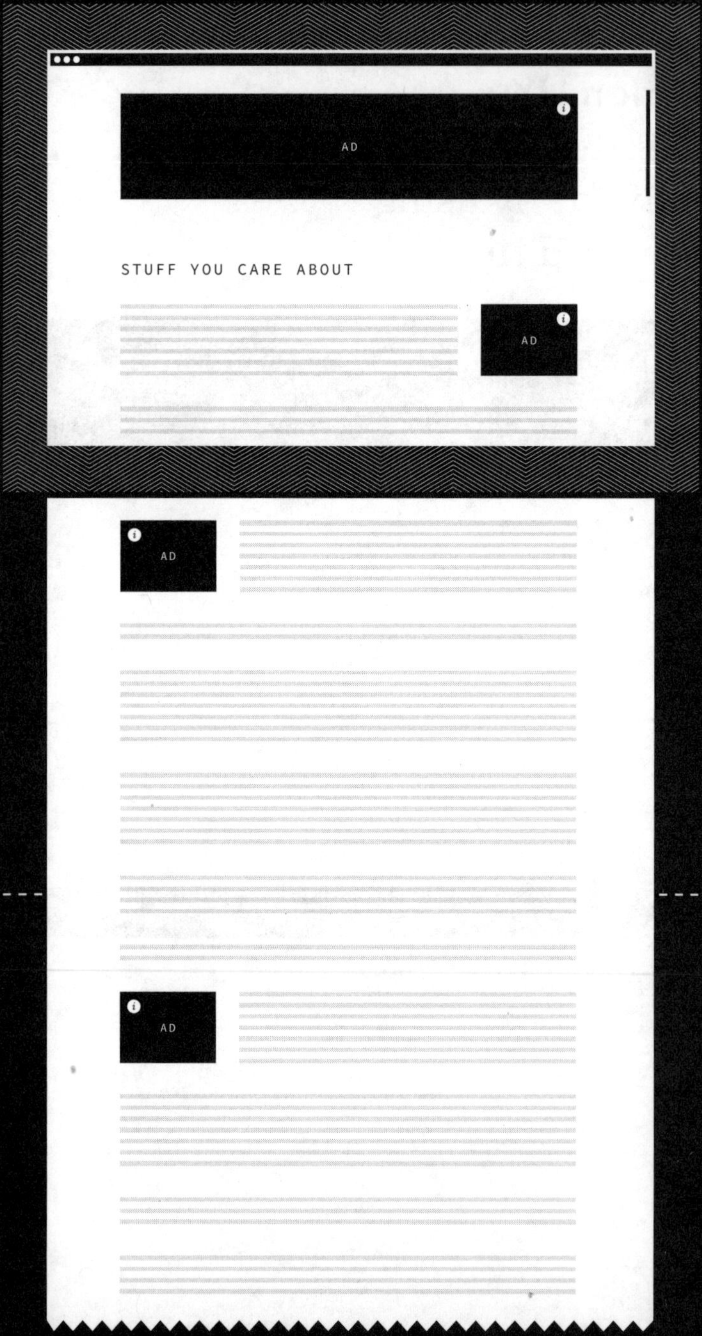

STUFF YOU CARE ABOUT

3.0

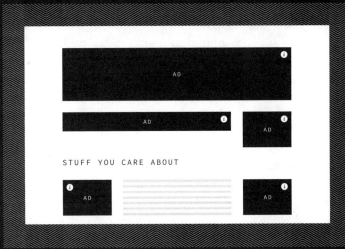

STUFF YOU CARE ABOUT

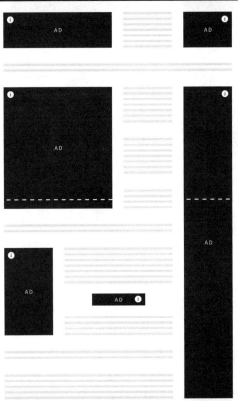

Chris Anderson be damned. A simple transaction that exchanges Coca-Cola's sugary drinks or McDonald's Big Macs for cash may not be the kind of old-guard transaction model looked upon admirably by some of technology's most influential; but even freemium and other creative techniques to exchange "free" goods and services for corporate gain have fallen by the wayside. Another traditional and dated transaction model that plagued the newspaper, magazine, and other old businesses of mass information has taken over: eyeballs for ads.

Free—a business strategy that's the result of many probable factors, among them: being unable to motivate customers with an immediate need to pay, creating a valuable service in a business sector that has traditionally been free, or making an effort to massively and rapidly grow the size and impact of technological products. These things glue many for-profits who build interfaces to the idea of giving it all away in order to survive the brutal, ultracompetitive electronic marketplace.

And despite popular new economy writings like Chris Anderson's book *Free*—which contains a variety of case studies and methods—tech's big players have largely fallen on a single way to provide free: ads, ads, and more ads. Although sometimes cloaked as sponsored stories, promoted posts, native advertising, or advertorials . . . they're ads.

Click here to cut down your belly fat by using this one weird tip. You won't believe what happens next.

Ninety-six percent of Google's thirty-eight billion dollars of revenue came from advertising in 2011.[1] Eighty-four percent of Facebook's five billion dollars of revenue came from advertising in 2012.[2] Ninety percent of Twitter's revenue came from advertising in Q4 of 2013.[3] Eighty percent of Yahoo's revenue came from advertising in 2013.[4]

They're some of the best-known of the bunch, but they're not alone. Those figures have and will fluctuate, but the current ad-based businesses—sometimes masked in PR with buzz terms like *data businesses*, or aligned with the old guard as *media companies*—dictate that the lion's share of their revenue will remain focused on the ads that pollute their otherwise valued content. Hopefully buyouts or valuable new product creation—such as Google's acquisition of the hardware company Nest, or Facebook's purchase of the virtual reality device Oculus Rift—will alter course by having other profitability far surpass ad revenue, but for now this is our reality:

Google at launch.

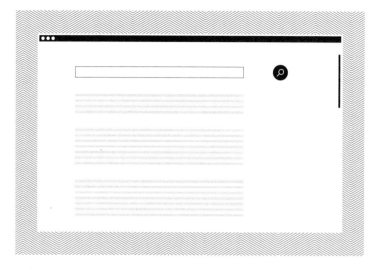

Google now.

◼ "Got the girl. Got the money. Now I'm ready to live a disgusting, frivolous life."[5]

Those are words of Stephan Paternot on CNN. On Friday the 13th, in November 1998, he watched the stock price of theGlobe.com—the website he cofounded in 1995 while a student at Cornell—increase by 606 percent in a Bear Stearns IPO that was Wall Street's largest first-day gain. By the next morning, it was valued at $843 million[6]. The promise of the website was to convert the massive traffic of his web community to sell personalized ads. However, the site couldn't get the traffic and user base of rivals like GeoCities, so the cofounders resigned in 2000, and the stock was delisted from NASDAQ in 2001.[7]

It's the kind of ad-based horror story that technology companies do everything to avoid. Most of today's popular ad-funded services originated with a product that solved a genuine need—how to find old friends, share ideas, or find out if the cute girl down the hall is single. Now publicly traded, many of these companies are following a simple way to fulfill their legal obligation to shareholders and avoid the death of similarly structured business plans. Companies like the departed DrKoop.com (ad-sponsored medical help) or the extinct theGlobe.com (ad-sponsored web communities) get us addicted to their interfaces. They shift away from the functional ideals of user experience design that made their services initially popular, and become more like sitcom television: get people to go brain-dead staring at a screen for as long and as often as possible.

"I have come to believe that advertising is the original sin of the Web." Ethan Zuckerman, one of the original creators of the pop-up ad, once said that in a public apology printed in the *Atlantic*. "The fallen state of our Internet," he says, "is a direct, if unintentional, consequence of choosing advertising as the default model to support online content and services."[8]

The pursuit of elegance has been long forgotten by short-term, revenue-seeking decision makers. A visit to some of their mobile webpages doesn't lead to the tidbit you need, but full-screen ads do pop up begging you to install their app in hopes that future notifications and a space on your app menu will get you to spend more time with their services.

Or—as practiced by some startups hoping to enter this elite space— they try to get on your smartphone so they can get permission to access your contacts list and spam blast everyone you've ever emailed that you're using their hot new addictive social network.

The general goal is to do whatever possible to keep more and more of us logged in and wired, dragging us back for more interface time because the more eyeballs, the more money they can sell their ads for; and the happier their shareholders, the longer their doors stay open. Solving user problems more efficiently is not a core part of the agenda. Addiction is. As the *New York Times* once headlined, "Yahoo Wants You to Linger (on the Ads, Too)."

In this perverse user experience model—reflective of one of the many negative outcomes of screen-based thinking—at the end of the day designers have a business mandate to prolong user goals, not to help us most elegantly or joyfully get done the things we need to do. Yes, corporations need to make money; yes, companies like Google have provided very useful tools for free in exchange for eyeballs; and yes, we can—and I have—found and shared valuable information more easily thanks to services such as Facebook and Twitter. But publicly traded companies with ad-based business models must eventually force their designers down a distinct path.

On the tenth anniversary of Google's IPO, the *Wall Street Journal* reported on the company's change in focus:

Just before Google Inc. went public 10 years ago, co-founder Larry Page said he wanted to get the search engine's users "out of Google and to the right place as fast as possible." Today, Mr. Page's Google often is doing the opposite: Providing as much information as possible to keep users in Google's virtual universe.[9]

What these companies have done is brilliant, fantastic, and has altered the way we live. But where they're headed as publicly traded, ad-first businesses is unnerving. Decreasing the time required to use these services equals profanity in earnings calls with shareholders; an increase in page views or time spent is rewarded in after-hours trading.

When Twitter's powerful tools allowed an increasing number of third-party services to elegantly extend Twitter's platform, for example—enabling people to consume and share Twitter content more easily—analysts reacted with concern. From Wells Fargo to BTIG, investment arms expressed caution because a quicker route to getting things done allowed 14 percent of Twitter's user base to avoid strategic ad placement.[10]

When companies place most of their profit eggs in one basket, metrics-driven results around ads can become more influential than the basics of good design.

■ "My feed is cluttered."

This is the first sentence of a 2013 Facebook researcher's Facebook post about her team's news feed findings.[11] The stream of thoughts, images, videos, and links your friends and advertisers share with you is at the core of the Facebook experience and can even alter your mood.[12] According to her team's research, the resounding feedback from people using their web service was that important and interesting content was buried in a cluttered feed of stories they were less interested in reading.

They redesigned.

They used tools to prioritize which things you'd be interested in reading, what people you communicate with most often, and what kinds of imagery you'll likely enjoy. The redesigned news feed was what Mark Zuckerberg called a "personalized newspaper."[13] A new design filled with more valuable content from friends also calls out sites that are more pertinent to your interests.

Then, Facebook reversed course. The new design disappeared.

Dustin Curtis, a technology writer and entrepreneur, reported that sources inside Facebook told him that the reversal occurred because people visiting the website on their desktop computers were, well, too efficient.[14] They were discovering what they wanted at Facebook, felt satisfied, and left the site faster than ever before.

"After an investigation into the problem by Facebook's data team," he wrote, "They discovered that the new News Feed was performing *too* well." It was great for user experience, but terrible for Facebook ad dollars. Less time on-site meant less advertising and a loss in revenue for the ad-based company.

A Facebook product designer argued back that Dustin's reporting was false. She wrote on her personal blog account that the new design had actually disappeared because it didn't work well for smaller monitors or netbooks.[15]

Even if her explanation is assumed true—and Facebook couldn't implement anything based on the tested and accepted practices of responsive design popularized by people like Luke Wroblewski and Brad Frost, which produces websites that flex, morph, and adapt to any screen size—the underlying relationship between time on-site and stock price still remains undeniable for any publicly traded technology company that has pursued this revenue model.

As a Morningstar analyst once wrote about Twitter's stock, "In our view, the most important growth levers for Twitter are growth in market share, users, and time spent."[16] Or as a Citigroup analyst boasted about Facebook before it went public, "It has a greater potential value than Google because it was beating the other giant in 'time spent.'"[17] For many of these companies, it's not necessarily about fewer or more ads, it's about interface addiction.

It's viewed as fantastic in annual reports when analytics show that users spend hours on these services; wonderful when a single user shuffles through dozens and dozens of pages. The ad-based interface is often measured on Wall Street like a drug—addiction good, moderation bad—but not in terms of human healthiness, happiness, or goals achieved. Acronyms like MAU—monthly active user—become more important than words like "joy" or "happiness."[18] Whether born of a revenue-first boardroom, a designer's intention, or our own frugality, the increasing time spent and addiction to the interface is not a good thing; it's largely taking us away from the things we actually should be doing.

When Vlad Savov of *The Verge* reflected upon the changes of Twitter, he wrote, "It now demands more from me—not more money, it's never asked for that directly, but the thing that money substitutes for: time. The original appeal and simplicity of Twitter have been diluted by superfluous additions like the Discover tab and a visual redesign that makes user profiles look almost indistinguishable from Facebook pages."[19]

Some younger startups that haven't yet been plagued by going public with an ad-based revenue model still pursue this Addiction UX in hopes of a higher valuation. Maciej Cegłowski calls it "Investor Storytime." It's "when someone pays you to tell them how rich they'll get when you finally put ads on your site."[20]

I'm all for services that provide us with insights, connect us with friends, and delight us with their content, but I don't believe it's our job as designers to get you addicted to their technologies.

I believe our job as designers is to give you what you need as quickly and as elegantly as we can. Our job as designers is to take you away from technology. Our job as designers is to make you smile. To make a profit by providing you something that enhances your life in the most seamless and wonderful way possible.

The path of addiction for profit pursued by some of our largest technology companies and encouraged by their investors is not good for us, or the next generation. Some of these services have become more addictive than alcohol or cigarettes,[21] and can make us feel worse about ourselves even when we use them.[22]

It's time for us to pursue a new course.

6. Distraction

"Will you marry me?"
"Sorry, I was sending Alice
a text. What'd you say?"

Clifford Nass passed away in 2013.

He had an infectious, radiant smile. A laugh that made the complex seem simple. He taught at Stanford and had a round, jubilant academic look to him.

Bill Gates once called Nass's scholarly work "amazing." But maybe more symbolically, Clifford was a professional magician. He understood people, and just seemed to want to see their Jon Evans just favorited your tweet smile.

Some of his former colleagues said he had the ability to make "any room a happier place."[1] His contagious joy combined with his curiosity about everything and made him sensational to watch in lectures and interviews because of his overwhelming excitement about, well, Retweet us.

Nass spent the latter part of his career, over twenty-five years, studying our proclivity to what the *New York Times* called in his 2013 obituary, "the increasingly screen-saturated, multitasking world."[2]

Fascinated by the multiple sources of media—email, chats, movies, text messaging, music players, Web browsing, etc.—and our tendency to use more than Please send 10,000 USD to collect your Nigerian inheritance of 300 million USD one of them at the same time, Nass studied the effects of this multitasking Archive on the human brain Archive with Archive those Archive that Archive have Archive been sucked into alluring, intentionally addictive, and distracting interfaces. We are taking time away from other people to dive deeper and deeper into interfaces, and he wondered A newer, better version is available what could be happening to our Update now minds.

Some have theorized that recent technological changes have created a group of people that thrive at this media multitasking. After many years of simultaneously managing buzzing emails, friend requests, pop-up notifications, text messages, and chat windows, a new breed of worker has emerged

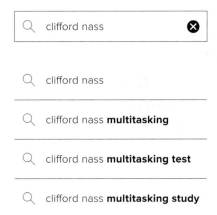

that flourishes in multitasking, one who thrives in an analyst-loving, DAU, MAU world.

So, with a team of colleagues, Nass studied people media multitasking, "a person's consumption of more than one item or stream of content at the same time."[3] What they discovered was so surprising that the findings became some of the most cited papers of Clifford Nass's entire career.

Nass and his team surveyed a set of 262 university students and invited the highest and lowest media multitaskers to a set of basic cognitive tests. The students Today's Ashley's Birthday! were showed things like Like collections of Like numbers Like and Like letters, Like Like Like Like Like Like and Like were asked to quickly filter by varying criteria like evens or vowels or consonants, while Nass and his team studied how their brains tried to tackle the task switching. What the researchers discovered was the opposite of what some expected. Poke

Where was I? "We, so far, have not found people who are successful at multitasking," Nass once told NPR about 24 of the cutest cats you've ever seen his research. "There's some evidence that there's a very, very, very, very small group of people who can do two tasks at one time but there's actually no evidence that anyone can do even three."[4]

And then, there was the insight that few saw coming.

The heaviest media multitaskers performed worse. They were not as good at filtering out +5 environmental distractions or irrelevant Tasty! thoughts from their own Level 252 mind. They were terrible at task-switching. "They couldn't help thinking about the task they weren't doing," Nass colleague, Eyal Ophir, wrote in a Stanford press release.[5]

"What this tells us is that if we're designing interfaces to encourage multitasking, or to support multitasking," Nass once told the Dave has endorsed you for sheep herding tech blog Gigaom, "we're actually Added to my professional network creating a worse thinking, poorer thinking, Congratulate less able to cope, less able to multitask group of people, and it's very worrying."[6]

This scientific rigor Endorse from a well-cited Stanford Endorse professor reflected what some modernists have been Endorse preaching in decades Endorse of art history as applied to an interface-happy Scroll world. The distracting interfaces that Scroll take you away from the important tasks at hand seem to be making you even less able to focus. Follow

So even though you think you're the exception—and that's why you keep checking your phone while reading this already distracted chapter—studies over and over seem to show that nearly all of us are incapable of focusing on more than one thing at a time.

The distraction is so pervasive Submit that even during one of technology's most-watched trials (Apple v. Samsung), the judge had to repeatedly remind attendees to get off their phones, even publicly shaming some by asking them to "stand up!" and pay attention to the billion-dollar trial happening in front of them.[7]

Then again, most of us are not even able to use technology and walk properly.

A separate team of researchers found that when we use technology and walk, we walk so oddly that the *New York Times* reported that it "could result in both immediate and longer-term physical consequences."

A third study Valencia with Favorite another Favorite group found that "participants distracted by Favorite music Favorite Favorite or texting were more likely to be hit by a Favorite vehicle Favorite in Favorite a virtual pedestrian environment than were Favorite un Favorite dis Favorite tract Favorite ed participants." Favorite Favorite Sutro Favorite Toaster Favorite Favorite Favorite

The addiction creates a ☺ distraction Loading that puts us in danger. And like second-hand cigarette ☺ smoke, ☺ digital interfaces also affect everyone around us, ☹ potentially putting them in danger as well.

This huh? *is* what? *our* excuse me? *brains* huh? *on smartphones.*

Maybe Like Favorite Reply Follow Connect Archive Save Close Submit Follow Favorite Reply Favorite Connect Favorite Submit Favorite Like Like Favorite we need Jason Humphreys. In half a mile, turn left. Then, turn right... Your destination will on be on the right.

Perhaps it was the Centers for Disease Control and Prevention's (CDC) warning that 1,000 people are injured and nearly *10 people die every day* in the United   States because they are distracted by their cell phones while driving. Maybe it was the studies that have shown a driver is *23 times more likely* to crash if he or she is texting while driving.[8] Or maybe it was just Jason Humphrey's gut   instinct that the ability to use a cell phone and be distracted by these services obsessed with getting our eyeballs to stare at their interfaces for as long as possible had likely negative consequences while driving 70 miles per hour on the highway.

Whatever the reason, Jason's survival instincts kicked in and guided him to take things into his own   hands on an interstate outside Tampa, Florida.[9] While on his daily commute, Jason carried with him for two years something that law enforcement called "amazing" for its   sheer size and power: an   enormous cell phone jammer capable of halting cell coverage for all those driving near him. The distracting interface disappeared.

When discovered, the FCC fined Jason $48,000 because his jammer also jammed the signals of emergency vehicles, and potentially even aircraft. But I don't blame him. After all, look how much cleaner these paragraphs are without distraction. Yes, his actions were illegal, and his tools were dangerous; but his fear was not irrational. Clifford Nass may not have blamed him either. However, we don't need to jam our cell phones.

There's a better way.

We can build better, more efficient, more elegant technology products that have no distracting interfaces at all. The best distracting interface is no distracting interface, and we can get there together.

7. Screen Insomnia
I love staring into a lightbulb! Me too!

They say if you want to understand women, listen to Oprah.

Oprah? The first female African-American billionaire. Awarded a Presidential Medal of Freedom.[1] Has donated more money to charities than almost any other celebrity ever.[2] Awarded an honorary doctorate from Harvard.[3] Host of *The Oprah Winfrey Show* for 25 years,[4] the highest-rated talk show of all time.[5]

Oh, that Oprah. My favorite Oprah contribution, *O: The Oprah Magazine*—fans just call it *O*—is still on newsstands today. Each issue features a full-color, vibrant, airbrushed image of the person whom their editors have deemed the most important of the moment: Oprah. Christmas? Oprah on the cover. War? Oprah on the cover. First black president? Oprah on the cover. Always, for 15 years, on every issue.[6]

A February cover asks, "Does your underwear need an overhaul?" In an October issue she "un-raps Jay-Z." Some of the more recent issues even feature two or three Oprahs on the cover because, let's be honest, we can never get enough.

Oh, *O*.

It's worked. One time, a German "exotic" magazine also named *O* tried to bring legal action over confusion on the name of the two magazines; but please, you can't pull that shit on Oprah.[7] Today, *O*'s annual circulation is around 2.4 million. It's one of the top 25-selling consumer magazines in the United States.[8]

To put Oprah into perspective, you'd probably need to look at an image of Earth from space. Really, take a look:

Ah, human progress. A visual articulation—from space, nonetheless—

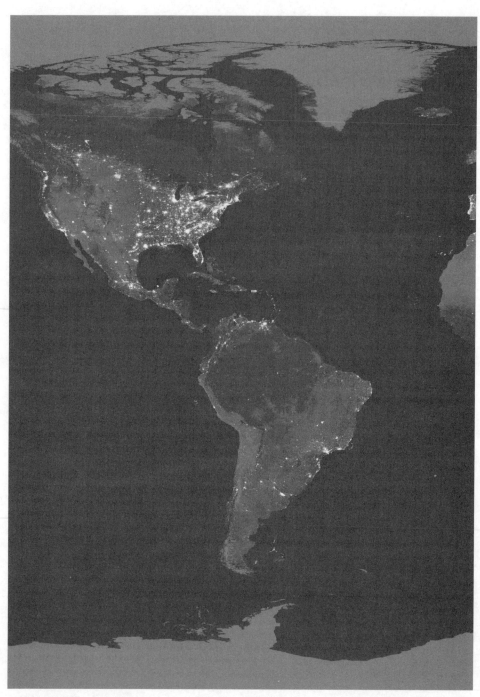

(Source: NASA)

of our achievements away from cave dwellings, kingdoms, and war; and toward peace, flying cars, and Oprah's forever expanding global commercial empire.

It's our beautiful home, but burning coal for power, we've polluted our air with CO_2.[9] Using fertilizers on our plants, we've polluted our groundwater with phosphorous.[10] And our technological progress has resulted in one of the most unusual, frightening, and commonly unknown potential health hazards as seen in the previous image: artificial light.

If you are a regular reader of O, you'd know this already.

A few years ago, a team led by Israeli scientists took one of these NASA images from space, and compared breast cancer rates to the amount of visible, artificial light at night in Israel.[11] It's important research because breast cancer is the most common malignant disease in their country.[12] It's also among the most common cancers in the United States,[13] scarily affecting about 12 percent of US women.[14]

The Israeli research team looking at the NASA imagery adjusted for factors known to skew breast cancer data, such as income and ethnicity. They also used data for lung cancer rates as another type of control because the primary cause for most lung cancer is believed to be smoking, not artificial light. (Smoking is estimated as the reason for 90 percent of all lung cancer deaths in the United States.[15] Don't worry, Oprah doesn't smoke cigarettes, though she did smoke weed once in 1982.[16])

What the team unraveled from their research is disturbing. It even made it into the pages of O:

They discovered that women living in the brightest neighborhoods— with enough light to read a book outside at midnight—were 73 percent more likely to suffer from breast cancer than those residing in areas where most late-night light is celestial.[17]

The connection is not conclusive, but suggests an unnerving correlation: the more artificial light, the more breast cancer.[18]

You know, if you want to understand women, listen to Oprah.

(Yes, I realize Rick Weiss wrote a better summary of this study for the *Washington Post*, but come on, how much more fun is it to quote O?)

What about men?

65

Well, a year later, the same Israeli research team compared artificial light levels at night to prostate cancer, this time across the world. And they found that the countries that have the most intense levels of artificial light at night tend to have the highest risk of prostate cancer.[19]

Now is a good time to ask: WHY IS THIS HAPPENING!?

Hold that thought. Grab your tablet, laptop, smartphone, or smartwatch, and stop reading this book until the sun has set. I'll wait for you.

Most of us don't really have a choice. We are naturally, chemically more

*This page
intentionally
left blank*

1 **Now, think about this: How soon do you want to fall asleep?**
I'm serious.

Think about how soon you want to curl into your soft, comfy
bed with those 1,000–thread-count sheets you just bought. Not
just when you normally sleep, but when you want *to sleep. Take*
a deep breath, assess, and decide how many hours or minutes.

2 **Once you've settled on a number, do a normal, everyday**
thing: turn on your smartphone or tablet with full brightness.
Swipe in and tap some stuff. Get lost in some of those
"important" notifications. Move things around and be wowed
by elementary animations and glowing lines, and wonder how
the geniuses at your cellphone manufacturer came up with
something that has worse typography than designs from two
hundred years ago.

3 **Then, while looking at the screen, ask yourself about a**
second number: How soon do you want to sleep now?
Stop cheating and reading ahead. I'll be here, I promise.
I'll even put a page break between this paragraph and the
next so you're not tempted. Go ahead. Just remember to
come back and not get lost in Oprah's Instagram feed.

Do it now.

alert when staring at our backlit, screen-based interfaces. Screens are a stimulant. Interfaces are a time-wasting drug. Want the opinion of Oprah's friend, Dr. Phil? How about the opinion of the more reputable former president of Harvard Medical School instead? "If light were a drug," Professor Charles Czeisler once said, "the government would not approve it."[20]

What? Let's rewind for a moment.

As far as we know, we've existed on Earth for roughly 200,000 years. While we evolved—or perhaps even back when we were the goo that evolved into our bodies now—we developed a natural circadian rhythm based on Earth's sunlight. In other words, our bodies do different things over the course of the day. You already know this because you get tired at night. You wake up in the morning. There are variances among us—we can't all be the hard-working biomachine Oprah embodies—but we all naturally follow a roughly 24-hour cycle.

With our ambitions high, we've fought sunset in all sorts of ways over time. Fire. Candles. Oil lamps. *The US Constitution wasn't going to write itself.* Those artificial light sources all probably affected our natural rhythms a little bit. But when we started developing brighter lights—like fluorescent lights, LED lights, or the lights emitting from our computers—that artificial light seemed to start doing something more dramatic to our bodies that scientists have been studying for the past few decades with surprising results.[21]

A few years ago, a research team at the University of Basel in Switzerland wondered how these different types of artificial light affected us at night.[22] So, they gathered a group of 16 healthy, drug-free men in their twenties who had regular sleep patterns. Then, they tested them for a few hours in different kinds of light temperature after sunset: a florescent light with a temperature of 2500k (slightly brighter than sunrise), an incandescent light with a temperature of 3000k (think of a classic yellowish lamp), and a florescent light with a temperature of 6500k (about the same as daylight).[23]

Their results likely mimicked your own findings.

Under 6500k light, the one like daylight, the subjects self-reported being less sleepy and their reaction times were dramatically faster when compared to the other light temperatures.[24] That bluer light temperature made the subjects most alert.

Why?

Relative Sleepiness adjusted to pre-light exposure (% sleepiness)

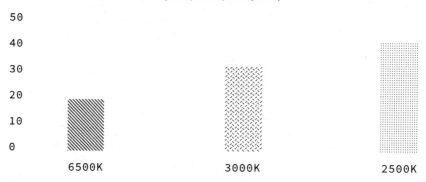

Melatonin adjusted to pre-light exposure

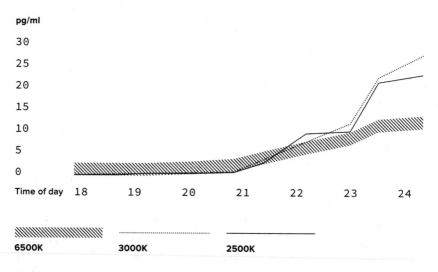

Perhaps because certain artificial light can suppress melatonin, a hormone that—among many probable things—seems to help regulate our sleep. Through saliva tests, the Swiss research team showed their test subjects produced 40 percent less melatonin when exposed to the 6500k light for a few hours.

What does this have to do with interfaces?
Well, odds are that a color temperature of 6500k or higher is used for the

screen of every device you own.[25] D65, as it's often called, is an industry standard for computer monitors.[26] We use that color temperature on screens because simulating daylight colors generates beautiful, rich colors on a computer display. In a balancing act of resolution, brightness, and contrast, many smartphone displays actually end up with an even higher color temperature. But when you look at an interface at those color temperatures at night, it seems to be leading your body to think it's daytime, suppressing melatonin, and affecting your sleep cycle. In other words, the backlight from watching 18 episodes of Breaking Bad on Netflix in full brightness in bed seems to be why you can't get great sleep—not because Tom Cruise's Oprah interview is still giving you nightmares.

The Federal Trade Commission (FTC), which exists "to enhance informed consumer choice,"[27] recently mandated that lightbulb manufacturers include a label "modeled on the Nutrition Facts label on food packages"[28] that includes the following chart about the color temperatures: Just as the calories you intake affect your health, so does the kind of light

Light Color

Correlated Color Temperature (CCT)

Warm White	Bright White	Daylight
2700K 3000K	4500K	6500K

you see. By mandating these labels, the hope is that if you better understand light temperatures, you won't do things like put a bunch of 6500k bulbs in your bedroom, accidentally tricking your body into thinking that it's daylight when you're headed to bed, thereby suppressing your melatonin and ruining your sleep.

Does melatonin do anything besides regulate sleep?

Well, many scientists believe melatonin does other great things for us, like help fight some forms of cancer, such as breast and prostate cancer. Studies have shown that when melatonin is introduced to those types of cancer cells, the cancer growth slows.[29] As the *Washington Post* once reported, "maybe it's better to stay in the dark."

"We can't say yet," Richard Stevens of the University of Connecticut Health Center in Farmington told the *New York Times*, "but the evidence is accumulating that light at night, and the consequent decrease in melatonin, may be a major driver of breast cancer."[30]

It all comes together.

Computers have D65 or higher screens; the high color temperature seems to suppress melatonin when used at night; and that suppressed melatonin might be throwing off your internal sleep cycle and possibly even preventing your body from fighting off some types of cancer. Like the idiocy of kamikaze insects that fly into lights for inevitable suicide, we might be hurting ourselves by staring into our backlit interfaces in the middle of the night, wondering if Cindy responded to our friend request.

She didn't, by the way.

In an effort to try to find out how we can use our screens at night, the Mayo Clinic ran a study to find what parameters could help. They found that very low brightness and holding devices far away from your face can help reduce the negative effects.[31]

But there's a much better way out than holding your phone at arm's length in bed. Our screen time can be greatly reduced if we embrace a path of No Interface. And I'd like to show you how we can build technology to get there.

Time for less interface, more sleep, and more O.

8. The Screenless Office
The best interface is no interface

Not long ago, our lives were filled with paper.

Gutenberg's Bible press capitalistically evolved in the Western world over a few centuries from a device to spread internationally influential moral teachings to typewriters, dot matrix printers, and fax machines spreading internationally influential corporate memos about low-hanging fruit, running it up the flagpole, and the bottom line.[1] According to the US Environmental Protection Agency (EPA), four million tons of office paper had been wasted in the United States by 1980.[2]

For some, even the American dream had become paper based.

Put in a good, honest, and hard day's work at a busy mail room on the ground floor of a beige office park—couriering messages in interoffice manila envelopes from one cubicle to another—and eventually you might just climb up the corporate ladder. Mail boy to the boardroom.

The opening of a 1982 *New York Times* editorial described the feeling of the time:

> **"New York is a city where dreams come true, where a girl named Barbra from Brooklyn can become a household name, where a mailroom clerk named Manilow can eventually make platinum records and lots of money, a city of limousines with gray-black glass in the windows and parties with paparazzi."[3]**

Move to New York City, work with paper, and one day you might just be the next Barry Manilow.

The paper-based mail room fantasy even dominated book sales. In 1981, Iris Rainer's *The Boys in the Mail Room*—a trashy, raunchy, homophobic story about a group of boys who rise from Hollywood's mail room to success in the industry—was the ninth best-selling paperback book in the United States.[4]

But with amazing, emerging technology in mind, some of us dreamed of something better. A different path. They thought the best paper was, well, no paper.

In 1975, *Businessweek* published "The Office of the Future," describing a distant, "paperless" world. The then-dreamers imagined fantasy scenarios about 1995 when a desk would be transformed from a resting place for piles of paper to a surface for a "TV-like display" with a typewriter keyboard that could access endless electronic file archives.

Following is a 1975 quote from one of those dreamers, George E. Pake, the former head of Xerox PARC:

> **"I'll be able to call up documents from my files on the screen, or by pressing a button," he says. "I can get my mail or any messages. I don't know how much hard copy [printed paper] I'll want in this world."[5]**

In 1980, the *Economist* printed its own take with "Towards the Paperless Office," and a business brief with a section about the "Death Sentence for Paper Shufflers."

From the imaginative latter, written twenty-three years before Skype:[6]

> **"He checks his mail by displaying it on the screen—President Clive Greaves in the New York office regrets he will not be able to attend the video teleconferencing session at 2pm (GMT) but will fax his revised forecasts beforehand."[7]**

They looked past the trends of the day and imagined something better.

But there were plenty of realists. Naysayers.

Oh, yeah? What about paper napkins, huh?? Or paper towels? Are you telling me you're going to replace toilet paper?! Those things will stay, along with my Wite-Out, carbon copy paper, and interoffice memos!

Sure. There will always be a number of people who can't see past the tools of the day—tools that could never go away, like paper—while searching for and shouting out exception cases. And there will always be people who are looking out for our "best interests," like, say, the National Security Agency (NSA).

In 1974, the United States government's most secretive agency started publishing a top-secret internal newsletter. The major general of the US Army called it "a new vehicle for the interchange of ideas."[8] It was a fascinating moment in the history of the NSA.

The publication discussed the inner workings and internal thoughts of their multidisciplined workplace. It had opinion pieces about employees' roles as collectors, analysts, and "cryppies," and the thinking behind some of the country's most well-kept secrets of code-cracking and encryption.[9] It was called *Cryptolog*. Recently, parts of it became declassified.

This is the cover of the April 1983 issue of *Cryptolog*:

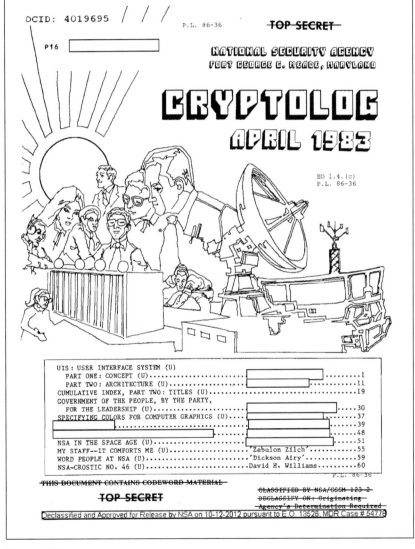

(Source: NSA)

And it opened with an editorial rant about the paperless office.

After they took an anecdotal "stroll through the local supply room," the editorial staff at the NSA reminded *Cryptolog* readers that a paperless world could never be realized because—as evidenced in their own supply room—people still care deeply about paper forms and memos, which is why "one can still hear serious debate about which brand of 'white out' does the best job."*

Clear, flawless logic.

"The next time you wander through your favorite supply room," they had warned, "take a close look at the tiers of forms arrayed there. Do you think they will ever go away?"

Here's the entire, magical editorial:

> The other day we saw a phrase that we haven't seen for a while: "paperless office." It was a popular term a while back, and was sometimes called the "paperless society." It was used to refer to that future day when all paper would be replaced by some other media, such as cathode ray tubes (TV) or other display devices.
>
> Just to see if something was happening that we hadn't heard about, we took a stroll through the local supply room. The shelves were still filled with paper supplies, and with things that make marks on paper. Looseleaf notebooks seem to disapper from the shelves as fast as the supply folks can stock them. One can still hear serious debate about which brand of "white out" does the best job. Erasers, paper clips, rulers, IN (and OUT) baskets, sheets of press on letters, scissors . . . the list goes on and on. Paper does not seem to be on the way out just yet. Not around here, anyway.

*white out: a "correction liquid." Sort of like a mini bottle of white paint that comes with a brush you can use to paint over mistakes on a piece of paper in case you accidentally write that you were born in 1992 instead of 1912.

There is a growing sentiment that we will never reach that paperless state. It is not, after all, a question of technology. In a recent survey of computer editing systems, the authors finished with the somewhat guilty admission that, in the preparation of their report, they had consumed just under a mile of paper. We have no statistics to support it, but we have the distinct impression that we are using more paper per capita, not less.

New technology does not have to replace the old; it sometimes finds its niche alongside the old. Office automation seems to be aimed at getting machines to write down, on paper, what used to be written down by some other method, on paper. Some people think office automation will use more paper, not less.

The next time you wander through your favorite supply room, take a close look at the tiers of forms arrayed there. Do you think they will ever go away?

With emerging technology in mind, some of the dreamers thought differently, but they had little luck in the beginning. For years, paper usage increased, and the naysayers grew confident in their opinions. Four million tons of office paper usage increased to six million by 1990, and seven million by the year 2000.

Then, roughly two decades after the miracle of WIMP (windows, icons, menus, pointers)—with slow-moving corporate policy shifts in place, a generational change in the workforce, and a few awkward years of email footers that asked you to "please consider the environment before printing"—paper consumption finally started to drop.

"Please consider the environment before printing."

As futurist Paul Saffo once said, "You can never go wrong by betting that change will go slower than everyone expects."[10]

Pounds of paper used per white-collar employee

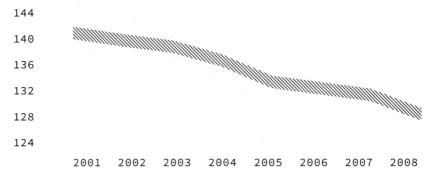

Paper usage in the office (Source: Osterman Research)

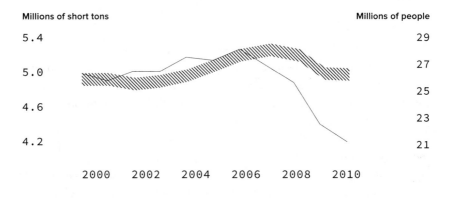

White collar employment   Office paper shipments

(Source: US Office of The Federal Register)

*Includes finance, insurance, real estate, professional and
business services, membership organizations

Measured by pounds per white-collar worker, the amount of paper usage in the office has been dropping every year since 2001.[11]

And so, as workplaces have finally embraced new processes for working without paper, the demand for paper has drastically fallen.[12]

As a result of finding ways to drop paper for digital, we can now search more easily, communicate more rapidly, and store incredible amounts of data painlessly.

But today, instead of paper, our lives are inundated with screens.

Your workplace isn't any good if you don't have at least two monitors on your desk. Your smartphone isn't decent if it's not at least five inches long. Your car is considered outdated if doesn't have a touchscreen. And if trends continue, your wrist will soon be unfashionable if it doesn't have a screen slapped on it, and your face will be outdated without an interface projected in front of your eyes by a face computer.

American children aged 0 to 8 are already estimated to be exposed to screens for over 2 hours a day.[13] Kids age eight to eighteen for an average of seven and a half hours a day.[14] And adults? We're exposed to screens for eight and a half hours a day.[15] Odds are that those numbers have increased by the time you've started reading this book.

The sad thing is, a lot of the screen time is a burden. A hurdle for our goals. As Don Norman wrote in 1990, when these digital interfaces were just beginning to take over our lives, "The real problem with the interface is that it is an interface. Interfaces get in the way. I don't want to focus my energies on an interface. I want to focus on the job . . . I don't want to think of myself as using a computer, I want to think of myself as doing my job."

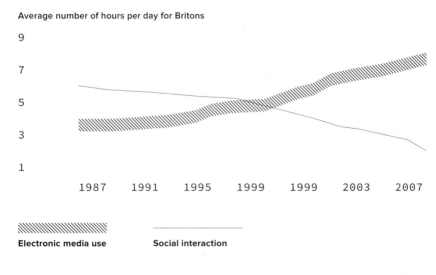

Average number of hours per day for Britons

Electronic media use   Social interaction

(Source: *Biologist*[16])

Interfaces have gone far beyond the workplace. They now steal us away from seeing, interacting, and talking to the people around us; they hinder our community-building and our intimate relationships.

At one time, our lives were filled with paper, so we dreamed of a paperless world. Now, instead, our lives are filled with screens. And I think it's time to dream of a screenless world. I sincerely think the best interface is no interface, and I'd like to show you how we can get there.

Let's end the confusion between UX and UI. Let's stop slapping screens on children's toys. Let's prioritize personal goals over addiction. Let's get our lives and our health back in balance by interacting with the real world instead of staring into a light, checking new notifications. Let's think beyond screens.

The best result for any technology is to solve meaningful problems in impactful ways.

The best design reduces work.

The best computer is unseen.

The best interaction is natural.

The best interface is no interface.

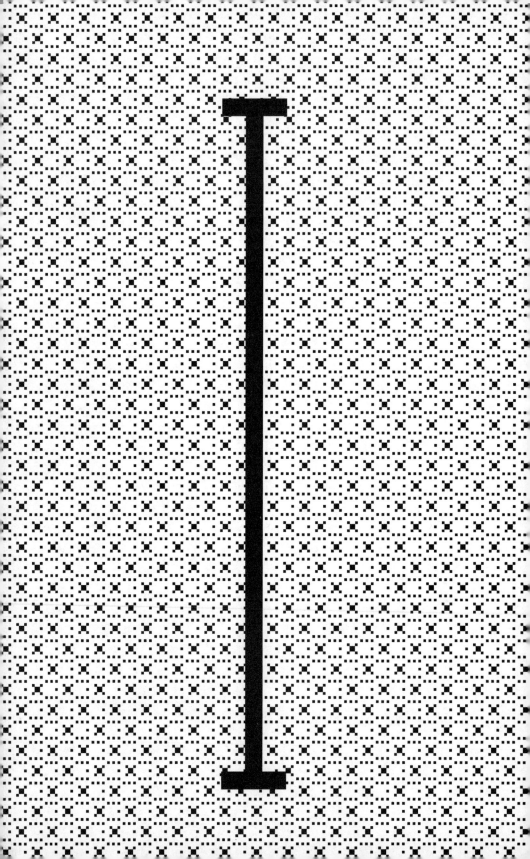

Principle One: Embrace Typical Processes Instead of Screens

9. Back Pocket Apps
This app goes perfectly with my skinny jeans

Embrace typical processes instead of screens. That's the first principle of NoUI. It sounds straightforward. However, screen-based thinking has become so deeply entrenched into our culture that the interface inundation has even led to unexpected psychological outcomes. But fear not—smart designers and engineers are working on variants of apps—yes, apps—that embrace our typical processes. Apps that can live in your back pocket.

A few years ago, a doctor by the name of Michael Rothberg reached out to a colleague with a request. He was confident that something medically undocumented had happened to him. Disturbed, yet curious, Dr. Rothberg told his friend Dr. Ashish Arora about his psychological event, and the two decided to design a survey for the medical staff at Baystate Medical Center, an acute care hospital in western Massachusetts, to locally measure the occurrence rate. Participation in the survey was unexpectedly high, and the results were astounding:[1] About 68 percent of the participants had exactly the same experience as Dr. Rothberg.[2]

Later, a nearly identical study in Indiana—conducted by a different group of researchers—attempted to measure the same phenomena with 290 undergraduate students.[3] The outcome? This time, 90 percent had experienced the same event as Dr. Rothberg. And it happened to those participants, on average, once every two weeks.[4]

■ I think that's you.
▢ *No, it's you.*
Are you sure?
I think so.
Maybe it's Jane. Jane is that you?
Oh, yeah, I think. Wait, no.
Frank?

Ringxiety.[5] Also known as phantom vibration syndrome (PVS). The twenty-first-century technological adaptation of Abbott and Costello's "Who's on First?" that plagued Dr. Rothberg . . . and still plagues almost all of us. Pager, smartphone, or smartwatch.

■ I'm on silent.
▢ *I thought I was.*

An imagined ringtone that makes you want to scream some 1843 Edgar Allan Poe in the middle of a movie theater when your phone isn't even buzzing:[6]

Was it possible they heard not? Almighty God!—no, no! They heard!—they
suspected!—they knew!—they were making a mockery of my horror!—this
I thought, and this I think. But anything was better than this agony! Anything
was more tolerable than this derision! I could bear those hypocritical smiles
no longer! I felt that I must scream or die! and now—again!—hark! louder!
louder! louder! louder![7]

Over 300 years before that Poe passage was written,[8] Leonardo da Vinci filled his encrypted notebooks with findings of everyday life and visions for the future. One of his passages—amongst sketches of flying machines and ana-tomical drawings of the human form[9]—was an unusual discovery about walls.

In the stains, paint chips, and various stones that made up the walls of his day, he saw something different. "Mountains, rivers . . . figures in quick movement," he wrote. "With such walls and blends of different stones it comes about as it does with the sound of bells, in whose clanging you may discover every name and word that you can imagine."[10]

Leonardo may have been one of the first to record[11] a visual and auditory form of the psychological state apophenia—an error in perception—called pareidolia. It's a form of pattern recognition encoded in us for survival gone haywire, where a false stimulus (like a sound, vibration, or image) is per-ceived as authentic.[12] Leonardo visually experienced it through stains on the wall. Edgar Allan Poe's character experienced it through sound after a mur-der.[13] It's how a Rorschach inkblot test works. And it's what Dr. Rothberg experienced when he heard phantom vibrations from his smartphone.

"In the case of phantom vibrations, because the brain is anticipat-ing a call, it misinterprets sensory input according to this preconceived hypothesis. The actual stimulus is unknown, but candidate sensations might include pressure from clothing, muscle contractions, or other sen-sory stimuli," reported the study by Dr. Rothberg and Dr. Arora.

✒ ✒ ✒ ✒

For us, the well-oiled machine of notifications hosted within smartphone platforms such as iOS or Android can be an unrelenting flood of app com-panies trying to use notifications to draw us to their interfaces. On a special day, like your birthday, it can be an endless stream of "Happy birthday!" notifications from services like Facebook, which by default reminds every-one to remind you it's your birthday. Even on a normal day, some of the more active users on Quora have reported receiving 150 to 500 notifications

Do you see a ringtone?

per day from all the applications on their phones.[14] Even though we can silence our phones and turn off notifications, an incredible number of us have become so accustomed to the inundation and so paranoid we'll miss an actual important event that we have hallucinations of buzzes and beeps when they don't even happen.

Your smartphone is begging you.

Activated by screen-based applications, addictive business models, and the structure of mobile operating systems, our smartphones crave to be outside our pockets and purses. *You have more friends on Facebook than you think. People have been looking at your LinkedIn profile.* Every ding, vibration, and ring is your smartphone screaming and begging: LET ME OUT! A day with our smartphones looks like this:

```
Unplug your smartphone from the charger, put in your pocket or purse,
pull it out to use the interface for a moment, put the phone back in your pocket or purse,
pull it out to use the interface for a moment, put the phone back in your pocket or purse,
pull it out to use the interface for a moment, put the phone back in your pocket or purse,
pull it out to use the interface for a moment, put the phone back in your pocket or purse,
pull it out to use the interface for a moment, put the phone back in your pocket or purse,
pull it out to use the interface for a moment, put the phone back in your pocket or purse,
pull it out to use the interface for a moment, put the phone back in your pocket or purse,
pull it out to use the interface for a moment, put the phone back in your pocket or purse,
pull it out to use the interface for a moment, put the phone back in your pocket or purse,
```

```
pull it out to use the interface for a moment, put the phone back in your pocket or purse,
pull it out to use the interface for a moment, put the phone back in your pocket or purse,
pull it out to use the interface for a moment, put the phone back in your pocket or purse,
pull it out to use the interface for a moment, put the phone back in your pocket or purse,
and plug it in to charge while you sleep.
```

As you read it, the same phrase repeated fifteen times may have felt redundantly silly; but Locket, a small New York City–based startup that makes a custom lock screen experience for Android, found that their roughly 150,000 users check their phones much more often.[15]

One hundred and ten times a day, in fact.

```
Unplug your smartphone from the charger, put in your pocket or purse,
pull it out to use the interface for a moment, put the phone back in your pocket or purse,
pull it out to use the interface for a moment, put the phone back in your pocket or purse,
pull it out to use the interface for a moment, put the phone back in your pocket or purse,
pull it out to use the interface for a moment, put the phone back in your pocket or purse,
pull it out to use the interface for a moment, put the phone back in your pocket or purse,
pull it out to use the interface for a moment, put the phone back in your pocket or purse,
pull it out to use the interface for a moment, put the phone back in your pocket or purse,
pull it out to use the interface for a moment, put the phone back in your pocket or purse,
pull it out to use the interface for a moment, put the phone back in your pocket or purse,
pull it out to use the interface for a moment, put the phone back in your pocket or purse,
pull it out to use the interface for a moment, put the phone back in your pocket or purse,
pull it out to use the interface for a moment, put the phone back in your pocket or purse,
pull it out to use the interface for a moment, put the phone back in your pocket or purse,
pull it out to use the interface for a moment, put the phone back in your pocket or purse,
pull it out to use the interface for a moment, put the phone back in your pocket or purse,
pull it out to use the interface for a moment, put the phone back in your pocket or purse,
pull it out to use the interface for a moment, put the phone back in your pocket or purse,
pull it out to use the interface for a moment, put the phone back in your pocket or purse,
pull it out to use the interface for a moment, put the phone back in your pocket or purse,
pull it out to use the interface for a moment, put the phone back in your pocket or purse,
pull it out to use the interface for a moment, put the phone back in your pocket or purse,
pull it out to use the interface for a moment, put the phone back in your pocket or purse,
pull it out to use the interface for a moment, put the phone back in your pocket or purse,
pull it out to use the interface for a moment, put the phone back in your pocket or purse,
pull it out to use the interface for a moment, put the phone back in your pocket or purse,
```

pull it out to use the interface for a moment, put the phone back in your pocket or purse,
pull it out to use the interface for a moment, put the phone back in your pocket or purse,
pull it out to use the interface for a moment, put the phone back in your pocket or purse,
pull it out to use the interface for a moment, put the phone back in your pocket or purse,
pull it out to use the interface for a moment, put the phone back in your pocket or purse,
pull it out to use the interface for a moment, put the phone back in your pocket or purse,
pull it out to use the interface for a moment, put the phone back in your pocket or purse,
pull it out to use the interface for a moment, put the phone back in your pocket or purse,
pull it out to use the interface for a moment, put the phone back in your pocket or purse,
pull it out to use the interface for a moment, put the phone back in your pocket or purse,
pull it out to use the interface for a moment, put the phone back in your pocket or purse,
pull it out to use the interface for a moment, put the phone back in your pocket or purse,
pull it out to use the interface for a moment, put the phone back in your pocket or purse,
pull it out to use the interface for a moment, put the phone back in your pocket or purse,
pull it out to use the interface for a moment, put the phone back in your pocket or purse,
pull it out to use the interface for a moment, put the phone back in your pocket or purse,
pull it out to use the interface for a moment, put the phone back in your pocket or purse,
pull it out to use the interface for a moment, put the phone back in your pocket or purse,
pull it out to use the interface for a moment, put the phone back in your pocket or purse,
pull it out to use the interface for a moment, put the phone back in your pocket or purse,
pull it out to use the interface for a moment, put the phone back in your pocket or purse,
pull it out to use the interface for a moment, put the phone back in your pocket or purse,
pull it out to use the interface for a moment, put the phone back in your pocket or purse,
pull it out to use the interface for a moment, put the phone back in your pocket or purse,
pull it out to use the interface for a moment, put the phone back in your pocket or purse,
pull it out to use the interface for a moment, put the phone back in your pocket or purse,
pull it out to use the interface for a moment, put the phone back in your pocket or purse,
pull it out to use the interface for a moment, put the phone back in your pocket or purse,
pull it out to use the interface for a moment, put the phone back in your pocket or purse,
pull it out to use the interface for a moment, put the phone back in your pocket or purse,
pull it out to use the interface for a moment, put the phone back in your pocket or purse,
pull it out to use the interface for a moment, put the phone back in your pocket or purse,
pull it out to use the interface for a moment, put the phone back in your pocket or purse,
pull it out to use the interface for a moment, put the phone back in your pocket or purse,
pull it out to use the interface for a moment, put the phone back in your pocket or purse,
pull it out to use the interface for a moment, put the phone back in your pocket or purse,

pull it out to use the interface for a moment, put the phone back in your pocket or purse,
pull it out to use the interface for a moment, put the phone back in your pocket or purse,
pull it out to use the interface for a moment, put the phone back in your pocket or purse,
pull it out to use the interface for a moment, put the phone back in your pocket or purse,
pull it out to use the interface for a moment, put the phone back in your pocket or purse,
pull it out to use the interface for a moment, put the phone back in your pocket or purse,
pull it out to use the interface for a moment, put the phone back in your pocket or purse,
pull it out to use the interface for a moment, put the phone back in your pocket or purse,
pull it out to use the interface for a moment, put the phone back in your pocket or purse,
pull it out to use the interface for a moment, put the phone back in your pocket or purse,
pull it out to use the interface for a moment, put the phone back in your pocket or purse,
pull it out to use the interface for a moment, put the phone back in your pocket or purse,
pull it out to use the interface for a moment, put the phone back in your pocket or purse,
pull it out to use the interface for a moment, put the phone back in your pocket or purse,
pull it out to use the interface for a moment, put the phone back in your pocket or purse,
pull it out to use the interface for a moment, put the phone back in your pocket or purse,
pull it out to use the interface for a moment, put the phone back in your pocket or purse,
pull it out to use the interface for a moment, put the phone back in your pocket or purse,
pull it out to use the interface for a moment, put the phone back in your pocket or purse,
pull it out to use the interface for a moment, put the phone back in your pocket or purse,
pull it out to use the interface for a moment, put the phone back in your pocket or purse,
pull it out to use the interface for a moment, put the phone back in your pocket or purse,
pull it out to use the interface for a moment, put the phone back in your pocket or purse,
pull it out to use the interface for a moment, put the phone back in your pocket or purse,
pull it out to use the interface for a moment, put the phone back in your pocket or purse,
pull it out to use the interface for a moment, put the phone back in your pocket or purse,
pull it out to use the interface for a moment, put the phone back in your pocket or purse,
pull it out to use the interface for a moment, put the phone back in your pocket or purse,
pull it out to use the interface for a moment, put the phone back in your pocket or purse,
pull it out to use the interface for a moment, put the phone back in your pocket or purse,
pull it out to use the interface for a moment, put the phone back in your pocket or purse,
pull it out to use the interface for a moment, put the phone back in your pocket or purse,
pull it out to use the interface for a moment, put the phone back in your pocket or purse,
pull it out to use the interface for a moment, put the phone back in your pocket or purse,
pull it out to use the interface for a moment, put the phone back in your pocket or purse,
pull it out to use the interface for a moment, put the phone back in your pocket or purse,

```
pull it out to use the interface for a moment, put the phone back in your pocket or purse,
pull it out to use the interface for a moment, put the phone back in your pocket or purse,
pull it out to use the interface for a moment, put the phone back in your pocket or purse,
pull it out to use the interface for a moment, put the phone back in your pocket or purse,
pull it out to use the interface for a moment, put the phone back in your pocket or purse,
pull it out to use the interface for a moment, put the phone back in your pocket or purse,
pull it out to use the interface for a moment, put the phone back in your pocket or purse,
pull it out to use the interface for a moment, put the phone back in your pocket or purse,
pull it out to use the interface for a moment, put the phone back in your pocket or purse,
pull it out to use the interface for a moment, put the phone back in your pocket or purse,
pull it out to use the interface for a moment, put the phone back in your pocket or purse,
pull it out to use the interface for a moment, put the phone back in your pocket or purse,
pull it out to use the interface for a moment, put the phone back in your pocket or purse,
pull it out to use the interface for a moment, put the phone back in your pocket or purse,
pull it out to use the interface for a moment, put the phone back in your pocket or purse,
pull it out to use the interface for a moment, put the phone back in your pocket or purse,
pull it out to use the interface for a moment, put the phone back in your pocket or purse,
and plug it in to charge while you sleep.
```

However, not everyone agrees with those usage numbers. The venture capital firm Kleiner Perkins Caufield & Byers (KPCB), which has backed Amazon, AOL, Intuit, Google, and a lot of other companies you might know,[16] would disagree with Locket. According to KPCB research, we actually tend to check our phones more often.[17]

One hundred and fifty times a day, in fact.

```
Unplug your smartphone from the charger, put in your pocket or purse,
pull it out to use the interface for a moment, put the phone back in your pocket or purse,
pull it out to use the interface for a moment, put the phone back in your pocket or purse,
pull it out to use the interface for a moment, put the phone back in your pocket or purse,
pull it out to use the interface for a moment, put the phone back in your pocket or purse,
pull it out to use the interface for a moment, put the phone back in your pocket or purse,
pull it out to use the interface for a moment, put the phone back in your pocket or purse,
pull it out to use the interface for a moment, put the phone back in your pocket or purse,
pull it out to use the interface for a moment, put the phone back in your pocket or purse,
pull it out to use the interface for a moment, put the phone back in your pocket or purse,
pull it out to use the interface for a moment, put the phone back in your pocket or purse,
pull it out to use the interface for a moment, put the phone back in your pocket or purse,
```

pull it out to use the interface for a moment, put the phone back in your pocket or purse,
pull it out to use the interface for a moment, put the phone back in your pocket or purse,
pull it out to use the interface for a moment, put the phone back in your pocket or purse,
pull it out to use the interface for a moment, put the phone back in your pocket or purse,
pull it out to use the interface for a moment, put the phone back in your pocket or purse,
pull it out to use the interface for a moment, put the phone back in your pocket or purse,
pull it out to use the interface for a moment, put the phone back in your pocket or purse,
pull it out to use the interface for a moment, put the phone back in your pocket or purse,
pull it out to use the interface for a moment, put the phone back in your pocket or purse,
pull it out to use the interface for a moment, put the phone back in your pocket or purse,
pull it out to use the interface for a moment, put the phone back in your pocket or purse,
pull it out to use the interface for a moment, put the phone back in your pocket or purse,
pull it out to use the interface for a moment, put the phone back in your pocket or purse,
pull it out to use the interface for a moment, put the phone back in your pocket or purse,
pull it out to use the interface for a moment, put the phone back in your pocket or purse,
pull it out to use the interface for a moment, put the phone back in your pocket or purse,
pull it out to use the interface for a moment, put the phone back in your pocket or purse,
pull it out to use the interface for a moment, put the phone back in your pocket or purse,
pull it out to use the interface for a moment, put the phone back in your pocket or purse,
pull it out to use the interface for a moment, put the phone back in your pocket or purse,
pull it out to use the interface for a moment, put the phone back in your pocket or purse,
pull it out to use the interface for a moment, put the phone back in your pocket or purse,
pull it out to use the interface for a moment, put the phone back in your pocket or purse,
pull it out to use the interface for a moment, put the phone back in your pocket or purse,
pull it out to use the interface for a moment, put the phone back in your pocket or purse,
pull it out to use the interface for a moment, put the phone back in your pocket or purse,
pull it out to use the interface for a moment, put the phone back in your pocket or purse,
pull it out to use the interface for a moment, put the phone back in your pocket or purse,
pull it out to use the interface for a moment, put the phone back in your pocket or purse,
pull it out to use the interface for a moment, put the phone back in your pocket or purse,
pull it out to use the interface for a moment, put the phone back in your pocket or purse,
pull it out to use the interface for a moment, put the phone back in your pocket or purse,
pull it out to use the interface for a moment, put the phone back in your pocket or purse,
pull it out to use the interface for a moment, put the phone back in your pocket or purse,
pull it out to use the interface for a moment, put the phone back in your pocket or purse,

pull it out to use the interface for a moment, put the phone back in your pocket or purse,
pull it out to use the interface for a moment, put the phone back in your pocket or purse,
pull it out to use the interface for a moment, put the phone back in your pocket or purse,
pull it out to use the interface for a moment, put the phone back in your pocket or purse,
pull it out to use the interface for a moment, put the phone back in your pocket or purse,
pull it out to use the interface for a moment, put the phone back in your pocket or purse,
pull it out to use the interface for a moment, put the phone back in your pocket or purse,
pull it out to use the interface for a moment, put the phone back in your pocket or purse,
pull it out to use the interface for a moment, put the phone back in your pocket or purse,
pull it out to use the interface for a moment, put the phone back in your pocket or purse,
pull it out to use the interface for a moment, put the phone back in your pocket or purse,
pull it out to use the interface for a moment, put the phone back in your pocket or purse,
pull it out to use the interface for a moment, put the phone back in your pocket or purse,
pull it out to use the interface for a moment, put the phone back in your pocket or purse,
pull it out to use the interface for a moment, put the phone back in your pocket or purse,
pull it out to use the interface for a moment, put the phone back in your pocket or purse,
pull it out to use the interface for a moment, put the phone back in your pocket or purse,
pull it out to use the interface for a moment, put the phone back in your pocket or purse,
pull it out to use the interface for a moment, put the phone back in your pocket or purse,
pull it out to use the interface for a moment, put the phone back in your pocket or purse,
pull it out to use the interface for a moment, put the phone back in your pocket or purse,
pull it out to use the interface for a moment, put the phone back in your pocket or purse,
pull it out to use the interface for a moment, put the phone back in your pocket or purse,
pull it out to use the interface for a moment, put the phone back in your pocket or purse,
pull it out to use the interface for a moment, put the phone back in your pocket or purse,
pull it out to use the interface for a moment, put the phone back in your pocket or purse,
pull it out to use the interface for a moment, put the phone back in your pocket or purse,
pull it out to use the interface for a moment, put the phone back in your pocket or purse,
pull it out to use the interface for a moment, put the phone back in your pocket or purse,
pull it out to use the interface for a moment, put the phone back in your pocket or purse,
pull it out to use the interface for a moment, put the phone back in your pocket or purse,
pull it out to use the interface for a moment, put the phone back in your pocket or purse,
pull it out to use the interface for a moment, put the phone back in your pocket or purse,
pull it out to use the interface for a moment, put the phone back in your pocket or purse,
pull it out to use the interface for a moment, put the phone back in your pocket or purse,
pull it out to use the interface for a moment, put the phone back in your pocket or purse,
pull it out to use the interface for a moment, put the phone back in your pocket or purse,

pull it out to use the interface for a moment, put the phone back in your pocket or purse,
pull it out to use the interface for a moment, put the phone back in your pocket or purse,
pull it out to use the interface for a moment, put the phone back in your pocket or purse,
pull it out to use the interface for a moment, put the phone back in your pocket or purse,
pull it out to use the interface for a moment, put the phone back in your pocket or purse,
pull it out to use the interface for a moment, put the phone back in your pocket or purse,
pull it out to use the interface for a moment, put the phone back in your pocket or purse,
pull it out to use the interface for a moment, put the phone back in your pocket or purse,
pull it out to use the interface for a moment, put the phone back in your pocket or purse,
pull it out to use the interface for a moment, put the phone back in your pocket or purse,
pull it out to use the interface for a moment, put the phone back in your pocket or purse,
pull it out to use the interface for a moment, put the phone back in your pocket or purse,
pull it out to use the interface for a moment, put the phone back in your pocket or purse,
pull it out to use the interface for a moment, put the phone back in your pocket or purse,
pull it out to use the interface for a moment, put the phone back in your pocket or purse,
pull it out to use the interface for a moment, put the phone back in your pocket or purse,
pull it out to use the interface for a moment, put the phone back in your pocket or purse,
pull it out to use the interface for a moment, put the phone back in your pocket or purse,
pull it out to use the interface for a moment, put the phone back in your pocket or purse,
pull it out to use the interface for a moment, put the phone back in your pocket or purse,
pull it out to use the interface for a moment, put the phone back in your pocket or purse,
pull it out to use the interface for a moment, put the phone back in your pocket or purse,
pull it out to use the interface for a moment, put the phone back in your pocket or purse,
pull it out to use the interface for a moment, put the phone back in your pocket or purse,
pull it out to use the interface for a moment, put the phone back in your pocket or purse,
pull it out to use the interface for a moment, put the phone back in your pocket or purse,
pull it out to use the interface for a moment, put the phone back in your pocket or purse,
pull it out to use the interface for a moment, put the phone back in your pocket or purse,
pull it out to use the interface for a moment, put the phone back in your pocket or purse,
pull it out to use the interface for a moment, put the phone back in your pocket or purse,
pull it out to use the interface for a moment, put the phone back in your pocket or purse,
pull it out to use the interface for a moment, put the phone back in your pocket or purse,
pull it out to use the interface for a moment, put the phone back in your pocket or purse,
pull it out to use the interface for a moment, put the phone back in your pocket or purse,
pull it out to use the interface for a moment, put the phone back in your pocket or purse,
pull it out to use the interface for a moment, put the phone back in your pocket or purse,

```
pull it out to use the interface for a moment, put the phone back in your pocket or purse,
pull it out to use the interface for a moment, put the phone back in your pocket or purse,
pull it out to use the interface for a moment, put the phone back in your pocket or purse,
pull it out to use the interface for a moment, put the phone back in your pocket or purse,
pull it out to use the interface for a moment, put the phone back in your pocket or purse,
pull it out to use the interface for a moment, put the phone back in your pocket or purse,
pull it out to use the interface for a moment, put the phone back in your pocket or purse,
pull it out to use the interface for a moment, put the phone back in your pocket or purse,
pull it out to use the interface for a moment, put the phone back in your pocket or purse,
pull it out to use the interface for a moment, put the phone back in your pocket or purse,
pull it out to use the interface for a moment, put the phone back in your pocket or purse,
pull it out to use the interface for a moment, put the phone back in your pocket or purse,
pull it out to use the interface for a moment, put the phone back in your pocket or purse,
pull it out to use the interface for a moment, put the phone back in your pocket or purse,
pull it out to use the interface for a moment, put the phone back in your pocket or purse,
pull it out to use the interface for a moment, put the phone back in your pocket or purse,
pull it out to use the interface for a moment, put the phone back in your pocket or purse,
pull it out to use the interface for a moment, put the phone back in your pocket or purse,
pull it out to use the interface for a moment, put the phone back in your pocket or purse,
pull it out to use the interface for a moment, put the phone back in your pocket or purse,
pull it out to use the interface for a moment, put the phone back in your pocket or purse,
pull it out to use the interface for a moment, put the phone back in your pocket or purse,
pull it out to use the interface for a moment, put the phone back in your pocket or purse,
pull it out to use the interface for a moment, put the phone back in your pocket or purse,
pull it out to use the interface for a moment, put the phone back in your pocket or purse,
pull it out to use the interface for a moment, put the phone back in your pocket or purse,
pull it out to use the interface for a moment, put the phone back in your pocket or purse,
pull it out to use the interface for a moment, put the phone back in your pocket or purse,
pull it out to use the interface for a moment, put the phone back in your pocket or purse,
pull it out to use the interface for a moment, put the phone back in your pocket or purse,
pull it out to use the interface for a moment, put the phone back in your pocket or purse,
and plug it in to charge while you sleep.
```

Your phone isn't just begging for attention a lot, it's begging "LET ME OUT!" every waking day. In an international poll taken by *Time* magazine, 1 in 4 people check their phone "every 30 minutes, 1 in 5 people every 10 minutes."[18]

Be careful not to rip the pocket of those skinny jeans.

But now, you've inadvertently downloaded the "Spiderman app." Don't worry, dropping your phone is common—popular even. According to the *Washington Post*, it's cool amongst suburban teens in Washington, DC. A sort of "subversive" trend, like a scar on your knee from a motorcycle accident. And if you know someone who hasn't been lucky enough to drop her phone into the "cat's water bowl," fear not. You can download literally hundreds of shattered glass wallpapers for free (or even purchase) to decorate the background of your smartphone to fit in.[19]

Just look at them. They're beautiful, really. Metal accented buttons. Lightweight and thin. Cutting-edge industrial design, manufactured with microprecision by specialized robots, and hand assembled in Chinese factories. But once the little gadget rears its head in the real world, and those notification wishes of your attention are finally fulfilled, the smartphone functions terribly as an everyday object in our hands. It's fragile, and even the most minor, everyday damage can be difficult to repair.

Don't drop it. Don't get it too wet. Oh, you touched it with sweaty hands?[20] Sorry, your warranty doesn't apply anymore.[21]

A recent survey found that 23 percent of all iPhone owners have a broken screen.[22] This is remarkable considering people in the United Kingdom and the United States tend to replace their smartphones every twenty-two months.[23]

Gadget blogs recommend smartphones because the metallic materials feel good in your hand, but then mention, oh yeah, "the phones are prone to scratches," so if you want it to last, "a case will resolve all of these issues."[24]

A broken iPhone

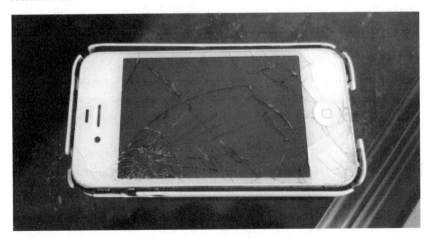

Wait, if you recommend a case that covers the materials of the phone, why are we talking about the materials of the phone?

Even some at the *New York Times* have drunk the Kool-Aid without critical thought. Why not buy a case? "Why pay hundreds of dollars for a phone and not spend a little bit more to protect it?"[25]

It's something the car industry has completely missed.

Now, this top-of-the-line model is really what you should buy. Oh, and if you're one of those people who goes to the gym, you'll want to buy this $5,000 case to prevent your sweat from utterly destroying your car . . .

Why has the fragility and water vulnerability of smartphones become commonplace and accepted? We know glass and metal don't do well in our cement cities. We know we sweat. Drop our phones. That it rains. Eighty-seven percent of all iPhone users have a case. Sixty-six percent of all Android users do.[26] To me, those case usage rates are a sign of failure in user experience design. A failure to embrace typical processes.

As smartphone manufacturers continue to spend millions in research to make phones thinner and thinner and lighter and lighter, and attempt to further and further reduce the absolutely-not-cumbersome edges around the screen in order to give gadget blogs something to drool over, most people just throw an ugly rubber case on them and don't even notice.

Then there's battery life. The Facebook group "I hate 'battery low'" has nearly 400,000 likes for a reason.[27]

The more mobile, the more connected we are to devices, the more and more important battery life becomes. Even in our most mobile place, an airport, we still don't have the resources in place to accommodate our devices' power needs. We huddle in corners and sit on the floor near bathrooms. The need to keep our devices charged has become a burden.

Don't worry, the *New York Post* has lent some advice: "If you frequently use your smartphone or tablet to do business while you're out of the office, it can be hard to sense exactly how much longer you'll be able to work before your battery dies and you need to recharge."[28]

True. Their solution?

"Battery Doctor is a mobile app that will tell you the amount of power and time left on your current battery. It will also give you suggestions on how to get more juice both when you need it now and in the future."

Oh, how I love screen-based thinking. So, in order to solve my battery problem, I'm supposed to launch another app to run on my battery-draining screen?

As mainstream phones keep getting bigger and bigger, it's harder and harder to even squeeze them in and out of your front pocket. Some thinner models made with aluminum can even bend with a little force.[29]

Hours of battery life vs. % screen brightness

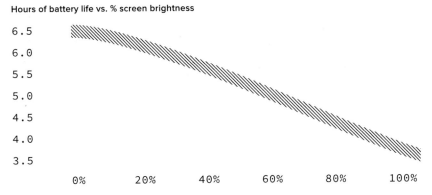

(Source: *Wired*)

Size of iPhone

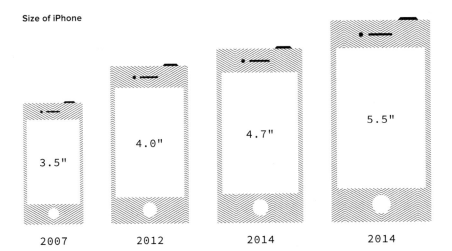

99

So I say, forget it. Stop taking your phone out of your pocket.

And no, I'm not saying, "If you don't have one already, go out and grab a smartwatch with an operating system designed around scrolling through annoying notifications on an ultratiny screen while your phone stays in your pocket."

Buzz.

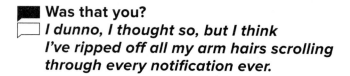

Was that you?
I dunno, I thought so, but I think I've ripped off all my arm hairs scrolling through every notification ever.

I say, put your smartphone away, forget that notification-minded smart-watch for a moment, and let technology completely fade into the background.

Sure, there are extreme ways of doing this. A designer at a technology conference once described to me his twenty-first-century vacation from the cries of his smartphone with wild-eyed enthusiasm.

> "Then, when you arrive, you toss your smartphones into a bucket . . .
> Your name, it's like, whatever you want it to be. . . . You can't talk about
> everyday stuff like work. There are no clocks on the wall. No watches.
> Watches are forbidden. . . . It's the best thing I've ever done in my life."

I've never been to the "summer camp for adults where grown-ups go to unplug, get away, and be kids again,"[30] that he was describing to me, so I can't guarantee that this designer, let's call him Craig, wasn't exaggerating when he told me about his latest grand adventure—but the annual cellphone-free event is real. Camp Grounded, run by Digital Detox, provided Craig with a getaway from tech to remember what it was like to live without hashtags and with human contact—bond, share, and have fun with roughly two hundred adults in the wilderness.

Craig was glowing from having paid money for someone to take away his technology. Take away his notifications. Take away his ringtone. Take away his phantom vibrations.

Yes, an adult summer camp in the wilderness does sound incredible, and breaking away from any addiction is a good thing; but we're not going to—and we shouldn't—toss our phones into a pile, douse them with gasoline, and watch their microchips melt. That's reacting to symptoms, not preventing the causes.

There's an alternate path. One that allows us to keep our phones in our pockets, that doesn't shun technology, that doesn't just push notifications onto our wrists. One that embraces the power of computing while pushing it forward to do something better. A few of the brightest in tech have already begun working on it.

⋰ ⋰ ⋰ ⋰

In early 2013, a startup called ProtoGeo released a smartphone app called Moves.[31] It was created to track your movement and record your aerobic activity, such as the number of steps you take each day.

Frankly, even at its release, the concept of tracking your movement wasn't that interesting. Cheap pedometers have been available for decades. Highly accurate GPS sport watches have been available for years. And smartphones already had hundreds of exercise-related apps.

But the Moves app had something different that stood out to me upon launch. Something wonderfully expressed in, of all places, its original app icon.* Something that I believe should be the starting point for more innovators in technology:

This app is designed for your pocket.

Unlike the buzzing and beeping of other apps begging you to play with them, this app, well, it likes your pocket. It lives there. It wants to be hidden. And it needs no additional electronic accessories.

It is a different way to approach a mobile experience and a fantastic design constraint. Here's how the app (still available) works: You do your typical thing. You walk. Run if you desire. Cycle if you must. While the

---

* Moves has been acquired by Facebook, and altered this original app icon.

phone sits in your pocket, it uses a few of your smartphone's sensors to collect information about how you move. No extra wearables to wear. The app just works in the background, using the phone's battery as little as possible.

As Rachel Metz said in the *MIT Technology Review* when it was released, "I'm convinced its simplicity represents the future of self-tracking."

It's a beautiful starting point to embrace our typical processes, but the Moves app falls short on the No Interface yardstick. The only thing it really does with all that wonderful data is dump it into a big old graphical user interface, leaving you searching through lists and dashboards for something meaningful.

We can go further. We can solve problems with our phones in our pockets.

✹ ✹ ✹ ✹

The *Wall Street Journal* reported that a British insurance company survey found that the average adult in the United Kingdom "misplaces nine items a day," that a third of respondents spend fifteen minutes a day trying to find lost items,[32] and that people are "most frustrated at losing their house keys."[33]

Cameron Robertson and Paul Gerhardt wanted to help us losers. Funded by Y Combinator[34]—a Silicon Valley organization that provides funding and resources to help founders get their ideas off the ground—the duo created the first generation of Lockitron, a deadbolt that connects to your smartphone. *Wired* raved on its release, "Unlock Your Home with Your Cellphone."

While it sounded exciting, the solution required a special deadbolt replacement and then asked an everyday action to drown in more cumbersome, phone-and-screen-based thinking that was no better than the old lock and key.[35]

1. Walk up to my apartment door.
2. Pull out my smartphone.
3. Wake up my phone.
4. Slide to unlock.
5. Enter my passcode.
6. Exit my last opened app.
7. Exit my last opened group.
8. Swipe through a sea of icons, searching for the app.
9. Tap the app icon.
10. Wait for the app to load.

11. Tap the unlock button.

12. Physically open my apartment door.

A year later, the Lockitron team redesigned their product, not by hiring a shallow-minded industrial designer to make the object shiner or a marketing team to make a stylish but incremental UI shift. Nope, they created a refreshingly new and more useful UX.

The first major change was to their custom deadbolt. They got rid of it. Instead, they made a cover that goes over your existing lock. No need for a new set of door keys.

More impressively, they also thought beyond screens, and eliminated the need for you to remove your phone from your pocket.

You still need to download and install their app on your smartphone, but once you set up the app, your smartphone can remain in its rightful place as a rectangular bump in your jeans. Using Bluetooth technology, the second-generation Lockitron app enabled your phone to talk to your deadbolt without an explicit digital interaction.* So when you're at your own door, Lockitron lets you in and welcomes you home without any need for you to even wake

---

* The first Lockitron did have near-field communication (NFC) capabilities, but unfortunately the market share for NFC was nearly nonexistent at the time.

up your smartphone. Their app didn't thrive off PVS or addiction—it created customer satisfaction by keeping your smartphone in your pocket.

This second-generation Lockitron raised $2.2 million on the crowd-funding site Kickstarter from potential customers.[36] An impressive amount for a door lock.

There are lessons to be learned from Lockitron's approach to its second-generation product. If we embrace our typical processes instead of graphic user interfaces, we can start to discover elegant solutions. All it takes is a little observation, empathy, and understanding.

Sadly, it seems like we are far from kicking the habit.

✦ ✦ ✦ ✦

Self-checkout machines are perceived as a potential big win for numbers-friendly, short-term, "Slap an interface on it!" –minded execs. They use touchscreen graphical user interfaces to shift work from store employees to customers like you. It's a strategy that sounds so alluring—reducing line lengths and labor costs—that the number of self-checkout lanes is expected to continue to increase, and the variety of businesses that install them is expected to grow.[37] You've probably seen self-checkout lanes at superstores like Walmart, Tesco, Sainsbury's, and Safeway.

But something unexpected has coincided with the rising popularity of these machines. It's gotten so bad that a number of chains have decided to close their self-checkout lanes and end their experiments immediately. The stores are losing money because self-checkout lane shoppers are regularly shoplifting.

ABC News, who reported on this "supermarket crime wave," reported estimates that theft at self-service lanes costs the typical American household over $400 a year (cost of stolen goods passed on to other customers). And that theft was "five times more likely" at self-checkout lanes than human-operated ones. Supermarkets Albertsons and Big Y have considered removing the machines.[38]

Maybe standing at the self-checkout lane causes us to instantaneously lose our moral compass. Maybe something about the screens makes us start inexplicably entering gourmet coffee beans as bananas into the self-checkout machine just to save two dollars.

But I think something entirely different is actually happening. Just ask Chris Matyszczyk, who wrote this for CNET:

> **"There's no line, so you figure you'll try it. You put your shopping basket down, then you begin to scan the items. That part generally works fine. But then there's the bananas. How much do they weigh? How much are they per pound? Which button are you supposed to press?"[39]**

The small increase in theft that correlates with self-checkout machines is probably because we're lost. We sometimes have no idea what we're doing. No matter what your cat appears to be doing on your iPad, touchscreen interfaces are not inherently intuitive.

The BBC reported that "48% of Britons think self-service checkouts are a nightmare, neither quick nor convenient."[40] In another study, nearly 60 percent of those in the United Kingdom who stole something from a supermarket did so because they "gave up trying to scan something that wouldn't register"[41] (the top reason theft occurs, according to that study).

In the United States, the *Wall Street Journal* reported that Walmart "discovered after increasing the number of self-checkout systems across its more than 4,000 U.S. stores that longer lines began forming at its staffed checkouts to deal with customers with more complicated and time-consuming transactions, such as shoppers who used coupons and price matching."[42]

As Farhad Manjoo once said, "the human supermarket checker is superior to the self-checkout machine in almost every way. The human is faster. The human has a more pleasing, less buggy interface. The human doesn't expect me to remember or look up codes for produce, she bags my groceries, and unlike the machine, she isn't on hair-trigger alert for any sign that I might be trying to steal toilet paper."[43]

And it's not just happening for checkout lanes. UIs are even appearing at places where we order food, like Jack in the Box, McDonald's, Burger King, Taco Bell, KFC, and Applebee's. Instead of people, customers are dealing with unintuitive, tedious, slow, and sometimes frustrating digital interfaces; and occasionally they're committing petty theft by accidentally tapping that they're adding a small bag of chips when they actually grab a jumbo gulp.

When McDonald's, for example, started seeing their sales slide in 2014, industry experts advised that the fast food giant focus on "food and branding."[44] What did they do instead? They installed touchscreens to attract younger customers. Joel Cohen, president of the Cohen Restaurant Marketing Group in Raleigh, North Carolina, said in response, "I'm just wondering if they're forgetting about their strengths, which are speed and convenience."[45]

What if, instead, we followed the first principle of No Interface? What if we understood our typical processes around payment and avoided using an interface?

This was the promise of Square's Wallet.

With the Square experiment, when you were within fifty meters of a store, your name and picture showed up on the cash register without you having to wake up your phone, or even open the Square app. When you activated their Pay with Square Auto Tab feature for a particular restaurant ahead of time, a low-energy Bluetooth technology signature from your phone allowed your Square account information to automatically pop up on the store's certified register application.

So did your order history. And since it started working within fifty feet, this actually allowed cafés to delight frequent customers by preparing a typically ordered item before they even walked up to the counter. When you picked up your desired item, your receipt was emailed to you instantly.

In the words of Jack Dorsey, cofounder of Twitter and Square,

"The customer can walk in the store, and the merchant actually gets a notification that the customer is in the store and that [he] had a cappuccino last time. So I can actually start making the cappuccino and say, 'Here David, here's your cappuccino,' and then it's done. It's super simple. And that's what builds loyalty. That's what keeps people coming back. . . . We see it with Starbucks. You go to the same Starbucks again and again, they know your name, they greet you with a smile, they know your order, it's amazing."[46]

Next time, leave your phone in your pocket. (Source: Square Wallet)

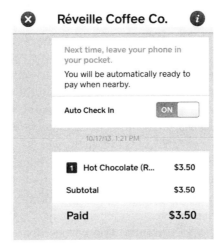

You wouldn't use the Auto Tab feature for everywhere, obviously. But at the places you frequent and trust, it could be a wonderfully elegant transaction that embraces your everyday habits.

Square's back pocket app allowed for faster and better service without costly and unintuitive self-checkout machines, asking you to pull out your credit card, or even forcing you to yank your phone out of your skinny jeans.

MasterCard's PayPass (launched in 2003)[47] requires you to pull out an object (credit card or key fob) and wave it at a special terminal to pay; JPMorgan Chase's Blink system (launched in 2005)[48] requires you to pull out their credit card and wave it at a terminal; American Express's ExpressPay line of cards (launched in 2005)[49] requires you to pull them out and wave them at a terminal; Visa's payWave (launched in 2007)[50] requires you to pull out an object (credit card or key fob) and wave it at a terminal; Google Wallet (launched in 2011)[51] requires you to pull out your phone and wave it at a terminal; Apple Pay (launched in 2014) requires you to pull out your phone and wave it at a terminal.

All of them are missing a higher standard in experience design.

To be fair, Square's technology does require some UI through their Wallet app to initially set up on the customer's smartphone. It also requires UI on the cashier's end to authenticate the order. But after the initial setup the customer doesn't have to deal with an interface—or even a wallet—just to order a latte.

As businesses figure out how to take advantage of the latest in tech, they often turn to *slap an interface on it!* as the answer but actually end up with worse customer experiences and costly mistakes. Although some news media outlets said grocer-chain Albertsons' decision to drop their touchscreen menu-happy self-checkout lanes was because of theft, the store went to the press to say they actually just wanted to bring back a better customer service experience. "We just want the opportunity to talk to customers more," a spokeswoman said about the move to drop their self-checkout interfaces. "That's the driving motivation."[52]

The same goes for Square Auto Tab. In the words of *Wired*, "the appeal was all about increasing human contact. By taking all the bits of paper, bills, and cruddy pieces of plastic out of the equation, a commercial transaction became more of a pure human interaction."[53]

As a startup trying to disrupt a global payments system, Square's Auto Tab provided magical experiences at small, locally-owned cafés, but to the remorse of its delighted loyal following and deep-pocketed investors, it struggled with the huge burden of mainstream adoption of its seamless Wallet app technology.*

That struggle might be because it embraced typical processes for consumers but not for businesses. This enormous undertaking—to educate enough cafés to understand the full power of their elegant system —proved too much for a small company. Even their biggest partnership—one to enable Square Wallet at Starbucks across the US—wasn't favorable for Square financially,[54] Starbucks employees weren't introduced to the system,[55] and worse, it never included Auto Tab. So with its biggest partner, on its biggest stage, Square Wallet was just another app at Starbucks that required you to pull out your phone, wake it up, find the app, launch it, and push a button to get a barcode that then had to be scanned.

(Shiver). *Please, let's keep those phones in our pockets whenever possible.*

Auto Tab remains an important moment in the history of computing because it started scratching the surface for something greater in experience design. Something extraordinary happens when we start imagining

---

* Square has declared it will take "everything we learned from Wallet" into apps like Square Order, a takeout ordering app.

screenless solutions. And what's wild is that these solutions are starting to become possible by keeping your smartphone in your pocket.

It's time to rethink our approach. Our smartphones are powerful computing devices capable of elegant solutions far beyond notifications and shallow pinches and zooms. We can start by avoiding screens and embracing our typical processes.

Let's continue with a closer look at one of the most accepted practices in creating new technology today: wireframes.

10. Lazy Rectangles

That's a great wireframe. We nailed it. We're going to make a billion dollars.

When the design process for new technology begins, it often starts brilliantly.

"What's good about that?" an elderly senior citizen is asked about her daily foot rub.

This path is fantastic.

"Hmph," a painter watching his paint dry is looked at with genuine curiosity, his techniques and typical processes well-noted.

It's journalistic. Qualitative. Without fail, enlightening.

It's a practice that can unmask new opportunities, uncover unknown yet common problems, illuminate regular routines, and find those things that are actually important to the end customer. And just a few weeks of these open-minded observations and conversations with customers is a marvelous first step that many smart people in technology use today to create something useful.

But it's certainly not the only smart first step taken in tech today.

Some start with history. Go beyond an Internet image search and—yikes—dust off old books for classic, beautiful examples where others have solved similar problems you're trying to tackle today. Like Jony Ive did with Dieter Rams's ideas of simplicity to inspire the forms for things like, oh, the iMac, iPhone, iPad, Apple Watch, and later versions of iOS.

Quantitative insights can be fantastic as well.

A smart analytics team can reveal patterns about customer behavior that may have been overlooked by everyone else in the organization. There's a good reason why McKinsey found that "companies championing the use of customer analytics are 6.5 times more likely to retain customers, 7.4 times more likely to outperform their competitors on making sales to existing customers, and nearly 19 times more likely to achieve above-average profitability."[1] Uh, because it's a great idea.

The lessons of analytics are often aggregated by wonderful means, as well.

Walls are covered in imagery. Mood boards are created around the emotional qualities of aspirational outcomes. User stories, personas, scenarios, and other means of aggregation provide an enormously useful guide into what must be accomplished to make something great for the customers.

But then, the creativity stops.

The amazing stack of unique problems is forgotten. The rich pile of specific insights disappears. Instead, from the unique opportunities emerges the expected. Organic insights are morphed into mechanical results. One-of-a-kind is turned into a square peg for a square hole. Because screens come before problems.

We do this:

And we do it again. And again. And again. No matter the client, the industry, or the problem we're trying to solve, the creative process for developing technological solutions repeats the lazy act of drawing a screen.

Where does the logo go? How big is it?

And in particularly polluted organizations, the more screens, the better the designer seems to be doing.

■ I pumped out a 32-screen flow today!
▢ *What!? You're the man!*

No, he's not. As designers, as makers of technology, we're here to solve problems in the most elegant ways possible. Our research allows us to identify new and unique problems to solve. Our creative drive to discover what motivates our customers is a fantastic way to start. But then, so often, we commit the common, terrible mistake:

Insight
+ insight
+ insight
+ insight
= screen.

Repeat.

We learn fascinating things, then we draw a lazy rectangle. We start asking what generic pattern libraries we should use, and toss in a parallax scroll . . . or whatever is trendy at the moment. Like the hamburger icon:

Bun

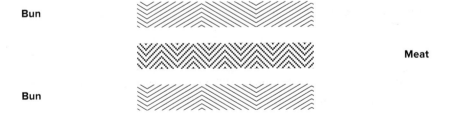

Meat

Bun

I'm the sexy rounded rectangle hamburger man with all the things you really need buried inside!

We end up asking questions like, "How can we help this 82-year-old diabetes patient using this form field?"

Ugh.

Unique problems don't have generic answers. Yes, in some cases a graphical user interface is a decent solution. But so often we throw away our best stuff, our opportunity to do something new and different, the very moment that marker hits whiteboard. Before we can even solve a problem meaningfully, we throw away the opportunity to do something better.

Digital products can do so much more than have a fancy front end.

Even if your company's core product is an interface, not everything that comes after has to be an interface. If things were that rigid, Apple Computer, the personal computer company, would have never become Apple Inc., the world's largest consumer electronics company. If companies didn't go after opportunities beyond what they do today, Netflix would still be mailing DVDs in red envelopes.

Great thinkers adapt. Great companies offer their customers the best possible solutions, whether they have a graphical user interface or not.

Alan Cooper—who brought user research to the software world back in 1992—once wrote to technologists, "Our most effective tool is profoundly simple: Develop a precise description of our user and what he wishes to accomplish."[2]

What he wishes to accomplish is rarely to use a menu, a drop-down, or other outcomes of lazy rectangles.

* * * *

In 1967, a group of pocket radio and TV manufacturers got together for the first annual Consumer Electronics Show (CES). It was a chance to show off the tech of the future—things like "$8 radios the size of a pack of cigarettes."[3]

By 1984, the annual event started gathering over 100,000 attendees. The growing audience at the technology trade show made it a destination at which to announce new products and services. In 1985, Nintendo revealed its first gaming console at CES. In 1992, Apple showed off its PDA, the Newton.[4]

At the show in January 2010, a car security company had a booth at CES to announce their new smartphone app. They said it "has many other capabilities beyond remote start," including helping people "pop the trunk." At

CES that year, which had attracted companies from around the world, their app stood out to the event's judges. It was awarded the "Best of Innovations Honors."[5]

From a wireframe perspective, it actually wasn't that bad.

On the home screen, five actions were clearly visible. The icons in the final design were even paired with text to help customers avoid any ambiguity. Those large five actions—lock, unlock, trunk, and panic—all seem like common, appropriate actions for an app that controls your car. It wasn't a beautiful interface, but the wireframe was coherent. Maybe the judges at CES were on point.

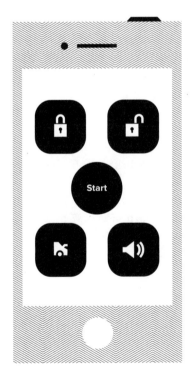

A simple wireframe of the app

Well, hold on to that thought for a moment.

Consider that we think this is decent because we're used to seeing things made with wireframes. Consider that we think this is good because we're used to screen-based thinking. And then consider an alternative path.

Let's actually look at the experience of using one of the functions from the app. Say, opening the trunk.

We already know one great way to start: Observation—watching people do the thing you're interested in improving in the environment in which they typically do that thing. It's almost too obvious.

If you watch an older man carry something to the trunk of his car, it's clear to see that his arms are full. His feet are free. He's carrying something heavy. He doesn't want to put down the heavy object, pull out his smartphone, tap and swipe, put away his phone, and then potentially throw out his back trying to pick up the heavy object again. Not too good news for our app makers.

I didn't make the observation. The Ford Escape design team did. In the "crossover SUV market awash with new models," Ford was hoping to create something that would distinguish its SUV from the others.[6]

Did they make an app with bigger buttons? Add voice commands so that their customers can stand in a parking lot shouting random commands at their trunk?

Nope.

They put a set of sensors under the bumper that can read a foot kick—a simple and easy action that works within the typical process of carrying something heavy to the trunk.

When the trunk opens from a foot kick, it feels like magic. No buttons to press. No interfaces to learn. Some 47 percent of Escape owners purchased this optional feature that attempted to work within the constraints of real life instead of pixel dimensions. As *Forbes* said, "That's a pretty robust rate for an option that hasn't appeared anywhere else before."[7]

Good design solves problems. Good experience design isn't about good screens, it's about good experiences.

There is so much screen-based thinking for cars. It's a screen-obsessed industry in which some companies pride themselves on awful touch screen center consoles. Where the most innovative companies say things like, "We started with a blank slate—17" of glass—which is the centerpiece of the interior."[8] Tesla, you have a fantastic company vision and beautiful cars, but a blank slate is not a 17-inch touch screen. It's dangerous to take a driver's eyes off the road. Let's solve real problems that embrace typical processes, not screens.

Look up.

When a foot kick breaks the electrical field via the two motion sensors at the back of trunk, the system knows to open the trunk. And if you're reading this caption to understand mechanical engineering, read another book. (Just kidding. I'm glad you're here.)

Even when a car isn't on the road, there are still legitimate problems to solve. Like having a boiling hot interior after your car's been sitting in a cement parking lot, baking from the sun. It can get so hot that according to NBC News, "more than 36 children die in overheated cars every year in the United States." Dogs left in cars are also fatal victims of the heat. The National Highway Traffic Safety Administration (NHTSA) found that "cars parked in direct sunlight can reach internal temperatures up to 131°F to 172°F (55°C to 78°C)."[9]

When in Australia recently, I ran across an ad for the Nissan Leaf. It took over an entire wall of the Sydney Airport. It read:

What If Your Phone Could Make Your Car Cooler?

I'm not making that up. It was part of a global ad campaign. You download Nissan's app from an app store, toss it into your sea of icons, and manually launch it when ready. Here's a screenshot of the app being advertised:

Leaf app with climate tab selected. (Image modified for clairty: text sharpened and logo removed).

How does it work? Here's Nissan's explanation:

> **Here's the scenario: It's a sweltering August day and you know you'll be getting in the car in 15 minutes. Use your smartphone or computer to remotely turn on the air conditioning and voila, you'll be entering a nice cool car.**[10]

Another great car misdirected by trying to solve problems with screens? The result of a lazy rectangle? Well, let's consider their scenario through open-minded observations. We know how.

It's a sweltering day, and your car is heating up in a parking lot. Wherever you are at the moment, you probably aren't thinking about how to babysit your car in the distant parking lot.

Say you're at the movies. After all, when things heat up in the summer, movie ticket sales do, too.[11] Pulling out a bright screen in a dark theater is probably not going to make the people around you very happy. Even CNN says looking at your phone during a movie is one of the "most annoying smartphone habits."[12]

Dude, turn off your phone!

What your car might look like on a hot day (Laitr Keiows / CC BY 3.0)

Even if people around you were OK with it, 15 minutes before the end of a decent movie, you probably aren't thinking about how your car interior is cooking.

Where you might be on a hot day (Source: NASA Goddard Space Flight Center / CC BY 2.0)

Can we again reduce the number of steps in a way that embraces a typical process? Here's a simplified view:

1.   **Leave car in hot parking lot and go inside movie theater.** — **Me**
2.   ~~Decide to return to my car~~.
3.   ~~15 minutes before I return to my car,~~
      ~~remember that my car could be warm.~~
4.   ~~Pull out my smartphone.~~
5.   ~~Wake up my phone.~~
6.   ~~Press my thumb to login.~~
7.   ~~Exit my last-opened app.~~
8.   ~~Exit my last-opened group.~~
9.   ~~Swipe through a sea of icons,~~
      ~~searching for the app.~~
10.   ~~Tap the app icon.~~
11.   ~~Wait for the app to load and try to find~~
      ~~the cooling action~~
12.   ~~Make a guess with the menu and tap "Climate."~~
13.   ~~Tap "Turn Climate Control On."~~
14.   ~~Wait 15 minutes~~.
15.   **Return to cool car.** ———————————— **My Goal**

Hmm.

To find someone coming up with an original solution unpolluted by lazy rectangles, we'd have to go so far back, we'd end up at a time when even the Internet wasn't regularly used. Back to 1991, when the online tech scene was so young there were fewer than 1 million websites worldwide. (For some context, there were 100 million[13] websites by 2007, and nearly a billion[14] by 2014).

That year, Mazda Motor Corporation released a new model of their luxury sedan called the 929. Being the fourth-largest Japanese automaker in the United States at the time,[15] they packed the 929 model with forward-thinking features in hopes of attracting new customers. The *New York Times* called the car "a snazzy new model."[16]

In this time before websites, before apps, before our lives were inundated by smartphones and -watches, before screens seemed like the solution to every problem, Mazda offered an optional feature in their 929 that attempted to tackle overwhelming interior car temperatures without any graphical user interface at all.

Clark Vitulli, then senior vice president and chief operating officer of Mazda Motor of America Inc., told the *Chicago Tribune*, "our goal is to become a world-class, premium motor car company, and you don't do that by being the cheapest or the most expensive, but by being distinctive and personal so that there's nothing else out there like your cars."[17]

Clark sounds like someone who cares about creating great experiences.

How did Mazda do it? They solved the problem elegantly by embracing the actual situation instead of what works best on a screen.

It goes without saying: Your car heats to unbearable temperatures when it's hot outside. So, Mazda installed one of the oldest and most common devices to check when it's hot: a thermometer. When the temperature crosses a certain threshold, a sensor acts like a trigger, letting the system know your car is heating up.

When that trigger is activated, small fans started to cool off the car. And since the sensor knew it was hot outside, it could be assumed that the sun was beating down on your car, so Mazda installed solar panels on top of the car to power the entire automatic ventilation feature. When you return to your 929, the system has automatically cooled down your car without using any gas, and perhaps just as importantly, no interface. By understanding the context, the 929 used the cause of the problem—the sun—as a solution to the problem.

Smart.

And when the temperature sensor detected that it wasn't hot outside, the 929's solar panels charged the battery.

Smarter.

But maybe not good enough.

In their tests, Mazda found that on a hot day (say, a sunny day with no shade in the Arizona desert), interior car temperatures could reach up to a ludicrous 167 degrees (75°C). Their system could make the interior temperature significantly cooler, but it tended to only reduce the temperature to a still scorching 140 degrees (60°C).[17]

The 929 did save gas because less air conditioning was needed to bring the car down to comfortable levels. And the system did so automatically, without a cumbersome experience for the driver. But the interior temperatures were still far from ideal. You would never want to leave anything sensitive to temperature—dog, child, goldfish, or gallon of milk—inside the car.

Eighteen years later, in 2009, Toyota took another shot at the same problem by leveraging the lessons of the 929.

An optional moonroof on their 2009 Prius slightly opened when it was hotter than 86 degrees outside.[18] Small fans then drew warm air out of the moonroof, and the whole system was powered by a solar panel on the roof of the car. Unlike the 929, the solar panel didn't power the battery on cold days, but Toyota did report better cooling results.

With a system based on modern components, Toyota claimed that indoor temperatures reached "near ambient" temperatures, which meant that if it was 90 degrees outside, the car wasn't too much hotter. (But not cool enough to keep your children in the car. Please don't keep your children in the car. Or an ice cream cake.) For the Prius, the feature was so popular that sales numbers for the optional feature exceeded even company estimates.[19]

The system—still available—isn't yet good enough to prevent heat-related accidents, but it's a fascinating feature and in high demand for good reason. Instead of asking us to learn a new interface, it works within our normal, everyday habits.

You're smart. You know how to look at a problem and understand the unique problems. You see the opportunities for improvement.

But if you're working on software, don't throw up a lazy rectangle as a solution. We so often miss the magic when we draw a screen and wonder how to fill it with generic elements, or cool new tricks, such as parallax scrolling or the hamburger button.

Instead, by understanding the context, by embracing typical processes, we can create more elegant solutions. Things that feel like magic.

Automatically opening trunks and cooling cars are just an early start. We can and should use machines to do things much greater.

Let's embrace typical processes, not screens. Let's aim for elegant solutions, not lazy rectangles.

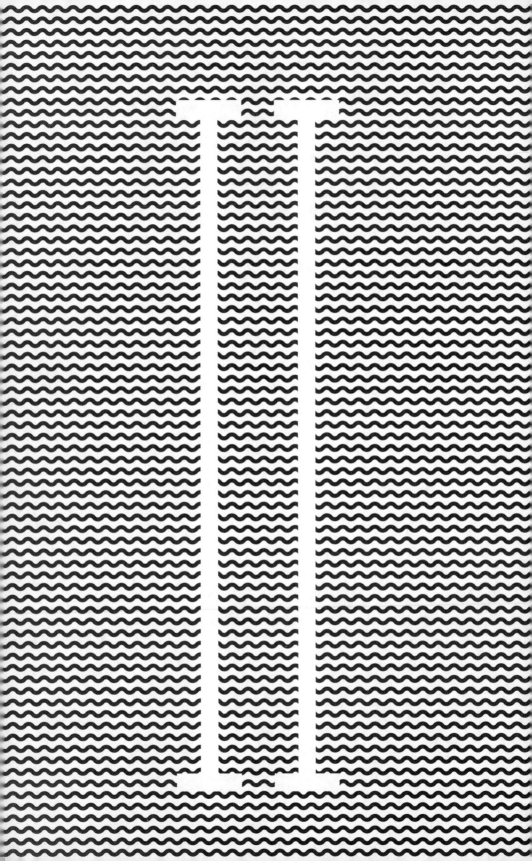

Principle Two: Leverage Computers Instead of Serving Them

11. Computer Tantrums
Your password must be at least 18,770 characters and cannot repeat any of your previous 30,689 passwords

The technology industry has not only been able to make huge improvements in the past few decades, it has also been capturing a growing amount of educational mindshare,[1] thereby producing an even stronger, deeper-thinking overall tech workforce. Computer science (CS) became the most popular undergraduate major at well-rounded Stanford University in 2012,[2] and by 2014, humanities programs at Stanford felt so left out they started offering joint majors in which traditional requirements for music or English were mixed with CS courses.[3] And at art and design schools around the world, interaction design programs—which teach young designers how to build great experiences—have sprouted up quickly.

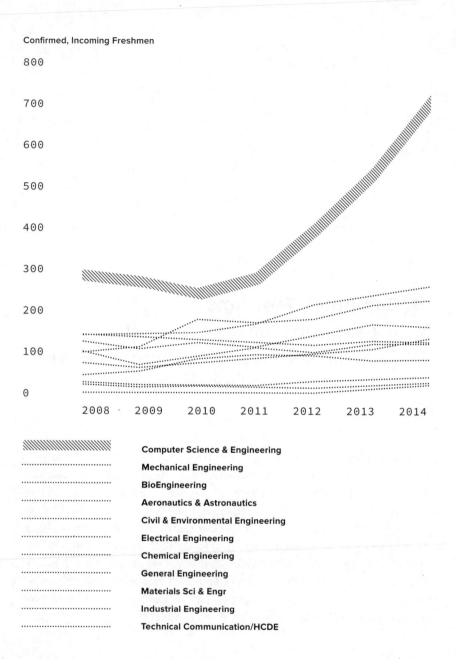

Confirmed, Incoming Freshmen

Legend:
- Computer Science & Engineering
- Mechanical Engineering
- BioEngineering
- Aeronautics & Astronautics
- Civil & Environmental Engineering
- Electrical Engineering
- Chemical Engineering
- General Engineering
- Materials Sci & Engr
- Industrial Engineering
- Technical Communication/HCDE

Major intentions for incoming freshman at the University of Washington.
(Source: University of Washington computer science department)

All of this momentum has done wonders for computational power. Just look at this 1997 work of art:

```
1. e4 c6  2. d4 d5  3. Nc3 de4  4. Ne4 Nd7  5. Ng5 Ngf6  6.
Bd3 e6  7. N1f3 h6  8. Ne6 Qe7  9. 0-0 fe6  10. Bg6 Kd8  11.
Bf4 b5  12. a4 Bb7  13. Re1 Nd5  14. Bg3 Kc8  15. ab5 cb5  16.
Qd3 Bc6  17. Bf5 ef5  18. Re7 Be7  19. c4
```

Beautiful, isn't it?

It marked a pivotal event in popular computing history.

In 1984, 13 years before it happened, it's important to understand that chess champion Garry Kasparov—the victim of the brilliance above—was under similar competitive pressure. The final, championship round in 1984 had lasted far longer than it ever had before—48 games with 40 draws against the reigning champion—and there was no end in sight.

Even earlier, when he was just 12, and his countrymen were the best at the game, Garry Kasparov was better; he won the USSR championship. At 16, he won the World Junior Championship. At 17, he was a grandmaster.[4] And by 1984, at 21, he had advanced to that final round of the 1984 World Chess Championship.[5]

It was so grueling, Kasparov lost 17 pounds[6] from the final round. The president of Fédération Internationale des Échecs (FIDE) ended the match for concern about the health of the chess players.

Kasparov was enraged about that World Chess Championship's first and only declared tie.[7] Ultracompetitive and thirsty for what was likely his eventual victory, he called the suspension an "under the table" deal portraying the chess establishment as fearful of his own ascension, telling a talk show host: Why would they want a "half-Jewish, half-Armenian" chess player rising to the top?[8]

When his 1984 championship match was resumed through a rematch in the (restructured) 1985 World Chess Championship, Garry took the world title at last and completed his deserved ascension to the top of the international chess food chain. It's important to understand his dominance, his unrelenting passion. But as unstoppable as he seemed, he couldn't have possibly seen what was coming in 1997.

On May 6, 1997, in front of a television studio of 500 people in New York City,[9] Kasparov had to rely on his genius mind to conclude a series of matches—the patterns he had seen before, and the strategies that had worked in his storied past. IBM's Deep Blue, the computer competitor that IBM offered $700,000[10] for Kasparov to beat, relied on 510 of some of the best processors of the day, running in parallel, that could analyze from 100 to 330 million potential moves per second.[11]

Promotional posters around New York featured a prominent image of Kasparov staring straightforward over a blurred chess board with a simple slogan: "How do you make a computer blink?"

Turns out, it was Kasparov who blinked.

When seeing his fate, Kasparov put his head in his heads, a vein from his forehead jutted out, and a look of frustration ran across his face. The intense, passionate Kasparov knew it before IBM's computer had even completed the game: He had lost to a machine. Garry knocked over his King in resignation and frustration, and walked away from the game and stage utterly distraught.

Not even the programmers who made IBM Deep Blue seemed to know it was coming. Over a decade after the 1997 chess match against Kasparov, an IBM engineer said the computer's fatal blow to Garry was a glitch.[12] An error. The computer actually didn't have the confidence to make a particular move, so it choose one at random. But maybe that's what made it human enough to beat a human after all.

Quick, what is 348202348920 times 128419024705729?

By 1997, we had already long ago surrendered that we could not compete with computers in straightforward calculations. We had also known for generations that machines could outmuscle us. Programmable cranes lifted concrete to build skyscrapers. We knew they could outrun us. Trains speeding over tracks were taken for granted. But to outthink us strategically . . . that was something new.

IBM's stock rose 3.6 percent[13] the day after Deep Blue beat Kasparov at a prized human skill: analytical thought. It was a pivotal event in computing history that gave us even more reason to admire the technology we created together.

In 1997, Deep Blue was classified as a supercomputer. It was celebrated and mythicized in magazines, and by computer and chess geeks alike. A piece of it was even moved to the Smithsonian National Museum of American History in Washington, DC, for attendees to admire behind glass.[14]

But today, Deep Blue's processing power would be, well, pathetic. Even compared against the computers we dread—our everyday, dusty old desktop systems that seem so impossibly slow we dream of tossing them out a third-story window and watching them smash into thousands of pieces on the sidewalk. Even against them, in some categories of computing measurements, Deep Blue doesn't stand a chance. The incredible human-developed algorithms inside Deep Blue gave it a foundation, but its processors empowered it with the rapid decision-making ability to beat Kasparov. Yet, an ordinary machine today can crunch data over 100 gigaflops faster than the one that had the ability to outthink the world's greatest chess player.[15]

So what are we doing with these machines today? How are designers of new technology taking advantage of the incredible computational power of machines so powerful they could clobber chess grandmasters?

We do this:

Your password must be at least 18770 characters and cannot repeat any of your previous 30689 passwords.[16]

That's a real error message from a recent version of Windows.

But the error message isn't interesting because it came from Microsoft. It's compelling because it's evidence of something much larger. Something that impacts all of us every time we use the almighty, powerful computer and all of its wonders that influence our everyday lives.

Hey, do you want to hear the most annoying sound in the world?

Built with incredible computational muscle, born with the ability to access its own exact location anywhere in the world, created with the innate thinking process to provide more timely and rich knowledge than an entire public library in a millisecond, formed to be able to remember a generation of enlightenment, computing devices have largely turned into this:

Waaaaaaaaaaaaaahhhhhhhh!!!!!

Like us at our worst: the terrible twos. A state of life when we are an emotional wreck, struggling with rules, and responding to unexpectedness with simple variations of a single word expressed through our limited vocabulary:

No. No! NO!

No, your username is not valid. No, Chase Bank online requires numbers in your name. No, your name isn't unique enough for Gmail—pick another name. No, you can't leave that blank, you need to give us your

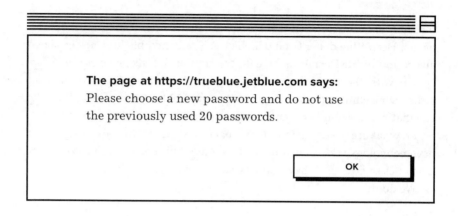

The page at https://trueblue.jetblue.com says:
Please choose a new password and do not use
the previously used 20 passwords.

OK

title—Dr., Mr., or Mrs.—it is MANDATORY at London Heathrow Airport to connect to Wi-Fi.

No, your password is not strong enough. No, it's not long enough. No, it needs an uppercase letter. No, it needs a punctuation mark. No, not that one. No, you cannot use one of your last 20 previous passwords on JetBlue.

No, dates have to be MM-DD-YYYY at the *New York Times* online archive, not MM-DD-YY. No, I don't care if it'll be a hundred years until that matters again.

No, these fields are required; do it now, or I will turn red with rage!

Oops! Your time has expired. Please hit refresh to reorder these concert tickets before they sell out. :)

Oh, I see. If we just add a smiley face and say "Oops!" it won't matter when we ruin someone's life by popping up an error message before saving the big presentation. And if you smile when stealing cookies as a two-year-old, maybe your cuteness will keep Dad from getting mad.

Error. You must accept the T&C to proceed.

These are not outliers. Not edge cases. These are reflective of common occurrences. And examples of our bizarre relationship with computers:

We. Serve. Them.

It's a cookbook. While we deservingly adore our age of bits, the incredible progress we have made, and the incredible impact it has had on our lives, we remain lackeys to bits and their needs.

We are forced to navigate complex databases to obtain simple information. We are required to memorize countless passwords with rules like one capital letter, two numbers and a punctuation mark. Spew out random facts for an algorithm like our childhood best friend's name. Most importantly, we're constantly pulled away from the stuff we actually want to be doing.

We serve computers.

It's sad. The thing we love doesn't understand us. It forces us to speak another language in order to communicate. It struggles with rules.

But there's a different way of going about it. A different approach to making computer software. One that takes advantage of the powerful machines of our day and lets them fulfill hopes and optimistic dreams. I say, let's reverse the relationship. I say, instead of us serving computers, let's have computers serve us.

This means inverting the paradigm. Finding a way for us to avoid things like form fields, and finding ways for them to more seamlessly fit into our lives. It's not about doing what's easy; it's about doing what's best.

This is a new age of technology, a time in which computers are adored for all their power and beauty. So let's focus on computer systems that can fulfill those expectations. Let's bottle all that excitement, the educated workforce, the market enthusiasm, and that incredible computing power to make something incredible, instead of tantrum-throwing imitations of two-year-olds.

Let's make systems that serve us.

12. Machine Input
I saved your life, and I didn't even need a password

Our powerful senses. They're complex and instantaneous—seeing, hearing, tasting, and so on—and taken for granted as the obvious and transparent ways for us to gather information. Rotten meat stinks. Sandpaper feels rough.

But when it comes to computers, we build them with a different information-gathering system. We use a methodology that fuels our bizarre relationship with them. We make them rely on *user input*.

It's a path that's forced misunderstandings and two-year-old tantrums. Perhaps *user input* is inspired from the breathtaking beauty of repetitious medical forms to be completed while we wait for a slow doctor, or those wonderful tax forms that ascertain how much money we owe to the government this year. Regardless of the source of inspiration, the awful information-gathering process we use over and over again with computers couldn't be more bizarre.

You look at a molded loaf of bread and, thanks to your senses, you can almost instantly conclude it's rotten after seeing mold and discoloration. Conversely, a common, modern computer system—sophisticated and advanced, able to crunch mathematical formulas in milliseconds, house terabytes of data, and access pedabytes more online—is asked to gather information using nearly the same methods it did way back in the early days of personal computing, when floppy disks weren't just the icons for saving files:

Sign in:

Username

Password

Or register:

Preferred username

Password

Password again

##########

CAPTCHA answer

Food:

Country of purchase* ▼

Type of food* ▼

Color of food*

Date of purchase*

☑ Agree to Terms & Conditions

☑ Subscribe to Newsletter

*Required fields

Submit

Ah, the joys of user input.

You know what? Fuck dropdowns.

It's time to teach our powerful machines to sense the world more like we do. The technology exists, it's prevalent, and yet it remains mostly unused in the consumer marketplace. It's a great way to have computers serve us. Make our lives better.

It's a path that industry visionaries have been working toward for decades.

✒   ✒   ✒   ✒

In the early 1990s, a growing number of computer geeks saw the future of computing as polygons painted with pixels. Snap on a pair of face computers, goggles, or headgear, and live your life through an interface that simulates real-life elements. "The goal of virtual reality is simple: it's total submersion. Complete detachment from reality," they would say.[1] Virtual reality, they believed, was the age to come. To them, it felt inevitable.

Sure, maybe it would become a world where people would be so addicted to the virtual that the real—potential conversations with other people IRL (in real life)—would cause panic and stress; but you know, that might not have been all that different from the world those geeks already lived in anyway. They saw the personal computer as a bearer of freedom, and their future should only be more dominated by screens.

In September of 1991, *Scientific American* printed a monumental essay that argued for an alternative future.[2] Titled "The Computer for the 21st Century," the article was far more than a critique of the virtual reality concept. In fact, you could say the essay is one of the most important pieces ever written about our relationship with computers. It wasn't the first time these ideas were discussed, but it was probably the most impactful presentation. And it could easily be argued that the essay is the butterfly's wings that eventually led to the creation of this book you're holding.

Author, genius Mark Weiser, I bow in respect.

Mark was part of a small group of researchers at Xerox PARC that explored the future of our lives with computers. The labs that had created the first graphical user interface. In the early 1990s, they were trying to predict the next wave of computing. They started experimenting with ideas to create invisible interfaces at a time before most people had even heard of the Internet; and email, well, was not even an understood phrase yet.

The future via 1991. (Source: Nicole Stenger / CC BY 3.0)

They looked back to see the future. They noted that in the 1950s many people would share the resources of one room-sized mainframe computer. Then, 30 years later, in the 1980s, each person had his or her own computer (partially due to *Xerox's own invention* of the graphical user interface). And, as they saw it, by the year 2000 that trend of increasing computing power per person would only grow further: each person would soon have many computing devices working for them. If you've got a phone, tablet, and laptop, you can already see some of their decades-old vision in action today.

Back then, Xerox's team defined new, ubiquitous computer sizes that should now sound familiar, like the Pad—their concept for a paper-sized computer. But at Xerox, they started to see something beyond more screen-based devices. "The most profound technologies are those that disappear. They weave themselves into the fabric of everyday life until they are indistinguishable from it," Weiser wrote in that 1991 essay.

Something was wrong with the interface. And Weiser started to figure it out all the way back in 1991. "More than 50 million personal computers have been sold," he wrote, "and the computer nonetheless remains largely in a world of its own. It is approachable only through complex jargon that has nothing to do with the task for which people use computers." The inventors of the graphical user interface were looking for a way to think beyond the ordinary graphical user interface.

It's not a far stretch to say that the team was scratching the surface of the woes of user input. The kind of input that today requires us to type into form fields, navigate crazy navigation, and type CAPTCHA words. The kind of input that makes us serve the computer.

Roy Want, also a member of the Xerox PARC team, was working on a new computer they called Tab—an "inch-scale computer" in Weiser's words, and vastly more invisible than the screen-based Pad. Along with some of the greatest minds of the day from around the world—Andy Hopper, Andy Harter, Tom Blackie, Mark Chopping, Damian Gilmurray, and Frazer Bennett—Roy Want worked on a kind of Tab computer that the larger group called the Active Badge.

The device was a small, 55 x 55 x 7-millimeter, 40-gram badge with no screen.[3] Using infrared, the badge "broadcasted the identify of its wearer" and acted like a "beacon." Receivers installed inside their office buildings would then automatically and continuously process those signals.

To see what was possible, the Xerox team wore the badges around the office and tried to use the data gathered to solve simple problems. So did collaborators at places like Cambridge, where at one point they had 200 badges in use. Different experiments allowed doors to automatically open to badge wearers and computer displays to boot up with personalized settings as a badge wearer approached. Since only corded phones existed at the time, one experiment with the Active Badge attempted to alleviate receptionists from having to hunt down employees when they received a call by instead having phone calls for a badge wearer be automatically forwarded to the corded phone inside the meeting room where the intended recipient was working.

Rerouting landline telephone calls is now laughable, ancient tech history. But something philosophically groundbreaking was happening with the Active Badge. Our historical relationship with computers was being reversed.

The Active Badge receivers inside these office buildings—the ones that constantly monitored the location of the badge wearers—were sensors. Kinda like your nose. Easily accessible, they seamlessly and continuously received one kind of information. Instead of relying on painful *user input* like form fields and website navigation, the computer system used automatic, sensory, signal-based *machine input*.*

Then, the computer understood what those data signals meant through

---

* I like the term machine input when discussing signals in software design because the phrase itself is an easily understood antithesis to the oft-used user input: "Hey guys, can we use machine input instead of user input here?" But if you hang out all day with mechanical or electrical engineers, just use the term signals.

code written to do what engineers call digital signal processing (DSP). Kinda like how your brain interprets what you smell.

And finally, the computer software acted upon that information based on an algorithm. Like how you decide to eat something because it smells good.

Computers opened doors. Computer displays customized themselves. Computers rerouted phone calls automatically with no dropdown menu, no awkward communication, and nothing inefficient between us and the machine. A beautiful alternative to the ugly:

Which room are you in?

Attic ▼

Log in with Facebook
Sign in with Twitter

Like our own senses, the Active Badge system was programmed to sense location. Instead of forcing an interface that made users serve a password database, the researchers made a computer system that served users in their natural environment. It formed a more fluid conversation between our human needs and the computer's calculations.

Let's change our conversation with computers.

Let's empower computers to observe the world beyond form fields. Let's give them the ability to sense our needs with sensors and other signals. Let's replace tedious *user input* with instantaneous and painless *machine input*—where the computer system finds the information it needs on its own—whenever and wherever possible.

As Weiser wrote, this approach may even help us reconnect with one another:

> By pushing computers into the background, embodied virtuality
> will make individuals more aware of the people on the other ends of
> their computer links. This development may reverse the unhealthy
> centripetal forces that conventional personal computers have

introduced into life and the workplace. ¶ Even today, people holed
up in windowless offices before glowing computer screens may
not see their fellows for the better part of each day.

Recently, a doctor sent me a product, created over a decade after the
Active Badge, that also followed this radical new paradigm: a headlamp
that helped him save more lives.

An emergency physician who also volunteers to do search and rescue,
he's sometimes called upon to save people trapped in caves—a situation
that happened in at least 25 different US states last year.[4] A rope snapped,
a person tripped, or a wrong turn was taken . . . and then the worst. An
adventure turned into claustrophobic loneliness as people were trapped
in caves with diminishing air, light, and hope.

The volunteer search and rescue job to save those people can require
squeezing into small crevices and searching for hours. And then, sometimes, having to drill out trapped, panicked survivors. Fortunately, a
small army of volunteers organized and trained through associations like
the National Cave Rescue Commission (NCRC) are there to help cavers.

Can technology help the noble effort?

The headlamp the doctor sent me is made by Petzl. The company has
its roots in caving, and after more than 40 years of making headlamps,
they could have just slapped an interface on it—so the doctor could check
Kim Kardashian's Instagram while saving lives—but instead they did
something that's unfortunately novel in technology today: They solved a
meaningful problem. And they did it by leveraging computers instead of
catering to them.

Although headlamps aren't unwieldily to use, they can require annoying adjustments for night joggers, hikers, and search-and-rescue workers
who travel through diverse terrain.

For example, they often need a high, bright beam to peer into deep,
dark caves and find survivors. But as they move quickly through unknown
routes to save the victim, that same level of brightness can whitewash a
handheld map.

To solve this problem, Petzl leveraged the power of computers. They put
a light sensor into their headlamp with a microchip that automatically and
instantly adjusts the intensity of light coming out of the headlamp based on
the amount of light sensed outside. The result? As *Gear Junkie* wrote, "You
won't blast your eyes with 300-lumen bounce back if you glance from that
proverbial cliff face above to a glossy map held in hand."[5]

And dimming the light at the right moments means the battery lasts longer. When you're out saving lives, the last thing you want to worry about is interfaces and batteries.

Sensors are one way to provide richer information for machines. They can seamlessly enable a machine to read the needs of the outside world without a submit button. And there are many ways to gather the signals that lead to machine input.

A global positioning system (GPS) radio can let a system know where you're located and calculate contextually appropriate actions. Bluetooth radios can let objects talk to each other to solve problems when they're near each other. A camera can provide color information so that a car can read traffic lights. Over a cellular or wireless connection, a phone in your pocket can automatically look up information to help you.

Let the computer do the search and filter the results. You don't need to deal with dropdowns when you've got powerful computing devices ready and willing to deal with your pain points.

When we think in this different way, when we begin to invert the prevalent computing paradigm of modern day consumer software, unseen opportunities to solve problems more elegantly and usefully become part of our design process.

Another example? Sure.

One of the most entertaining, hardest-hitting National Football League (NFL) linebackers in the 1990s was Junior Seau. At 6-foot-3-inches and 248 pounds when drafted in 1990 by the San Diego Chargers, he was a giant amongst giants.[6] His athleticism and talent made him one of the most enjoyable players to watch, but his selfless personality made him an inspiration. Unlike the tech millionaires and billionaires revered for making apps that cure micro-boredom through addictive virtual farms, Junior actually gave back to the world in a meaningful way.

He opened his restaurant on Thanksgiving for families of domestic violence who had no where else to go. With his charity, the Junior Seau Foundation, he gifted over four million dollars to underprivileged kids so that they could have opportunities they wouldn't otherwise, like the ability to attend college.

George W. Bush awarded him the Volunteer Service Award in 2005, bestowed upon those who dedicate thousands of hours to volunteer service.

Beyond opening his wallet and donating his time, he was known as a smiling, friendly person to friends, family, and the fans who adored him.

"He didn't think he was better than anyone else. I think that's why a lot of people in Oceanside [California] liked him," one fan said on a San Diego television station.[7]

And when another fan, drunk and a bit crazy, jumped out of his seat, leaped, and tackled Junior on the field while he was in full uniform on the sidelines of an NFL game—well, Junior got up, wished the fan "Merry Christmas," and just laughed the whole thing off.[8]

On a separate night, when a military officer nervously introduced himself to Junior at a small bar, Junior inverted the flattery: He thanked the officer for his service, paid for his dinner and drinks, and serenaded him by playing "Brown Eyed Girl" on a ukelele.[9]

His smile so infectious, his attitude so fun-loving, his heart so open to giving all made his suicide shocking. On May 2, 2012, Junior Seau fired a gun into his chest.[10] A shocking, awful, stomach-dropping moment for the many lives he blessed.

In the autopsy, coroners discovered that Junior had chronic traumatic encephalopathy (CTE), a degenerative brain disease. CTE is believed to be caused by repetitive head trauma, in Junior's case, from the many hits he endured while playing football.[11] The brain disease—symptoms include "memory loss, confusion, impaired judgment, impulse control problems, aggression, depression, and, eventually, progressive dementia"—appears to have altered Junior's demeanor from selfless joy to inescapable depression.[12] The sport through which he brought us joy removed his.

Sadly, his case appears to be part of a larger pattern. Thirty-three of the first thirty-four brains of deceased NFL players studied at Boston University showed signs of CTE. After a few years of testing, the league has even admitted in federal court that "it expects nearly a third of retired players to develop long-term cognitive problems and that the conditions are likely to emerge at 'notably younger ages' than in the general population."[13]

Head trauma appears to have serious consequences. For football players at a collegiate or high-school level, where medical personnel are not as trained as they are in the NFL, the health repercussions are more frightening. Considering college football players who are eager to make an impression rarely even report head trauma, the solutions don't seem easy. A survey of 730 elite college football players found that the players report only 1 out of every 27 concussions.[14]

So, should we create a mobile app to solve the problem?

Well, the CDC has one. It's got a cheesy design and is basically a brochure with lots of buttons and menus.

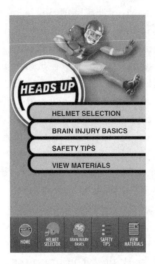

Screenshot of CDC's app (Source: CDC Heads Up App)

Yay!

Actually, I applaud the CDC for making that app. The information is important. And having it on a mobile device could be crucial to some-one trying to help a potential victim or select an appropriate helmet to reduce potential trama. As the welcome screen says, "This app will help you learn about helmet safety, as well as learn how to spot and what to do if you think your child has a concussion or other serious brain injury." That's a good thing.

But when MC10, a flexible sensor manufacturer, worked with Reebok, they aimed for a more elegant solution: the Reebok Checklight. It relies on signals through machine input, and a network of sensors to help detect head trauma when it happens, instead of the menus, tab navigation, and guesswork of user input after the fact. That's better.

Consisting of an accelerometer and gyroscope made of flexible mate-rials, the Reebok Checklight is just a skullcap—something many football players already wear under their helmet—with an LED light on the back.

It fits comfortably, continuously trying to sense any impact to your head without asking you to reset your password every 60 days.

Like a traffic light, Checklight gives feedback through red, yellow, and green LEDs. Intermittent flashing green means it's on and working, yellow means the system believes there is a moderate level impact, and red means there's been heavy trauma to the head. This is not a replacement for proper medical diagnostics—the system can't definitively tell you if a concussion has occurred[15]—but it's an extra data point that can help coaches, parents, and athletes make the right decisions about returning to the field, seeking medical attention, and informing football athletes of potential head trama, possibly before reaching the unfortunate fate of Junior Seau.

This is the kind of tool we can focus on when we forget the interface. When we stop thinking about which screen can do what, and instead focus on solving a problem with as little interaction as possible. And when we solve a customer pain point in a way that actually utilizes the power of the immense progress we've made in computing, well, that's tech worth celebrating.

Let's change our conversation with computers. Let's change the way machines gather information. Let's empower technological solutions with seamless machine input. Let's stop using dropdowns whenever possible. By finding simpler ways of collecting information alone, we can stop serving computers, and have computers serve us.

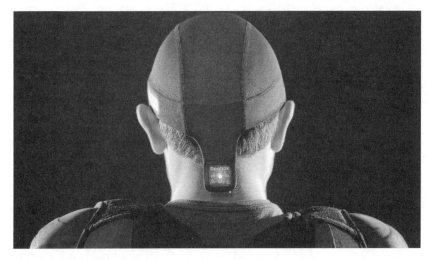

Reebok Checklight (Source: Reebok)

13. Analog and Digital Chores
I know, I suck at life.

You say you'll do it. Then, you don't.

You say, give me another chance—*this weekend, I promise!*—and then you don't do it again. This perpetual disappointment can be frustrating for you, your coworkers, your friends, and the people you love.

But don't feel bad. I understand. Call it privileged. Call it entitled. A lot of us can actually relate to you.

After all, your excuse is the number-one self-reported reason why nearly 70 percent of Australian women aren't doing what they want to in life,[1] why Michigan teens haven't gotten a driver's license,[2] why overstressed Americans don't deal with their stress,[3] and it's even the most self-reported reason why nearly 60 percent of men in the UK don't shower in the morning.[4]

You're too busy.

It even occurs for those with devout faith. The big conclusion of a recent five-year, 20,000-person, 139-country study of Christianity? Christians feel that they are just too busy for God.[5]

The feeling isn't unwarranted. In the United States, we are working more hours than has ever been statistically recorded. Some corporate lawyers are working 15 hours a day. Some schoolteachers work 80 hours a week. The United States is one of the only countries in the world where the government doesn't require companies to give you any time off.[6]

So yeah, you didn't take out the trash. Clean the car. Go for a jog. Brigid Schulte's book *Overwhelmed: Work, Love, and Play When No One Has the Time* was recently in the top 10 on the *New York Times'* Best Seller list for a good reason.[7] Volunteering, one of the most important things we can do for our communities, hit a 10-year low in 2013.[8]

We all have a lot going on; we all wish we could do more for the people we care about; and none of us really want to spend our free moments doing those mindless, embarrassing, strange, or painful chores we feel obligated to get done and don't enjoy.

"There are things you can do individually, though, to save energy," Barack Obama told a crowded room in Springfield, Missouri, when running for president in 2008. "Making sure your tires are properly inflated. Simple thing."

Oh, sure, I'll just do one more chore.

While the country at the time was in the midst of two wars in the Middle East, we were looking for simple, non-time-consuming ways to stop handing our hard-earned gasoline dollars to the Middle East, where oil-bearing countries could be potentially harboring or aiding distant, hardly understood enemies. And the answer to our worries was . . . put more air pressure in our car tires?

Barry, I'm sorry, I've got to take the kids to soccer practice right after work . . . I don't really have time for my car tires.

During that election, the opposing Republican party—whose nominee John McCain was using the slogan "Drill, baby, drill!" in support of North American oil drilling—mocked the town hall meeting in Springfield, Missouri. Conservative radio personality Rush Limbaugh said, "This is unbelievable. My friends, it's laughable, of course. But it's stupid! It is stupid."[9] And the party sent out tire pressure gauges to supporters with the words "Obama's energy plan" printed on them.

At least, on this particular issue, Barack Obama's campaign statement was accurate. Having the appropriate tire pressure makes cars more efficient. They use less gas, which means we could reduce some of our foreign dependency on oil. In fact, the US Department of Transportation has estimated that five million gallons of fuel are wasted every day—yes, every day—because of Americans with improperly inflated car tires.[10]

And by being more efficient, we would pollute less, thereby reducing global emissions. The wrong air pressure in our tires would mean more air pollution in our lungs and more pollution in our drinking water.

And if that's not enough to convince you the correct air pressure is important, it also has safety consequences. The Society of Automotive Engineers estimates that about 260,000 accidents each year involve improperly inflated car tires. The National Highway Traffic Safety Administration

(NHTSA) found that you're three times more likely to be in an accident if your tires are underinflated.[11]

Interesting and timely, but Obama's speech wasn't going to solve any of this.

It couldn't. Because it wasn't (and still isn't) an information problem. Yes, many people don't understand the merits of proper tire pressure, but that's not the heart of problem.

It's not a social issue, like marijuana legalization or gay marriage, which can be discussed and debated to convince minds. This is more like the dishes in your sink, or a dirty toilet bowl. This is an experience design problem. You don't have the time, and even if you did, you're probably not going to do it because it's an annoying chore.

Say you actually find the time and set forth to properly inflate your car tires. Once you find a gas station with an air pump, the burdensome experience continues not with delight, but with a feeling that you're being scammed. Many pumps require you to pump quarters into a coin slot to buy air from a machine.

Then, you bend over, squatting on the ground near your car tire, and you deal with showing the world another kind of coin slot: your butt crack coming out of your jeans.

And, as a little icing on the cake, as you attempt to rush through the embarrassing squat on the oil-stained ground, the air machine you just dumped all of your pocket change into might even be deceiving you about how much more air you need to buy. A study by the NHTSA found that 34 percent of low-volume gas stations had air machines with gauges inaccurate by 4 or more pounds per square inch (PSI) when trying to fill car tires that need a common 35 PSI.[12]

Yeah, I'll get that done next weekend.

Some who understand the consequences of not properly inflating their car tires just don't care enough to do anything about it. I don't blame them: Nobody wants to be squatting at a gas station with a plumber's crack pumping quarters into a lying machine to buy air. We just don't have the time.

So, what does a major tire manufacturer do about this problem? Well, don't worry, Goodyear has made an app. It has allowed people to do amazing things like, um . . .

"Print and email brochures."[13]

Make sure you add a share button! Yeah, one for Google Plus, too.

Fortunately, Goodyear's Innovation Center in Ohio has been working on something that leverages technology to solve the real problem. They're thinking beyond screens, and imagining a world of no interface that follows the first principle by embracing our typical processes, and also the second principle to leverage technology to serve us.

It's straightforward, really. They've created a tire in their labs that senses air pressure while you're driving. And if the tire pressure is low, it opens a tube that fills the tire back up to the ideal air pressure while you're moving. You just drive your car, and your tires fill up with air if they need it. They don't take you away from what matters, they don't take up your time, they don't add an additional chore, they just operate on their own. A simple system helping you avoid something you don't want to do that greatly benefits all of us.

The technology caters to your needs, so it all happens automatically, behind the scenes. Have no time? Worry not. It's not a tedious screen-based app, it's a machine input that works for you. As genius cofounder of Google Larry Page once said, "I'm kinda lazy, and having the computer do things is good."[14]

Whether self-inflating becomes an industry standard, or unpredictable market forces halt Goodyear's efforts before they hit your local O'Reilly's, the Goodyear project is a signpost on a journey that embodies the kind of thinking we should all be building toward. When we focus on leveraging systems that work for us within our typical processes, we can forget all that time spent on getting people to enter the right password, and instead focus on solving problems that do things like save us gas, money, and the environment for generations to come.

We're forgetful, fragile, and busy. Instead of adding another chore, computers can do the things we don't want to do, that we don't know we should do, and that we aren't able to do behind the scenes.

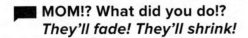 **MOM!? What did you do!?**
They'll fade! They'll shrink!

A teenage daughter in another room, not visible on camera, screams with despair.

▬ I LOVED those jeans![15]

Those quotes from a recent Whirlpool washing machine commercial embody the first-world, Orange County crisis of the multibillion-dollar, international appliance industry.[16] She's afraid her mom will do something wrong with a machine that's designed to clean clothes and ruin her new pair of designer jeans forever.

Yeah, her mom is from a fictional commercial, but it's hard to blame her, nonetheless. According to *Good Housekeeping*, the average American family does eight loads of laundry a week,[17] and the washing choices aren't obvious for loads of random, varying clothes. Please consider these actual controls on a top-selling washing machine:

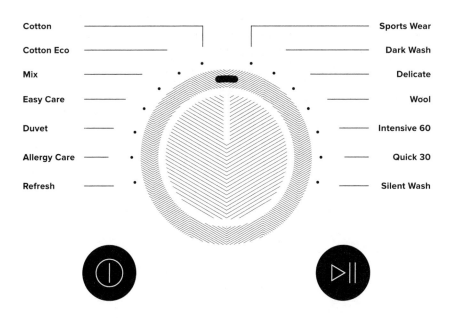

Controls for one of the most popular laundry machines today.

Finally, you make the time to do laundry, and now you don't even know which button might completely ruin your clothes.

So, if I played basketball in this cotton T-shirt, do I select *Cotton*? Or is it *Sports Wear* because it smells terrible? Wait, but isn't the purpose of a washing machine to wash my clothes so they don't smell? What does *Sports Wear* do differently? Oh look, there's *Silent Wash*. That could be good, too, because I don't like how loud this washer gets sometimes. Then again, there's *Quick 30*, which might be nice because quick is good, right? I've got things to do. Actually, wait, I sometimes get allergies—like 55 percent of all Americans[18]—maybe I should choose *Allergy Care*?

As some appliance companies have gone slaphappy with interfaces, the problem has gotten even worse as some models adopt touchscreens with pages and pages of options and bizarro apps that control them.

So what do consumers do with all this choice?

Well, colleagues who have done user research in the appliance industry have reported to me that time after time they get the same result: People have no idea what the buttons on their appliances actually do. An informal survey found that 58 percent of men in the UK don't even know how to use a washing machine.[19]

You don't have the time. There are more important things to do than read an instruction manual about the differences between *Easy Care* and *Delicate*. Yes, when you've paid $1,000 or more for a machine with just one purpose, you're entitled to better expectations.

washing machine what does	🔍

washing machine what does **permanent press mean**

washing machine what does **spin do**

washing machine what does **rinse hold mean**

For people using a dishwasher, the results are worse. I've been told by industry insiders that research indicates we often keep a single cycle button pressed forever. *Forever.* No matter what dishes have mom's spaghetti stuck on them (or not) there's always the same cycle button pressed on the dishwasher.

Are we pathetic because we can't figure out which cycle to use? Do we suck at life?

Nah, struggling with choice is actually a basic and observed part of human psychology that's an understood element in good design thinking. The burden and anxiety caused by the need to make choices has been confirmed time and time again. Like the study in which people were offered 30 randomly selected chocolates and ended up being less satisfied and more regretful than when they were offered only six randomly selected chocolates.[20] Or the discovery that the more retirement mutual funds employers offered to their employees through the investment firm Vanguard, the less and less those employees participated.

This has been explained by Barry Schwartz, the author of *The Paradox of Choice: Why More Is Less*, in his 2006 TED talk:

> **Why? Because with 50 funds to choose from, it's so damn hard to decide which fund to choose that you'll just put it off until tomorrow. And then tomorrow, and then tomorrow, and tomorrow, and tomorrow, and of course tomorrow never comes. Understand that not only does this mean that people are going to have to eat dog food when they retire because they don't have enough money put away, it also means that making the decision is so hard that they pass up significant matching money from the employer.[21]**

For appliances, is there anything simpler than buttons?

Of course. And some of the more experience-focused appliance makers are working on it. They're moving past the woes of user input and using signals to enable machine input. To save us time. To put the burden onto the machine that is designed to help rather than the instruction manual.

When Whirlpool showcased the teen jeans drama—"MOM!? What did you do!?"—they were advertising a sensor-based washing machine. The machines they introduced in 2013, the Duet Washer and Dryer, used sensors to determine the size of the load in the washing machine, and with that information the washer then used the appropriate amount of water and detergent.[22] And the dryer had moisture sensors to make sure your clothes were actually dry before it stopped running.[23] Neat.

But before those sensors went to work, you still had to choose a cycle from an enormous wheel of options . . . and a touch screen. Perhaps as a slave to the paradigm of bullet-point shopping—where websites and stores sell products based on bullet points, not experiences—appliance companies often feel the pressure to add a few more buttons and gizmos to get a few more bullet points that attract a few more sales despite any advances in actual experience.

Oh, look, this has 12 buttons and a touch screen! It must be the best.

But more impressively, Whirlpool's dishwashing division has created a button to end all buttons: A "sensor cycle." Wanna keep one button pressed forever? Sure. Press the sensor cycle, and sensors measure "temperature, soil level, and load size."[24] The dishwasher determines every setting so that your dishes come out perfectly clean each time, whether they're lightly stained wine glasses or plates heavily stained by Mom's spaghetti.

✁ ✁ ✁ ✁

Today, there's a new kind of chore. A new set of numerous, mindless errands embedded into our already overwhelmingly busy lives.

Over the past decade, these tiny requests have been culminating into a larger and larger ball of more and more of our time, taking us farther and farther away from spending more time with our friends and family, or allowing us the free time to make our communities stronger by volunteering at places like the downtown homeless shelter.

These tasks are the result of graphical user interfaces that assume constant, demanding attention is the expected norm. They are the byproduct of screen-based thinking. First-world errands for the almighty computer and the apparent productivity software we have to manage.

From their roots in delight and harmlessness—"You've Got Mail!"—they've grown into an endless stream of to-dos and checklists. As our lives continue to become increasingly digital, these tasks have exponentially increased because the standard paradigm in making new software is that we serve the computer, that we live to click. As each old-world thing turns digital, the software has more requests for you.

On a given day, you could have software updates to download and install, passwords to reset, notifications to attend to, files and folders to sort, messages to archive, social media requests to confirm, calendars to update, credit card balances to check, information to verify, storage space to manage and monitor, documents to back up, messages to reply to, photos to upload, flights to check in . . .

These are digital chores. The maintenance of our digital lives.

Oh, a new version is available? Yes, I'd love to download it for the next few hours.

By clicking here, yes, I'll be boarding that flight tomorrow that I purchased for that exact date for that exact route for $1,000 that has a $150 cancellation fee even though you're going to resell my ticket to another person if I don't check-in. I'd be delighted to let the computer know.

These digital chores are nightly, weekly, and monthly errands that can feel just as mundane and forced as taking out the trash. Sometimes, they have worse consequences than traditional chores. Previously, you forgot to do the laundry and had to wear an old shirt. Now, you forget to accept a request, and your friend may not be your friend anymore. You forget to change your password, your account can get hacked, and you lose your private pictures, or maybe even your friends all get porn in their inboxes attributed to you.

No, I swear, that's not my dick pic!

Rarely do these digital chores involve creating or contributing to the world. Rather, they're mostly made up of us serving the computer. We seek alluring, aspirational moments like Inbox Zero—a state of having an empty inbox because you've deleted, moved, or archived them all—which many desire and few attain. But for what? For happiness? The improvement of society? Nope, for the computer. For the interface. So that a count in a numerical badge floating above your application icon can diminish and eventually disappear. So that the application notifications go away. So that your most important documents are preserved. So that your account stays current. So that you don't get hacked.

In this digital errand world of operating system settings, folders, badges, and notification centers, one of the absurdities of the job is that the more digital chores you do, the more new digital chores may arise. Reply to an inbox full of messages? You'll probably get a lot of replies back, and your temporary state of Inbox Zero will quickly become aspirational all

over again. In other words, the better you are at email, the more emails you get.

Back up your photos? Now it's time to rethink that cloud storage. Saving and preserving your memories can mean massive file management.

Update your mobile operating system? Oh, well, all your applications need to be updated now, too. They don't work with the new system, duh.

The whole process feels like getting done with the laundry and having your clothes come out of the dryer dirty again.

Wait, why do my socks smell even worse now?

Fortunately, not everyone is convinced that this is the right path.

By taking advantage of things like an application programming interface (API) that allows software to talk to software, or by embracing a simple type of machine input—such as Wi-Fi or Bluetooth radio—some designers and engineers are rethinking software in NoUI ways.

In 2006, a startup called TripIt wanted to be the service that helped people manage their travel, in their words, "to enable the perfect trip." And in pursuing that goal they attempted to remove a digital chore that was a typical process for frequent travelers. See, travelers were getting emails from airlines like United, and then going through the mindless chore of entering that flight information and the rest of their trip itinerary at the correct times into their preferred calendar program, like, say, Google Calendar. So, TripIt—embracing their mantra "automagical"[25]—created an email address to which you could forward any travel information, like an email about flight, hotel, or rental car, and TripIt would automatically compile your trip itinerary. Your travel information just showed up in your calendar. People described it as "magic."

Eliminating a digital chore? That's a good thing. Making your customers feel like your service is magic? That's a great thing.

In 2010, they took it a step further. With user-granted email permissions, TripIt made an algorithm that finds travel-related emails when you get them—say, emails from Marriott or JetBlue—and automatically puts them in your calendar.[26] No need to forward or even open your email. The software worked invisibly in the background, automatically eliminating a nonsensical digital chore for you.

The movement to link software to software and create subscription-based services that make the computer serve you is still in early stages. So, it's mostly executed as a single feature of a larger resource, as when Dropbox introduced "background uploading"[27] in 2012 that automatically backs up photos from your smartphone to Dropbox when you're connected to Wi-Fi.[28]

The philosophy is embraced by more manual, hackerish services such as IFTTT (if this, then that; pronounced like "gift without the *g*"),[29] which allows you to create recipes so that if something happens in one digital space, you make something else happen in another digital space. (Like if you get a phone call from an important client, they get a text that you'll call them back soon.)[30]

These invisible kinds of subscription-based applications point toward a refreshing future. Instead of more gadgets, more software to manage, and more digital chores to take care of, these background robots will remove your digital chores. The computer will serve your needs.

Look, you're busy. We all are. We'd all love a few extra hours to see the people we love, to enjoy life, and to contribute to the world. When it's possible for computers to free us to be more productive, well, let's take that option. Let's have the almighty computer serve us.

Principle Three: Adapt to Individuals

14. Computing for One
You're spécial

Buried in the chapters, consumed in the pages, and gone astray in the paragraphs, I realize now that I got lost and must apologize. So, it's time for me to finally look up and honor the great thing that has been right in front of me this entire time: You.

I love that shirt you're wearing.

It's so . . . you.

That whole outfit. Something about it just screams—with a kind of understated elegance that shines through the ordinary—your unique, amazing inner spirit. It's far beyond fashion.

You're spécial.

So much so that AutoCorrect replaced *special* with *spécial* in the previous sentence and I didn't even bat an eye. You need the emphasis. You deserve it. That laugh. Your approach to life. It's become so obvious to those around you, that way you bring joy into our lives.

Sure, admiration from an author you don't know—speaking via a relationship of words on a page—may seem silly, but the reality is actually undeniable: You're one of a kind, and you always have been. By the way, what are you doing next weekend?

Sadly, your wonderfully distinct qualities have been dismissed by CBS's *60 Minutes* as some kind of generational, Millennial hiccup driven by childhood influences. "Who's to blame for the narcissistic praise hounds now taking over the office?" Morley Safer once asked.

An opinionated *Wall Street Journal* columnist answered: "You had a guy like Mr. Rogers," he told *60 Minutes*, "he's telling [preschoolers], 'You're special, you're special' . . . And for doing what?"[1]

First of all, it's *spécial*. And ignore him. In another time he probably would have ranted about those kids with their cool leather jackets, fresh bell bottoms, hip carpenter's jeans, or even hot Zubaz pants.

Look, I'm flattered you've even gotten this far in this book; not just because about one in four Americans tend not to read any books at all,[2] but because I think if we spent some real time together, one-on-one over coffee, or maybe a few beers, I could really learn from you.

Let me put it another way. If I had met you earlier, you could have helped me make this book better. You would have corrected mistakes and added knowledge to shallow sentences.

Think about you for a second. You have lived a unique life surrounded by a unique set of things that has shaped you with a unique perspective on the world. And from your life, I guarantee there's so much you could share, and I could learn.

Oh yeah, *that's* unique.

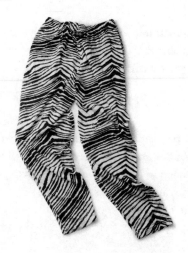

You have your own set of preferences, desires, and interests. Your own favorite color. Your preferred route home. Your favorite food. Your own way of talking. Your own way of writing. Your own friend group. Your own schedule. Your own style of working.

And I wouldn't have you any other way.

You're spécial.

This reality, I'm sorry to say, isn't what we typically embrace when we make most software today—despite the billion-dollar valuations, optimistic NASDAQ NDXT-like indices, and promises of grand TED talks shot from nine camera angles.[3] We don't make a separate digital interface for each and every unique person. Within the constraints of modern front-end software development, that would be an endless, gargantuan task.

Sometimes, antithetically, graphical user interfaces are even despairingly based on a single person's view of the world; in other words, not yours. And as for more experienced software designers making graphical user interfaces on collaborative teams, we've tended to draw common screen elements based on blurry, qualitative averages.

Sigh.

Your special qualities and unique life instantly fade away as the boxes, lines, and form fields of digital, screen-based interfaces come to the forefront. Your routines are washed out by an art director's stylistic preferences based on trends from a single moment in time. Your uniqueness is forgotten.

This flawed course to making digital products is actually very difficult. Because of accepted routines and years of practice, the methods of building a graphical user interface from the outside seem well established; but despite repeated tools and methods, actually achieving success when aiming for the average—trying to score a pop hit—is incredibly difficult.

There's a good reason why, despite the millions of mobile apps available, a tiny percentage (only about 500 of them) account for more than 80 percent of all downloads.[4] Or why—contrary to the press-driven hype—most people download, um, zero mobile apps every month. Yeah, zero per month.[5]

I'm gonna get so rich off this app!

That seemingly practiced task of developing an app typically requires a fair amount of money, open-minded leaders, great research, deep insights, a team of really smart people, and even a little luck. Innovation is really about understanding you and your needs, and digital product failures come easily when the creators of technology don't understand you and your needs. Making one digital interface that will satisfy an average is very hard, and in the end, interfaces are often representative of no one.

I'm sorry.

It makes you wonder why nearly every industry—from car insurance to soft drinks—is spending millions of dollars[6] in a near-impossible pursuit to make an interface that just dismisses your individuality and eccentric personal habits by putting you into a generic box.

Worse, most software immediately starts losing whatever value it adds to your life the moment you start using it. The features built for the average may have surprised and delighted you when you first used an interface, but over time their generic facelessness become more and more stale.

Install and Discover   **Small gains with fixed toolset**

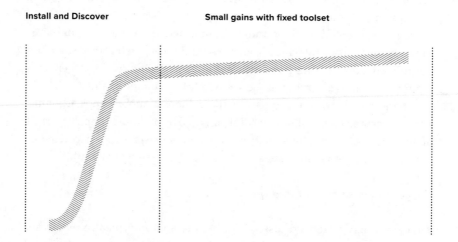

A visual gesture of your time spent with typical software (not based on numerical findings)

Sadly, the obvious way for an interface to give you another leap forward, another set of tools and features to delight you, is to have its designers and engineers spend an incredible amount of time and effort to redesign it. And when they do, you will be faced with the pain of learning all over again how to interact with that new interface. Some things will work better for you, and some things will be worse for you. Buttons will move and disappear. Menus will change. *Wait, where's the . . . ?* Ugh. Interfaces are not a great way to embrace you, your uniqueness, or your evolving preferences.

Chin up. There's a way out.

Some forward thinkers have started to take an opposite approach. They spend their lives studying unique patterns in the unceasing pursuit of solutions that are best for what's most important: You.

New doors are being opened by applying robust techniques previously used for tasks like trying to predict chaotic stock prices in financial markets. A new symbiosis between individuals and technology is just beginning, something that can create such seamless experiences that when the methods are applied to products thought to be at their peak, those products have been completely transformed. These people are working on ideas to create things that can continuously adapt to you.

One method which empowers this kind of system is the ability to find recommendations through mountains of information. Learn from history. Track your patterns and others' preferences to make matches about what you might need and want based upon millions of data points. However, for tens of thousands of years, information capture was done through rudimentary techniques that could never accumulate enough data to provide insights about what might be best for you.

About 40,000 years ago, information was captured through, well, cave drawings.[7] Five thousand years ago, it was pictorial language carved into clay-like rocks. About 1,000 years ago, we started gathering information through printed books. The printed book is the best of this short list of capture solutions, but as poet Fremont Rider (the understudy of Melvil Dewey, the creator of the Dewey Decimal system) identified in 1944, "By the year 2040, Yale University library will have, at the present rate of growth, 200 million volumes to house, requiring 6,000 miles of shelving and 750,000 drawers for the catalog index."[8] The storage capacity is unsustainable.

In 1990—when the personal computer had become a regular part of our homes, the Internet was a few years shy of going mainstream, and Michael Keaton was still Batman—Peter J. Denning had incredible foresight into the new medium, and saw its power and capability to do something no information-storage medium—caves, clay, or paper—could ever offer. While working at a NASA research lab that year, Peter published the paper "Saving All the Bits." Here's the first paragraph:

> **I often hear from colleagues in the earth sciences, astronomy, physics, and other disciplines that after we start up an expensive instrument or complete a massive computation, we must save all the bits of information generated by the instrument or the computation. The arguments for this practice are, first, that the cost of acquiring the bits is so great that we cannot afford to lose any of them, and, second, that some rare event might be recorded in those bits, and to throw them away would be a great loss for science. Sometimes these points are made with such vehemence that I am left with the impression that saving the bits is not merely a question of cost but is a moral imperative.**[9]

Inspired by the idea that we might someday know what to do with all that data, some computer companies started collecting huge amounts of it. And as they did so, overwhelming market demands provided a catalyst for the standard 40-megabyte[10] hard drives of the day to increase in size and decrease in price per byte. So, eventually, the annoying pop-ups you had to close, the error messages that bothered you, the times your software crashed, and your clicks on the good stuff were stored cheaply, easily, and in large quantities.

People like Gordon Bell—through his MyLifeBits project at Microsoft Research Silicon Valley Laboratory—started collecting information about their own lives to beat memory loss.[11] Over time, the digital medium's incredible ability to remember built up to what today we call "big data."

Enter the world of the data scientist to find relevant meaning in all that digital data, to power solutions that adjust to your wonderful uniqueness. To think of you.

What do you want to eat tonight? What's the best way home? Data science is one way we can find meaning in all that cheaply stored information—whether big data or even small, relevant, searchable sets—and develop real insights and accurate answers to valuable individual questions. It could completely change the way we think of technology.

If we know you well enough—that is, if we have the appropriate data set, ask the right questions, and use the correct lens to interpret what we observe—we can potentially give you what you need, when you need it, and all without you even asking. By looking at you, the people like you, and how you compare with larger masses, we could understand what works best for

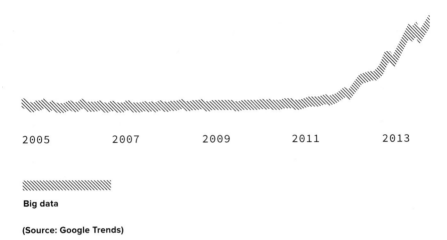

2005   2007   2009   2011   2013

Big data

(Source: Google Trends)

you, how you're different. And if we used those tools to tackle meaningful problems, the approach could positively impact your everyday life.

This combination of cultural insight, transparent but moral data collection, predictive analytics, machine learning, computational thinking, and the statistical confidence to take action is a huge undertaking, both politically and technologically. But when the time and money are allotted for it to happen in the right way—morally, transparently, and intelligently—the possibilities are endless. And when we leave the interface behind, we can make technology that adapts to a unique you. That way you smile. That awesome shirt. Finally, embrace you.

As Stanford professor Andrew Ng once said, "Sometimes I actually think that machine learning is not only the most exciting thing in computer science, but the most exciting thing in all of human endeavor."[12]

So, what kinds of things have already happened using these powerful and fascinating tools? What have we done so far in this new frontier of statistics that has the ability to center experiences around you?

Some of the top talent at the world's great universities—Harvard-educated economists and PhD and master's degree graduates from McGill,[13] Carnegie Mellon, the Indian Institute of Technology,[14] the University of Chicago, and MIT—are working on the enormous, complex, financially viable problem of creating quality in processes like RTB (real-time bidding) for the larger picture of relevant text and banner ads, and all so you can see annoying, deceiving ads that are relevant to your browsing history.

"The most coveted employee in Silicon Valley today is not a software engineer," the CEO of Redfin once told *Business Week*. "It is a mathematician. The mathematicians are trying to tickle your fancy long enough to see one more ad."[15]

Wait, what?

Unfortunately, with short-term dollar signs in their eyes, motivated by what we *can* do rather than what we *should* do, unimaginative online advertising has consumed the talent of some of these new statisticians. But don't worry, not everyone is chasing a simple, shallow paycheck.

"The latest and greatest."

Smart and experienced people at the most influential technology companies across the world know that "the latest and greatest" is tech's biggest lie, a grand possibility diluted by reality. Like the way a political bill for universal health care that could have a huge positive impact on the welfare of a country is washed down to meaninglessness by backroom deals, favors for campaign donors, and paranoia around Gallup polls . . . the same things happen in tech.

Wonderful solutions, beautiful products, and revolutionary ideas die over the politics of egomaniacal vice presidents, half-witted Steve Jobs wannabes, and others who undeservingly have happened to stick around. Those who have gained enough clout at the local bar to fill a C-suite with stupidity, shortsightedness, and a desire for job security reinforced by no new ideas whatsoever. While there are great executives and visionary corporate presidents, sometimes smart people with amazing accomplishments are at the whim of leaders who have unwarranted power to make decisions distant from actual operations, and an ocean away from understanding real customers and what they need.

This is the way Xerox's original invention of the graphical user interface was laughed out of the boardroom. Or how about Knight Ridder's iPad-like device—nearly two decades ahead of its time[16]—which was so disliked by the newspaper company's executives that they quickly dissolved the internal, forward-thinking group that created the product.

Tech workers aren't fired for being safe; but while remaining safe, tech companies die.

Look at our user base. Blackberry will always be the world's most popular smartphone. Let's not change anything.

So while we sometimes recall and retell technological history through effortless tales, the reality is that many meaningful technology accomplishments at the most influential companies are the result of successful internal political wins, a slow climb of convincing the right people in the right place at the right time that a good idea is actually good. What you see as a consumer is not truly the latest and greatest, but instead what managed to squeeze through the available channels, and somehow convince enough influencers in the company that they wouldn't get fired for agreeing to approve it.

Taking a leap forward to make a service that understands you? Avoiding bland, sameness averages for unique, individualized experiences? Well, friend, that ambitious goal is certainly *not* safe.

In 2006, Jonathan Goldman, a PhD graduate in physics from Stanford working at the professional social network LinkedIn, wondered if, by studying you, the service could suggest connections you might know. Could he create an interface of smart connections built around you and your friends rather than putting you in a box as part of a generic database?

Even at LinkedIn, where data scientist celebrity DJ Patil, um, coined the term "data scientist" with Jeff Hammerbacher back in 2008, the concept of creating platforms that adapted to your wonderfully distinct qualities seemed foreign just two years earlier.[17]

According to Patil, outspoken stakeholders in the company were said to have been "openly dismissive" of Goldman's concept. Engineers on staff reportedly "seemed uninterested" at the notion.

Trying to get his idea passed through the ranks, Goldman found a friend in CEO Reid Hoffman, and was able to eke out a tiny pixel box the size of a small ad that enabled Goldman to try his People You May Know feature. It would crunch huge amounts of data to provide a truly personal suggestion of other people you might want to connect with on LinkedIn.

The result? The small window devoted to understanding your uniqueness—minuscule compared to the size of dozens of other features on the

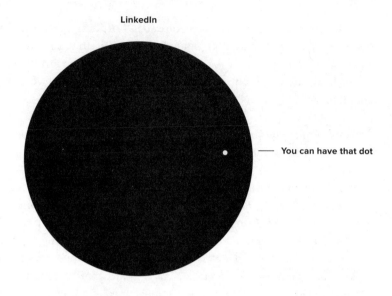

LinkedIn

—— You can have that dot

site—"generated millions of new page views." And for the company at large, that tiny move toward using data in a meaningful way shifted LinkedIn toward massive growth.

What could happen if we expanded the idea further?

Others have explored similar kinds of techniques for movie recommendations and links for similar product recommendations—and these big undertakings have had enormous value for each of their companies—but I believe we can accomplish much more by doing one simple thing: thinking beyond the graphical user interface.

Imagine building a graphical user interface like decorating a wall. You put a picture here, hang a shelf there. You can move the objects around, perhaps even introduce a different photo for each person who walks into your home; but no matter what you do, your options are fairly limited. You have a given space and a given set of tools. The objects are fixed.

But what if there were no wall? What if we shifted the primary experience from the concrete to the abstract? What if instead of spending all that money and time on a static interface that will look outdated in a year, we spend the resources on a learning algorithm that can adapt a service in any way needed?

When tools like machine learning and data science are lifted from the shackles of a static, small, pixel sandbox, we can use insights to change

Starts learning about you   **Adapts to you**

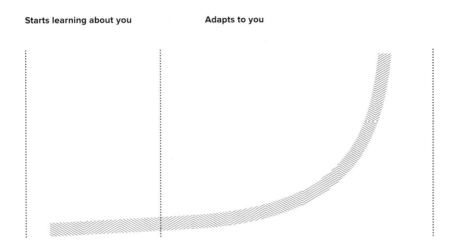

**Another visual gesture of a different kind of software experience
(not based on numerical findings)**

everything: Rapidly adjust for you. Make things that fill your life with the kind of joy and laughter that you've provided for others. Diminishing rate of return over time? Nay, increasing returns.

Sound nuts? It is. This near future of brilliant technology is barely even understood by those pursuing it. Sound amazing? It is. Turn the page to learn more.

15. Proactive Computing
In the future, I'll talk
to my computer!

Over 60 years ago, an eight-year-old boy named Jack Weeks was playing in his garage when he opened a large box and discovered something his father had been hiding from the world: a head.[1]

It had been there since the start of World War II.

His father John was an engineer at Westinghouse, then a prominent appliance company in Mansfield, Ohio. The company was known for its clothing irons and ovens, but John and some of his colleagues were more passionate about something else: a massive male figure who was a towering seven feet tall and weighed nearly 300 pounds;[2] a frame so large Westinghouse paraded him around the 1939 New York World's Fair to greet attendees at the Westinghouse Pavilion.

At the optimistic futurist event, which that year took place shortly after the height of the Great Depression, his sheer size felt to some like a positive glimpse of things to come. So were his funny lines like, "Hey, toots!" and his amusing stories. And the funny way he smoked cigarettes. And his fun dog, Sparko. But maybe most impressive was his ability to respond to voice commands. And then, one day, after the second World War broke out, Westinghouse dismantled him and Elektro the seven-foot-tall robot took a pause from the fame.

John, who had worked on his wiring, took Elektro apart and stored him and his dog Sparko at home. John's son Jack eventually discovered the head and torso in their basement, and made a friend of Elektro. He would dress him up, and wheel him around to play games like cops and robbers.

Shortly after the war ended, when Jack was a little older, Westinghouse decided to recollect and reassemble Elektro to put him back on tour. John even joined him as they entertained people at county fairs and department store openings.[3]

Elektro, who had the look of a 1930s B movie robot, wasn't Westinghouse's first or only robot. And Westinghouse wasn't the only company

(Source: **Ian McKellar** / CC BY SA 2.0)

exploring human-like robots—but something about Elektro's appearance and behavior made him stand out. His bronze-painted brushed aluminum shined from head to toe. His large, rectangular chest had a circular hole that contained a light that illuminated after each word Elektro's assistant spoke into an attached telephone receiver and showed there was no human inside.[4] His legs looked as though they were assembled from two pipes meeting at the knee, a construction that allowed Elektro to walk very slowly in a straight line upon a particular voice command. His rounded art deco head that could turn side to side and up and down had ears, eyes, nose, and a mouth, but only his mouth had real utility; it could move up and down linearly as Elektro told recorded stories out of his speaker. He also had a small air gauge inside so that he could smoke cigarettes and quickly blow up balloons.[5]

Elektro wowed crowds with what some believed was the pinnacle of the future of computers, a human-like robot we could speak with. At one point, he became part of an amusement park, and his opening and closing jaw helped him play a part in two movies.

In the 1940s, seeing Elektro respond to simple vocal requests, walk, and even smoke on command made the future of interaction with machines seem obvious:

Hello, computer.

Today, it still sounds fantastical. The mythical presence is most often seen in science fiction fantasy movies where dialogue with the computer works seamlessly for the script and storyboard because the computer simply becomes another character in a screenplay. Hal, or *Her*, is desired and revered by the general public in offhand discussions about life in the future, and drawn up in future scenes by *Popular Science*-esque magazines that influence enthusiasts about the direction life with technology is headed. Although seamless dialogue with our machines is a simple crutch for screenwriters and movie directors—embarrassing in *Rocky IV*, captivating in *Moon*, and entertaining on stage with Elektro—it hasn't unfolded as we once envisioned, though we've certainly been trying . . .

Consulting my tea leaves. Here's what I found on the Web . . .

Siri is one of many flawed attempts to make this conversational avenue of science fiction come alive as a modern-day robot assistant. Probably because of well-placed marketing and novelty, Siri was briefly a popular tool, with reports indicating that over 60 percent of the latest iPhone owners used Siri on their smartphones once a month.[6] Eventually, the usage flatlined to reports of 85 percent of users ignoring the tool entirely.[7] Those statistics are bound to change again as the technology is rebranded and redesigned, but they are reflective of something else that is fundamentally wrong with our current approach to voice input, smartphones, or seven-foot robots.

Voice recognition companies like Nuance—which has powered Siri, Samsung's S Voice, and other hugely popular services—have made great strides in the field. Their work has been impressive. But the experience with these services often begins with something akin to a computer relic:

```
C:\>_
```

Like one of those old command prompts where anything you type seems possible, but actually only DIR and other bizarre words will lead to any action, voice input can be a guessing game of a limited set of possibilities with a powerful machine, not knowing what will do what.

175

OK Google, umm . . . no, I meant, um . . .

Hey Siri, uh . . . actually, could you, uh . . .

Hi Cortana, let's see . . . how about . . . eh . . .

While voice input works at the World's Fair, in science fiction movies, and on television commercials because of planned stage performances and well-written character-based storytelling, the magic of conversing with a computer—despite over 80 years of trying—often falls short in the real-life experience of saying brand names and guessing commands with a computer on a crowded subway train. We often think of these attempts as a path toward making a system that will grow and learn for us, but it's not a direction that has worked well.

Microphones could be a seamless machine input in many ways. They could, in theory, inform your phone to turn up your phone's ringer when it senses you're inside a loud room. Or, at beeping crosswalks, trigger vibrations to inform the blind that they can safely cross the street. But voice recognition using the microphone—an actual conversation with the computer—is a long way off.

Perhaps one day we'll finally perfect an Elektro-like robot or Nuance-like voice input and talk with our computers seamlessly, but what if we aimed for something other than voice input? Instead of the extremely difficult act of trying to recreate human dialogue, we should aim for something that has a richer experience. What if instead of trying to build *reactive* conversations with the computer, we instead aimed for *proactive* help with our unique, individual needs? What if instead of single moments of input, a service worked continuously to help us with our varying individual needs?

What if we shifted from the ideal of "Hello, computer" to the idea of "Thank you, computer" and made systems that adapted to our spécial instead of responded to our voice with cheeky dialogue? What would that look like?

Well, that's a lot of questions. Let's start with something simple. Say, the temperatures you prefer in your house.

When I first saw the Nest thermostat in 2011, I thought they had just slapped an interface on a thermostat and called it "innovation."

Much like voice commands to robots, a graphical user interface on its own creates a reactive system that can't see what's ahead, can't understand you, and just tries to stay afloat, hoping that you'll prevent it from

drowning into meaninglessness by tossing an input lifesaver and pulling it toward your goals.

Nest Labs escaped this screen-based thinking result by utilizing a bit of data science. Pulling in information from sensors that measured temperature, humidity, far-field activity, near-field activity, and ambient light, algorithms were created so that it studied your indoor climate needs and habits. It learned when you woke up and when you tended to be out of the house, along with the temperatures you preferred over the course of the day.

Eventually, the entire experience adapted for you. It fell into an auto mode where it set the temperatures you wanted throughout the day without any further input from you. The primary experience shifted from a reactionary user interface to a proactive NoUI solution.

Fixated on a primary task, and using sensors and information for solely executing that task of changing house temperatures, Nest gained the trust and desire of consumers. By 2014, when Nest Labs was acquired by Google for $3.2 billion, Morgan Stanley estimated they were selling 100,000 thermostats a month.[8]

While those numbers are impressive, there's so much more we could do than just predict what room temperatures you prefer. In building proactive systems, some people are already working at the edges of machine learning and developing products that aim for the holy grail of achievements: keeping us healthy and alive.

A common environment created to enable the sick to heal currently takes its precautions via scrubs, sinks, sign-ins, and sounds.

Yes, sounds. The voices of the machines, the bells, beeps, and dings of medical equipment, create a symphony of sounds to which doctors and nurses must be attuned. But those sounds have been failing us. People have been dying unnecessarily.

In the 1920s, a new form of poetry emerged from the dadaist art movement, one that was created in response to the violence of the First World War. This new form of poetry was sometimes expressed with multiple voices shouting over one another in various languages. These non-sensible verbiages were an art form intended to create a compounded mess of sound that mimicked the sounds of war.[9]

Boomboom, Boomboom, Boomboom!

Sadly, today's emergency room can have a similar, bizarrely compounded mess of sound. Unpredictable flats and out-of-tone mechanized, sometimes indiscernible beeps and buzzes may blast up to 150 alerts per day.[10] And these alerts aren't status updates or button presses or social site pokes; they are the machine communicating to the health-care worker that a life needs urgent care.

Beepbeep, Beepbeep, Beepbeep!

In 2011, Liz Kowalczyk of the *Boston Globe* wrote a groundbreaking, fascinating, and sad investigative article about how poorly designed and programmed hospital machines may have led to hundreds of unnecessary deaths.[11] The *Boston Globe* found "more than 200 hospital patients nationwide whose deaths between January 2005 and June 2010 were linked to problems with alarms on patient monitors that track heart function, breathing, and other vital signs."

A problem well worth solving.

"I don't understand 'Siri, I'm not feeling to [sic] well.' But I could search the Web for it!"

Take non-ICU (intensive care unit) patients, who might be monitored by busy nurses at intervals of every four to six hours only. How might you help this kind of health care setting in a NoUI way so that alarms aren't missed and patients in need get the care they deserve?

First, embrace typical processes.

Just as Russian theater director Constantin Stanislavski taught his acting students to live and breathe the characters they were playing—what we now call *method acting*—role-playing in technological systems can lead to elegance and effortlessness in a path to achieving goals.

So, put yourself in the shoes of the people using the system most often. Be a method designer to discover their typical processes.

From the point of view of a patient, the primary user, a typical process is to lay in a hospital bed, preferably in whatever position is most comfortable. From the point of view of a health-care worker, the secondary user, her attentions are often divided, trying to provide various kinds of care over her assigned area. The system should work within these typical processes.

Second, leverage computers instead of serving them.

Instead of asking the patient to paste a set of electrodes onto his chest hair (ouch), use machine input to seamlessly gather the information you need to solve the problem within the typical processes, such as a sensor that sits underneath the hospital bed mattress and can read heart rate, respiratory rate, and movement without ever touching the patient.

And, lastly, as we're now learning, adapt to individuals.

Instead of using generic alarms that can go off for a large variety of reasons, study the patterns of each unique patient, compare those patterns to the patient's history, larger known patterns that typically indicate certain outcomes, and other informed data sets to make individualized alerts. Be proactive about the information. When the patient is about to need a certain kind of help, such as breathing issues, alert a health-care worker who can help with that exact need, like someone with pulmonary expertise.

That's a NoUI system for the patients. And fortunately, these are all parts of an existing product: EarlySense, a contact-less patient monitoring system used in some top-end hospitals today.

The EarlySense EverOn sensor is remarkable. Tucked away underneath a patient's mattress, the sensor picks up on heart rate and respiratory rate, as well as movement without any physical contact with the patient. It's not an add-on, it's part of the experience: It helps the sick sleep better and be more comfortable all day long.

The predictive nature of the system—which can be set up so that an appropriate doctor and/or nurse gets a message when a patient needs attention—means no extra alert noises to distract health-care professionals or disrupt a patient's rest, just regular communication channels between the system and a clinician based on an individual patient's needs.[12]

And since it's studying your patterns, the alarms that do go off are fewer, more accurate, and more targeted. In tested environments, traditional monitoring systems can blast 120 alarms—many of which "do not require clinical intervention"—while EarlySense lets off only about two more-targeted, more-appropriate alerts.[13]

And those alerts can happen hours before the patient is even in need. A study led by a researcher from Brigham and Women's Hospital and Harvard Medical School found that "when tracking adverse clinical events for patients monitored by the EarlySense device, we found the monitor was able to identify hours ahead of time most of these events."

Instead of chasing Hollywood's fantasies to make faux personal experiences, transitioning computing from reactive to proactive can actually have huge individual benefits. Our preferences can be matched, and our health care can be better attended for our exact needs. Gaining the kind of confidence to take action is extremely difficult, but when focusing on well-defined problems, proactive computing can be incredibly powerful.

✦ ✦ ✦ ✦

In April 2013, one of the world's greatest basketball players took one dribble toward the hoop and then crumbled to the ground. The basketball season for Kobe Bryant, the Lakers superstar, came to an instant end. He ripped his achilles on a pivot, and fell to the floor. It was a grade 3 rupture . . . there is no grade 4.[14]

Kobe left the game limping, and cried in an interview after the game.[15] Some questioned whether he would ever play basketball again at the same level. Upset Lakers fans soon started to point fingers.

The Lakers' then head coach Mike D'Antoni took a lot of the heat. Online polls showed fans identified D'Antoni as the reason Kobe got hurt: He played an aging Kobe for too many minutes. After 17 seasons in the NBA, Kobe ranked second in most minutes played up to that point in that NBA season.[16]

The real cause of Kobe's injury is hard to predict with the limited information. But the result of that kind of injury was transparent. In the

NBA, losing a superstar dramatically alters a season. The Lakers were swept out of the playoffs. The team lost millions of dollars in potential revenue.[17] The fans had to wait at least another season to see success.

Later that year, in September 2013, the NBA announced that it would start installing a camera system in the catwalks of all 30 stadiums.[18] The system from sports information leader STATS LLC, called SportVU, was used as machine input to automatically track the players' movements. Among many things, they monitored defensive impact, the speed and distance of each player, and his number of passes.[19] The players wouldn't have to wear any extra gadgets to enable the system, and they didn't have to download any apps to empower it; the cameras would work seamlessly and invisibly while the players did their typical thing during each game.

To put it technically:

There are six computer vision cameras set up along the catwalk of the arena—three per half court. These cameras are synched with complex algorithms extracting x, y, and z positioning data for all objects on the court, capturing 25 pictures per second.[20]

For fans, the data from the cameras gave them new ways to admire their favorite players. TV broadcasters will get new stats to show during games. More importantly, for team doctors, SportVU provided an opportunity to avoid Kobe-like injuries. "The longest contracts we have are not our players," Dallas Mavericks owner Mark Cuban once said. "They are our support and health staff."[21]

By combining that SportVU data acquired during games with OptimEye (phone-sized GPS wearables) on players during practice, some teams have changed how injury in the NBA is approached. "We have an opportunity to take these players and be totally proactive," said Alex McKechnie, the director of sports science for the Toronto Raptors.

In Toronto, McKechnie introduced unique training programs for each player's one-of-a-kind physiology based on the data, so that they can play more minutes and stay healthier longer. Programs that are adapted to individuals—an idea that dropped injury rates in Toronto so low that they were the least injured team in the 2013–14 NBA season.

Everyone reading this book is different. You have your favorite way of getting things done. Your own approach to things. And a world of NoUI can embrace that reality. We can transform your primary experiences with computers from reactive interfaces to proactive solutions.

The Challenges

16. Change
You hate this book?
Thank you.

A lot of people won't like this book.

I don't blame them.

Some of those people have built robust processes around making screens and graphical user interfaces, and over the years they have gotten really damn good at it. Maybe they've sold those ideas to clients for lots of money, shared those ideas at conferences or in classrooms around the world, and built their reputation around being experts in screen-based thinking. That's how they earn their living; maybe that's even how they made a fortune.

So for me to say that what they are good at doing, what pays their bills, is actually the wrong way to go is definitely not going to rub those people the right way. It's going to make them dislike this book, NoUI, me, and the phrase, "The best interface is no interface."

I get that. That's part of questioning the norm. Asking the industry to go in a different direction means backlash.

So I'm ready for potential online bashing and blog post hating: No to NoUI essays. "It depends" mockery. Dismantling of chapters.

I welcome it. This idea is relatively new, and when someone writes something thoughtful in response to this idea of a screenless world, it pushes the idea further and further to maturity and eventual mainstream adoption. When someone finds a flaw in the concept, it forces me (or you) to discover a smarter way to execute NoUI. Or if there is no good alternative, it forces honesty about NoUI limitations. If the editor of this book never deleted five thousand words from a chapter and wrote me, "Golden, you're gonna wanna kill me when you see the next cut," this book would have been worse. Thoughtful critical thinking pushes us forward.

This book is a collection of founding principles written in a manner to convince, encourage, and inspire. To present a simple philosophy that can produce brilliant technology. But being at times fun, whimsical, and sarcastic, it may offend. The hope, of course, isn't to see a tech titan fall, or a smart designer on the street; it's to push the industry forward. I like you, and I want us to be better at what we do. It's not easy though, and there are many things about this forward-looking idea that worry some people.

It would take years to write about every NoUI edge case that raises questions about the NoUI concept, but I wrote this section to attempt to address at least some of the popular concerns, and warn you about the paths to avoid as we begin to build a NoUI world.

17. Privacy
The machine will "learn" about me? No thanks.

Technology legal agreements. They pain us so much that when we see them, we often look the other way. We ignore them though they're in our direct line of sight, and turn a shoulder when they're front and center. When directly asked to confirm that we read them, we lie.

I have understood . . .
Check!

I have read . . .
Continue!

I will obey . . .
Submit!

In fact, you've probably already spent more time reading this chapter than you ever have spent reading a technology legal agreement because doing so is digital torture.

Want Wi-Fi? Oh sure, it's free. Just step right up, now. Step right up, son, and see the one, the only, the ad-free legendary speeds here! Now, first, I'll just have you lie down on this shiny guillotine . . . !

The rope is pulled . . . Latin phrases . . . !

The blade falls . . . impossible-to-follow run-on sentences . . . !

The crowd gasps . . . all caps for emphasis . . . !

Free Airport Wi-Fi

By using the Airport's free Wi-Fi High Speed Internet Service, you agree to be bound by the following terms and conditions, which are a binding agreement between you and this airport. You represent that you are of legal age to agree and be bound by this agreement.

Personal Use Only
You must use the service and technology provided to you for the sole purpose as described here. You must immediately notify us of any unauthorized use of the Free Wi-Fi or any other security breach.

◄   Page 1 of 213   ►

☐ **I have read, understood and agree to: Airport Wi-Fi Terms and conditions as well as to the Privacy Policy**

Continue

Your head and your rights roll away in a confusing mess.

IF THESE LAWS APPLY TO YOU, SOME OR ALL OF THE ABOVE DISCLAIMERS, EXCLUSIONS, OR LIMITATIONS MAY NOT APPLY TO YOU, AND YOU MAY ALSO HAVE ADDITIONAL RIGHTS.[1]

Above? Oh, that's just one nonspecific, legalese phrase from the iTunes terms and conditions—an ever-evolving document that's about the length of 56 printed pages,[2] so absurdly overwhelming and long that roughly 500 million of us have dealt with it like a waterboarded confession.[3]

There's probably something we should read about our privacy in that long, mundane, and exhausting document, but there's also a good reason mental impairment can cause false confession.[4]

In Redmond, Washington, where they've reported that 1.1 billion people use Microsoft Office,[5] they've even included text in their software license agreement to play "good cop" and let us know how we should read their own confusing text:

THE ADDITIONAL TERMS CONTAIN A BINDING ARBITRATION CLAUSE AND CLASS ACTION WAIVER. IF YOU LIVE IN THE UNITED STATES, THESE AFFECT YOUR RIGHTS TO RESOLVE A DISPUTE WITH MICROSOFT, AND YOU SHOULD READ THEM CAREFULLY.[6]

"Read them carefully." Sure, that sounds fun.

Say we attempted to swim out of the mental drowning, and we actually carefully read privacy policies starting with just the websites we visited. How long would it really take all of us to collectively read those privacy policies?

About 54 billion hours.

The answer comes from Carnegie Mellon researchers Lorrie Faith Cranor and Aleecia McDonald, who set out to explore the real cost of lengthy and complex privacy policies in the United States. Amongst their measurements, they had 212 participants "skim" for "simple comprehension" the privacy policies of some of the most popular American websites. Combining that information with a variety of other data, such as individual browsing habits from Nielsen, they estimated how long it would take the typical American to read the privacy policies of the websites they commonly visited. What they discovered is that the torture is extensive.[7]

OK, if I use this fork, I can probably dig out a tunnel in 2.25 million days.[8]

189

Assuming that we read privacy policies like it was our job (for eight hours a day), Cranor and McDonald estimated it would take the individual American 76 work days to read the privacy policies of the common websites they visit. And that doesn't include apps. Extrapolated out to the population of the United States, according to their research, it would take up about 53.8 billion hours for the country to read the privacy policies of just the websites they frequently visit.

The financial cost of all that tedious reading?

If paid just 25 percent of our salary to read the privacy policies, it would cost us $781 billion in time. And, yes, we're still just talking about only the websites you frequently visit.

Terms and conditions are long, boring, complex, expensive, painful, and another step between us and our goals. But as more and more new services emerge, and our data exists in more places, the more important those policies become.

Think back to when you signed up for Friendster. Or MySpace. Or Facebook. Or Instagram. Or Ello. Or that other hot new service.

First, you just share the interesting basics at convenient times. Then, things accelerate. Trust grows. You tell your friends. You see each other more often. Share everything. Always. Anything. You love the feedback. Wear your heart on your posts. You get hooked. You get so many likes and favorites. It becomes a passion.

And then the social network you've been dating changes its privacy policy and all your secrets leak out. Your cousin tags you, Mom sees your photos from Spring Break at Destin, Florida, and your karaoke medley of Queen hits goes viral. Shit. All of a sudden, you're a privacy advocate even more afraid of Latin and all caps.

Due to its popularity and historically poor execution on privacy, Facebook is a common modern target in the social world for privacy advocates. So Facebook recently did what anyone would do. They had an engineering team—which is probably great at writing code—add something to their site that they thought would reduce the fear: a cartoon dinosaur.

"Our team looked at a few different characters, saw the dinosaur and just thought he was the friendliest and best choice," a Facebook engineering manager told the *New York Times* in 2014.

To better explain their privacy policy, Facebook created a mascot to explain where your posts are going to end up.

What?

This is a time of privacy madness, a bizarre tipping point when the largest social network has chosen to use a cartoon dinosaur to explain their ever-changing privacy policy settings,[9] when a US privacy savior has been banished to Russia, and when an enormous American search engine has caused so much paranoia about privacy that it has gone on tour in Europe to convince its citizens that their own courts are misguided about privacy.[10]

Meanwhile, back in the United States, according to Pew Research Center, 68 percent of Internet users believe that our current laws are "not good enough in protecting people's privacy online."[11] And as we jump from service to service, our data and our personal information lie in multiple servers we may have forgotten.

It's like having 20 ex-wives or -husbands running around town with the ability to reveal your most embarrassing secrets to the world.

Some say these worries are a soon-to-be passé issue. That once the next generation grows up, all these privacy concerns will fade away like 1956 paranoia about Elvis Presley's swinging hips.[12]

"As younger people reveal their private lives on the Internet, the older generation looks on with alarm and misapprehension not seen since the early days of rock and roll," says a subheader from New York Magazine.[13]

The chief privacy officer at the computer security company McAfee (the antivirus guys) has concurred. "Younger generations," she once told USA Today, "seem to be more lax about privacy."[14]

But despite your struggles with your daughter's Instagram, studies have shown the opposite: Privacy actually does matter to teens. Given all that is shared—photos, videos, animated GIFs—the idea that the upcoming generation does not care about privacy seems false. After all, with more on the table, there's more to lose.

Your teenage daughter may not have anything to hide from the government, but she probably doesn't want her friends (or enemies) to get that video of her chicken wing dance moves from Aunt Eleanor's wedding. As Molly Wood from the New York Times once wrote, "The second generation of digital citizens—teenagers and millennials, who have spent most, if not all, of their lives online—appear to be more likely to embrace the tools of privacy and protect their personal information."[15]

That's probably why the concept of quickly exploding messages on services like Snapchat are popular among teens. A recent Pew study revealed 51 percent of American teens (aged 12 to 17) have avoided certain apps "due to privacy concerns" and 59 percent of American teenage girls disable location awareness out of fear of being tracked.[16]

Similar results have shown up in research by top universities. At Harvard's Berkman Center, researchers collaborating with Pew found that 60 percent of American teens had manually set their Facebook profiles to private (friends only) before it became the default option.[17] In a collaborative study from UC Berkeley and the University of Pennsylvania,[18] researchers found that "large percentages of young adults (those 18 to 24) are in harmony with older Americans regarding concerns about online privacy, norms, and policy suggestions."[19] Obnoxious over-sharers stand out, but the average teenager seems to place the same value on privacy as her previous generation.

If, going forward, we continue to evolve our technological experiences, and we step into a No Interface world in which technology is built to understand your needs, collecting data about your preferences can be a powerful tool. It can allow systems to achieve currently unfathomable advancements in technology that change the way you live. But to truly succeed, those new products and services need to be created with ethical policies desired by this generation and the next.

So, how do we end the waterboarding? How do we fix the problem of legal agreements so that we can take this leap forward?

Should we force users to scroll to the bottom of a privacy policy before allowing them to continue to install a program in hopes that'll make them read the legal terms? More all caps so everything seems more important? A pop-up warning that they should really read the terms? A more robust checkbox confirmation method? Better typographic formatting?

Nope. Instead, embrace reality: It's mental torture, and the average user is probably never going to read legal agreements.

Not long ago, a company called PC Pitstop shipped a popular piece of software called Optimize. It scanned the entire contents of your personal computer—your personal documents, your images, your music, and more—to identify any common problems that could be slowing down your computer.

For scanning software like Optimize, which could be potentially sifting through your sensitive password or bank information, privacy is hugely important. Curious about how long we're comfortable sitting in the boredom gas chamber to actually read our rights, PC Pitstop secretly altered their end user license agreement (EULA) to include a section about how to get a free cash prize, just in case anyone actually had the pain tolerance to read that far into the document.

Months passed. Thousands of sales. No one cashed in.

But then, on one surprising day, after over three months and nearly

3,000 sales, a customer contacted the company to claim the prize. He received a well-earned $1,000 check.

Maybe it was an unethical experiment, but their discovery revealed a pattern.

A few years later, a UK retailer indulged a similar curiosity. Gamestation, which at the time sold new and used video games, inserted a special clause into their sales contract with online customers: They asked you to sell your soul to them. Seven thousand five hundred people agreed to the clause, probably unknowingly handing over the rights to their souls.[20]

Quick: What's the average time someone actually spends looking over the terms and conditions of software? Seventy-four work days? Ten work days? Five? How long do you think we're willing to spend on the torture rack?

Roughly one and a half to two seconds.[21]

Make it stop! I'll check the box! I agree! My troops are hiding behind the mountain!

Most of us would make terrible spies.

That number comes from Tom Rodden, a professor of computing at the University of Nottingham,[22] who has found that we tend to spend just a few forgettable moments considering the agreements we check off every time we install a snazzy new app, 15 times less than we spend watching a 30-second television ad for toilet paper.

Americans' Concern with Transparency about Data Usage

Very much	80%
Somewhat	
Only a little	
Not at all	
No response	

(Source: "Big Data: Seizing Opportunities, Preserving Values," Executive Office of the President, White House 2014)

Even if some of the smartest people in tech legal managed to triple the amount of time people spent reading terms and conditions, you'd still only be at six seconds of reading per agreement.

Instead, a greater return on our efforts might occur with improving other things in the experience that could help us manage our privacy.

For one, the bland settings menu.

In 2014, President Barack Obama called for a "90-day review of big data and privacy." Over 24,000 people were surveyed about a variety of issues. One of the most striking findings was that 80 percent of the respondents were "very much" concerned about transparency of data use.[23]

That same year Microsoft released their first version of Cortana, a voice assistant. There are a lot of interesting things to discuss from their initial work, but one thing that stands out, believe it or not, is their settings menu. I'll recreate it here for you:

Contana settings:

Cortana suggestions

On

You'll no longer get suggestions, reminders, alerts, and ideas from Cortana. We won't delete anything in Cortana's Notebook.

☑ **Track flights or other things mentioned in your email.**

Steve

change my name

Change the name Cortana uses for you, or how Cortana pronounces it.

☑ **Have Cortana call me by my name.**

What's so striking? The simple, straightforward, transparent, plain English. The understandable explanations under switch buttons. The ability to change your name with ease, and no need for a cartoon dinosaur. With potentially 80 percent of the US population concerned about transparency in data collection, an easily understood settings menu—including such things as a simple checkmark for "Track flights or other things mentioned in your email"—can be much more powerful in gaining trust than forcing someone to scroll through a legal agreement.

Transparent and ethical data collection is a fantastic foundation for privacy. Much more so than LATIN IN ALL CAPS.

In the pursuit of trying to create elegant, No Interface experiences, technology companies will probably need to collect a bit of data about you to make sure they're doing the right thing.

Say, for example, a startup wanted to make a NoUI experience that made the lights in your bedroom mimic a gentle sunrise just before your alarm clock went off. To make it work, the startup would probably need to know only when you have your alarm clock set. Not your contact list, who you follow on Twitter, or your LinkedIn connections.

Going overboard on data is a good way to lose trust and make customers run the other way, like when it was revealed that the social network Path was secretly copying your smartphone's address book onto their servers. Yes, they fixed it, and apologized profusely,[24] but they had to pay the Federal Trade Commission (FTC) an $800,000 fine,[25] and it damaged their public image forever.

Or when Jay-Z made a deal to give his *Magna Carta . . . Holy Grail* album away as a free app, but the app didn't play any of his music until you gave away your address book information, your call log, access to your social media accounts, the ability to send messages on those services, your email account, and, unbelievably, a whole lot of other things that had nothing to do with listening to Beyonce's love talk about his Yankees cap.[26] Facing privacy ridicule, Jay-Z himself tweeted "sux must do better."[27]

World's best apology.

All that said, to deliver what you need and when you want it, more advanced NoUI systems may need to learn about some of a user's general preferences.

Say, for example, you built a back pocket app that attempts to discover a customer's food preferences to provide him with a custom-tailored food delivery service. He may have flown by the EULA—*Yes, I agree!*—

and given you permission to gather information about his favorite foods from some of his other public channels.

Eventually, through social media posts and shared articles, your software may start to see a pattern around cupcakes. And when your system gains enough confidence that he loves them, you might decide to give him a free delivery of the best cupcakes you can find.

He gets the cupcakes, loves the treat, and now tells everyone about your amazing service.

Cupcakes . . . ? For me!?

Even though you knocked his socks off, his data about loving cupcakes is still his data. And you should treat it that way. So the app could automatically forget detailed information after a period of time. The act of forgetting that sounds like blasphemy in a world of tech businesses built on advertising, but it is a great way for a reputable company built around data to gain trust.

That event could trigger after success. Perhaps after delighting him with the cupcake delivery, the system could jot down that it successfully delivered a dessert, forget all about the cupcake-specific data, and start again, looking for a new pattern that's not dessert related.

We got dessert, now what?

Inactivity could be another automatic trigger to erase any stored information. If he hasn't utilized the system in a long time, his food data could automatically clear. With so many services out there trying to grab our attention, knowing that a system collecting more general information will just forget everything it knows about you if you don't use it for a long time might ease the resistance to trying out the new software in the first place.

He could even explicitly tell you how long to collect his data. The mobile app Glympse, for example, lets you share your GPS location with a specific set of people within a defined time period.[28] You're walking to meet your friend, you set a 20-minute timer to share your location, so he sees you when it's relevant, and then shares no data when it's not relevant.

Or, an easy "let's start over" button could exist on a physical object or graphical user interface to clear all saved data at any time.

For richer transparency, granular controls could be offered within a list of conclusions, including the observations that led the system to those conclusions, that allow a user to remove those findings. Maybe something like this:

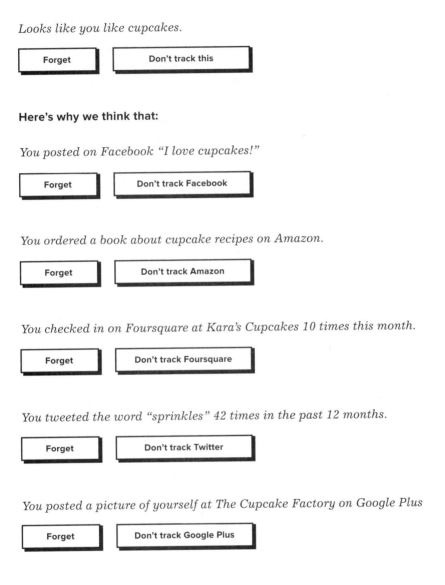

Looks like you like cupcakes.

| Forget | Don't track this |

Here's why we think that:

You posted on Facebook "I love cupcakes!"

| Forget | Don't track Facebook |

You ordered a book about cupcake recipes on Amazon.

| Forget | Don't track Amazon |

You checked in on Foursquare at Kara's Cupcakes 10 times this month.

| Forget | Don't track Foursquare |

You tweeted the word "sprinkles" 42 times in the past 12 months.

| Forget | Don't track Twitter |

You posted a picture of yourself at The Cupcake Factory on Google Plus

| Forget | Don't track Google Plus |

Buttons are ugly, and graphical user interfaces aren't aesthetically elegant. But having explicit controls sitting in the background of a complex system that you can directly manipulate is one way of easing any potential user fear and creating a relationship of trust. The graphical user interface in this case is not the experience; it's just there for advanced privacy settings.

Look, we're not going to sit around and spend hours reading through legal documents we don't understand. It's first-world torture. We're eager to get things done and live our lives. But privacy is really important, and when taking technology to the next step we should consider good methods for providing the kind of control—automatic or manual—that lets everyone keep their secrets safe while enjoying the elegance of a system that provides you with what you need.

The best interface is no interface, but that leap forward in technology needs to value privacy or it won't have success.

18. Automatic
Automatic solutions are terrible. Look at Clippy!

Automatic solutions sound so wonderful.

Everything just magically gets done. And machines do it all on their own. They give us what we need, when we need it, and how we need it. The computer becomes a mind reader for our preferences. Science fiction becomes reality.

Robot vacuums. Autopilot. Self-driving cars. *Back to the Future* power laces.

A lot of NoUI thinking lends itself to making these kinds of automatic solutions. They aim to feel like pure delight. Like magic. Where technology should be in the twenty-first century.

But when it comes to actually implementing an automatic solution, a lot of people get scared. Some designers shiver. Some engineers run far, far away. Some project managers laugh when I draw one on the whiteboard. Some executives tell me I'm nuts. They assume it's impossible. Some even tell me to leave the meeting room.

And you know what?

They *should* be scared. Because automatic solutions—even partially automatic—are really hard to do correctly.

You need a lot of valid data to prove intention. You need a lot of confidence in your data analysis to know when to take an action. The wrong information, or using the wrong lens to look at that information, can lead to a bad reading and a terrible result. Even if the stakes are low, an undesired result that's off the mark might be so creepy that it alienates customers and invalidates their belief in your product.

But when we overcome the immense barriers, when we have a rich understanding of the environment, and apply models that work beyond ideal situations, we can create something special. Something people love. Because when automatic solutions work well, they have a history of doing very well in the marketplace. Some of them have become an invisible yet embedded part of our lives.

The mathematician Heron of Alexandria, born in roughly 10 AD, wrote books about his visions for the grand machines of the future. Surprisingly, they weren't filled with wireframes for apps, but inventions that could help humankind become more efficient by utilizing air, water, and steam pressure. Among his inventions, he drew a steam engine nearly fifteen hundred years before one was realized, and two designs for an automatic solution that wouldn't become a real product until 1960.[1]

In that year—nearly two millennia later—brothers Lee Hewitt and Dee Horton released a working version of one of Heron's dreams: an automated door. Frustrated by the effects of high winds on swing doors at their store in Corpus Christi, the brothers started their own door company that sold the world's first automatically opening doors.[2]

Today, the Horton Automatic sliding doors are replicated all over the world. When you walk up to a grocery store or hospital, the doors often automatically open. When health-care workers rush a patient into a hospital from an ambulance, the doors just slide open.

Um, I know how automatic doors work.

The experience isn't a shocking, please-leave-the-meeting-room, techno-utopian vision, but an expected, boring solution. It isn't something we marvel at, revere, or even consider special; it's become an automatic solution we just count on. And that, honestly, is a great thing.

These seamless, automatic solutions sometimes take decades (or a few millennia) before they are reliable enough to become part of our everyday lives. They're not easy, but they're remarkable when they work. They set a high bar for technological success.

In 1953, not long after getting into a car accident with his wife and seven-year-old daughter, John W. Hetrick filed US patent 2,649,311 for what is considered the prototype for the first car air bag. German Walter Linderer filed a patent for a similar system a year later. In 1967, Mercedes-Benz started working on air bags for their cars, and a handful of other car manufacturers made incremental improvements in the years following.

But it wouldn't really be until Allen K. Breed's air bags were tied to a crash-sensing system—US patent 5,071,161—that the solution became standardized. By 1998, the automatically deploying air bag was so reliable that it became federal law in the United States that all consumer cars and light trucks sold had to have driver and passenger safety air bags.[3]

An automatic solution that puts a soft barrier between me and my steel-framed car? Obviously, a great thing. So convincing, it's the law. It's estimated that air bags have saved more than 10,000 lives[4] by acting in a millisecond of time in which you're not able to wake up your phone, swipe, and tap an app to launch an inflatable bag between you and your car.

Driving is one of the most dangerous things we do on an everyday basis. And cars are also the location of another embedded automatic solution that is one of the most insane, risky ideas that we don't even bat an eye toward today: automatic transmission.

"Did you ever realize how many steps it takes to drive a car with a conventional transmission? Watch closely . . . after 19 distinct manual operations, she's finally under way."

That beginning of an ad for Oldsmobile's 1940 "Hydra-Matic"—the first automatic transmission—sounds like the beginning of this book. Advertised as "simplicity itself," the commercial for the automatic solution they called "Motoring's Magic Carpet" showed how manual controls—like the clutch— have become unnecessary.[5] "This is said by engineers," the *New York Times* wrote in 1939, "to be the most revolutionary development in motor cars since the invention of the self-starter."[6]

By 2013, fewer than four percent of new cars sold in the United States had manual transmission.[7] Even Lamborghini, a car lover's car, has started making models with automatic transmissions.[8]

The market loves great automatic solutions.

They're not easy. They may even take a decade or two to perfect. You may even get thrown out of a conference room suggesting the notion. But don't underestimate their power: Automatic solutions that work well can become a seamless part of our lives.

19. Failure
What happens when it all falls apart?

Oh, those fools.

Listen, don't buy a refrigerator. Because once you get one you'll start buying perishable items. And before you know it, your refrigerator will be broken, and you'll have a bunch of spoiled, awful-smelling meat on your hands. Refrigerators don't last forever, so don't be foolish.

Don't start taking showers, either. You'll start getting used to having one in your daily routine, and one day if your water stops running, well, you'll have this terrible habit that relied on running water and you won't remember how to clean yourself in a good old-fashioned tub. No one needs to clean with a fire hose above his or her head.

Lightbulbs? Ha! Use candles, because if you rely on the government's bureaucratically created electrical grid to automatically deploy to you just the right amount of electricity, well, I don't know what to tell you my friend, you're living in a dreamland.

What would you do if it ran out? If it stopped working? If it failed? Then what would you do? You'd be a running-water-loving, cold-food-eating, electricity-hogging idiot!

Those dated thoughts may sound insane to you now, but in more modern times we've had our fears.

Y2K: *Oh no, two digits!*

Online banking: *My money in cyberspace!?*

Leaping into the unknown is scary. And relying on a new means of getting things done means the fear of failure will be prevalent. Examining that fear of failure—a consideration of edge cases—can be limiting and often unproductive during early production ideation, but it is essential to consider when putting together the final stages of anything.

Some of the largest and most ambitious projects in recent human history have ended in disaster because of an inability to see important details upon executing the ideas. Chernobyl had a meltdown that contaminated its workers and the land around it. The *Titanic* crashed. The *Challenger* space shuttle exploded.

Those are major, tragic failures, but the possibility of even modest failure should never be overlooked—no matter how small the system. When making tools to be a part of our everyday lives, any good system should consider and anticipate failure.

Many of the NoUI examples mentioned in this book have found various useful ways to deal with failure. Even mundane automatic sliding doors commonly offer a physical "push to open" backup option in case of rare electrical failure.

Some devices have added sensors to prevent failure. Although infants should always be placed in the backseat, the impact of a rapidly-inflating, quickly-ejected air bag can injure the smaller bodies of older children sitting in the front seat. To prevent that potential failure, many air bag systems now use several additional sensors—such as weight, seating position, and seat belt use—to determine whether the air bag should be deployed.[1]

I personally root for sensors and predictive systems to help solve failure in real time, such as those General Electric (GE) has mentioned in their move for an Industrial Internet. Marco Annunziata, chief economist at GE, explained in his TED talk:

> We've developed a preventive maintenance system which can be installed on any aircraft. It's self-learning and able to predict issues that a human operator would miss. The aircraft, while in flight, will communicate with technicians on the ground. By the time it lands, they will already know if anything needs to be serviced. Just in the U.S., a system like this can prevent over 60,000 delays and cancellations every year, helping seven million passengers get to their destinations on time.[2]

But for some of the examples already mentioned in this book, the makers are using a simpler technique to handle failure: graphical user interfaces. As a backup. As a secondary experience. That shift from primary to secondary is one smart way to use training wheels toward a No Interface future.

Nest, a learning thermostat, always has a graphical user interface available front and center. If your preferences and habits have changed, you can always go up to it and just turn the dial to the new indoor temperature you prefer. It's always ready to learn again.

Lockitron, the back pocket app that unlocks your deadbolt, has a set of controls on the Web and through its app. If you log into your account, you can, for example, manage who has access to your deadbolt. That back end system can also help you orchestrate more complicated activities, such as giving an Airbnb guest access to your home for just a few days without the need to change your deadbolt and keys.

The Petzl headlamp that automatically adjusts the amount of light needed for optimal performance in deep, dark caves comes with desktop software. The headlamp works without requiring you to install anything, but if you happen to not like the built-in automatic settings, you can use the desktop interface to customize levels of brightness.

EarlySense has a sensor that can read important information about a patient's health status, learn about the patterns, and inform the correct health-care worker at the correct time. But for a complex hospital environment, EarlySense also offers detailed software so that health-care workers can see additional important information to make any necessary case-by-case decisions by examining spreadsheets of data collected.

TripIt, which removes the digital chore of syncing your calendar with your travel information, has a website and app. The backup interface allows you to modify trip information in case the "automagical" syncing got it wrong.

Aiming for a screenless world, well, that's fantastic. But as we go forward in that direction, we may find that screens are a decent backup option for those edge cases when all hell breaks loose.

Talk of failure can slow ideation and start an endless, paranoid debate when discussing the abstract in early product stages. But when actually readying something for the real world, we shouldn't always rely on the intended solution. Failure is always a potential outcome, and any good system considers how to deal with that failure in an effective way: predictive analytics, sensors, or even graphical user interfaces.

20. Exceptions
Less is sometimes more

The goal of this book is to be enriching and entertaining to guide you toward a new direction in user interface theory in a way that doesn't sound as painful, dreadful, and nauseating as *user interface theory*. Maybe it's even enjoyable enough to read that you'll pass this tech book along to someone else and have him enjoy it, too.

To get here, I've spent a few thousand hours sketching, thinking, and scribbling. And inevitably, via software like Scrivener, iA Writer, and InDesign, I've spent quality time getting chummy with the very thing I'm fulminating about to bring this book to your hands: Form fields. Menus. Dropdowns.

Puke.

But if it weren't for those interfaces, you wouldn't have this book. Absolutes are hardly ever absolutely true.

"The best interface is no interface" doesn't mean the *only* outcome should be no interface, it means the *best* possible outcome is no interface. Insisting that NoUI is the only viable solution would be utterly stupid.

Having an aspiration goal, a point of view, and a design philosophy means you have a mechanism for filtering ideas—a principle to build a process around. Less isn't always more, but "less is more" is an effective Modernist design philosophy.

The best interface is no interface is a path toward achieving technologically elegant experiences. It's about moving past screens and trying to implement principles that can lead to a wonderful experience. It's about people first. We have enough tedious and inefficient solutions—let's aim higher.

Of course, there are exceptions.

For one, computers can summarize task-oriented or information-heavy content; but consuming for pleasure via screen, well, there's no need to rid ourselves of that joy. You can certainly make an experience more elegant by cleaning up a cumbersome streaming video application, but I can't imagine how you'd enjoy a Benedict Cumberbatch movie without some kind of screen.

We probably also need some kind of interface for major digital decisions. Buying a cup of coffee or paying for a taxi ride can be NoUI, but if you're making a massive house payment online, I think it's safe to say that providing a button or two is a good idea when confirming a $200,000 home loan.

Same goes with governmental decisions. Tax codes shouldn't be written by quiet software based on big data. We need empathic leaders making explicit choices. And militarily, it goes without saying that we don't want an automated Stanley Kubrick doomsday device that accidentally obliterates the world.

Yeehaw!!

And some of the things people love to do, like cooking, hiking, or watching a sports game, they would never want a machine to do for them. The whole point of the efficiency is so that we can enjoy more of what we love.

No, this isn't a complete list of exceptions, simply an acknowledgment that, like any rule, there *are* exceptions.

The real power of "the best interface is no interface" is as a call to action. As a philosophy. It's not about flat design or skeuomorphic. Web or mobile.

This is about aiming for the best outcome of NoUI. One that doesn't distract us or try to get us addicted, something that embraces the way we live and aims to make it better quietly and elegantly. For technology to become embedded in the fabric of our lives instead of a distraction away from what really matters.

Conclusion

21. The Future
Wow, this is boring

One day, I hope you think this book is utterly boring. Passé. And that you hear about the idea of screenless solutions and yawn.

The best interface is no interface? Wake me up when you have something interesting to say.

Because if that day comes, remember to celebrate: You'll be living in a better time. Not one drowning in screens with intentionally addictive interfaces that distract us from one another, but one in which typical processes are embraced. When computers serve us, instead of us serving them. When technological systems are continuously adapting to our individual needs. A day, probably a few decades from now, when children dress up as their grandparents on Halloween by sticking smartphones to their faces.

Look, I'm like grandpa who stares at his giant phone all day.

That day will be joyous. I hope that today's marvel becomes tomorrow's mundane. That NoUI is like watching a rerun of *Friends*.

But that day may not come. This book is a journey into just one possible future. Some of the companies I have mentioned for taking us toward that future may have already disappeared by the time you've read this book. If there's enough dust on the cover of your copy, some of the examples in this text may feel ancient. I hope the ideas in this book aren't forgotten, but end up as stepping stones to something far greater—a future in which the best case of a graphical user interface has been understood as no interface.

Along the way will be battles to be fought inside companies and class-rooms, privacy issues to tackle, and other unforeseen hurdles. But when the philosophies settle, the debaters come to agreement, the doers under-stand how to get it done, and the business plans start to fall into place, we could have something utterly revolutionary in our hands.

And when that revolution finally comes to fruition, we may think of it as the most boring, expected solution. *No screens? Tell me something I don't know.*

Here's hoping for that boredom.

Appendix A:
Endnotes

Chapter 1
Why Did You Buy This Book?

1 John Pavlus, "A Tale of Two Newspaper Interfaces," *MIT Technology Review*, March 13, 2013. http://www.technologyreview.com/view/512486/a-tale-of-two-newspaper-interfaces/

2 Karis Hustad, ""Netflix Rolls Out Updated, Smarter TV Interface," *Christian Science Monitor*, November 13, 2013. http://www.csmonitor.com/Innovation/2013/1113/Netflix-rolls-out-updated-smarter-TV-interface

3 "Apple TV: A Simpler Interface, Easier Access to Media Through the iCloud" *Washington Post*, March 8, 2012. http://www.washingtonpost.com/business/economy/apple-tv-a-simpler-interface-easier-access-to-media-through-icloud/2012/03/08/gIQARVivzR_story.html

Chapter 2
Let's Make an App

1 "Apple iPhone 3G ad - There's An App For That (2009)," YouTube, Last accessed August 2014. https://www.youtube.com/watch?v=Mc-pV2YYOAs

2 Simon Hudson, *Bumps for Boomers: Marketing Sport Tourism to the Aging Tourist*, 2011, (Oxford: Goodfellow Publishers), p.14

3 Apple in 2009 started using the phrase, "There's an app for that" in TV ads to show off the multitude of apps available for iOS devices through its popular App Store, which opened July 2008.
Brian X. Chen, "Apple Registers Trademark for 'There's an App for That,'" *Wired*, October 11, 2010. http://www.wired.com/2010/10/app-for-that/

4 "According to a joint report by UNICEF and the United Nations, of the 783 million people still without safe drinking water, the majority live in countries that are not among the world's poorest."
Joan Rose, PhD, "Clean Drinking Water: UN Goal Met Five Years Early" Water Quality and Health Council, April 5, 2012. http://www.waterandhealth.org/clean-drinking-water-goal-met-years-early/

5 "The tally found that 610,042 people were homeless on that night, reflecting a drop of nearly 4 percent from 2012 to 2013, the agency says."
Bill Chappell, "Number Of Homeless Declines Again, But Gains Aren't Universal," NPR, November 21, 2013. http://www.npr.org/blogs/thetwo-way/2013/11/21/246589487/number-of-homeless-declines-again-but-gains-arent-universal

6 "When we hug or kiss a loved one, oxytocin levels drive up."
"What Is Oxytocin?," *Psychology Today*, Last accessed August 2014. http://www.psychologytoday.com/basics/oxytocin

7 "This week in my App Smart column,"
Kit Eaton, "App Smart Extra: Apps to Improve Your Singing," *New York Times*, February 15, 2013. http://gadgetwise.blogs.nytimes.com/2013/02/15/app-smart-extra-apps-to-improve-your-singing/

8 Bob Tedeschi, "App Smart Extra: A Weather App That Works," *New York Times*, May 20, 2011. http://gadgetwise.blogs.nytimes.com/2011/05/20/app-smart-extra-a-weather-app-that-works/

9 "If you have any money left to invest, a program from Bloomberg offers a wealth of basic stock market data and news on the iPhone for free."
Roy Furchgott, ""App of the Week: Dial M for Meltdownn," *The New York Times*, January 25, 2009. http://gadgetwise.blogs.nytimes.com/2009/01/25/If-You-Have-Any-Money-Left-To/

10 "Apps, apps, and more apps—tens of thousands of them at our fingertips, and some, like Facebook, YouTube, SitOrSquat—are truly life changing."
Jennifer Jolly, "5 New apps That Will Change Your Life," *USA Today*, May 3, 2014. http://www.usatoday.com/story/tech/columnist/2014/05/03/5-new-apps-that-will-change-your-life/8571485/

11 See my screenshots from a CNN.com search: https://www.dropbox.com/sh/ntfhibch27kvpep/PkhxvS6YSc

12 "Stuck in Snow? There's an App for That!,"," CNN, February 13, 2014. http://newday.blogs.cnn.com/2014/02/13/stuck-in-snow-theres-an-app-for-that/

13 Samuel Burke, "Moody? There's an App for That!,"!," CNN, December 19, 2013. http://edition.cnn.com/videos/tech/2013/12/19/cnn-pkg-burke-mood-app.cnn

14 Jason Miks, "Staying Safe in Danger Zones? There's an App for That," CNN, October 8, 2013. http://globalpublicsquare.blogs.cnn.com/2013/10/08/staying-safe-in-danger-zones-theres-an-app-for-that/

15 "Remote Sex: There's an App for That," CNN, April 25, 2013. http://edition.cnn.com/2013/04/26/tech/innovation/fundawear-orig-ideas/

16 Rafael Romo, "No TP? There's an App for That," CNN, June 17, 2013. http://edition.cnn.com/videos/tech/2013/06/17/pkg-romo-venezuela-shortage-app.cnn

17 Tory Dunnan, "Need to Pray? There's an App for That," CNN, May 3, 2013. http://edition.cnn.com/videos/bestoftv/2013/05/03/prayer-tech.cnn-universal-pictures

18 Mike Mount, "Sending Top Secret Information? There's an App for That," CNN, February 26, 2013. http://security.blogs.cnn.com/2013/02/26/sending-top-secret-information-theres-an-app-for-that/

19 "Need a Concierge? There's an App for That," CNN, October 3, 2012. http://edition.cnn.com/2012/10/01/travel/personal-concierge-app-guide/index.html

20 "On Health Kick? There's an App for That," CNN, September 27, 2012. http://www.cnn.com/video/data/2.0/video/health/2012/09/27/health-minute-weightloss-apps.cnn.html

21 Laura Koran, "Ordination on the Go? There's an App for That!," CNN, July 17, 2012. http://edition.cnn.com/2012/09/27/health/mental-health-apps/

22 "What's #Trending: Want to Know How Attractive You Are? There's an App for That!," CNN, April 30, 2012. http://earlystart.blogs.cnn.com/2012/04/30/whats-trending-want-to-know-how-attractive-you-are-theres-an-app-for-that/

23 Eoghan Macguire, "Save the Whales? There's an App for That," CNN, April 23, 2012. http://edition.cnn.com/2012/04/22/world/whale-iphone-app/index.html

24 "Dead? There's an App for That," CNN, April 18, 2012. http://www.cnn.com/video/?/video/us/2012/04/18/dnt-in-qr-code-tombstones.wlfi&iref=allsearch&video_referrer=

25 Paromita Shah, "Opinion: Being Arrested? Yes, there's an App for That," CNN, March 17, 2012. http://inamerica.blogs.cnn.com/2012/03/17/opinion-undocumented-immigration-being-arrested-app-for-that/

26 Sanjay Gupta, MD, "Are You Sick? There's an App for That!," CNN, January 16, 2012. http://edition.cnn.com/videos/bestoftv/2012/01/16/exp-are-you-sick-theres-an-app-for-that.cnn

27 Karin Caifa, "New Year's Eve: There's an App for That," CNN, December 30, 2011. http://www.cnn.com/video/data/2.0/video/bestoftv/2011/12/30/nr-new-years-apps.cnn.html

28 Shanon Cook, "Sting's Career? There's an App for That," CNN, November 16, 2011. http://marquee.blogs.cnn.com/2011/11/16/stings-career-theres-an-app-for-that/

29 John Abell, "Stalking: There's an App for That?," CNN, October 28, 2011. http://edition.cnn.com/videos/politics/2011/10/28/am-abell-apps-stalking.cnn

30 Peter Taggart, "Want to Be a Priest? There's an App for That," CNN, October 17, 2011. http://religion.blogs.cnn.com/2011/10/17/want-to-be-a-priest-theres-an-app-for-that/

31 Karin Caifa, "Can't Sleep? There's an App for That," CNN, September 16, 2011. http://edition.cnn.com/videos/tech/2011/09/16/caifa-sleep-and-relaxation-apps.cnn

32 Karin Caifa, "Wedding Plans? There's an App for That," CNN, June 12, 2011. http://www.cnn.com/video/data/2.0/video/living/2011/06/12/caifa.wedding.planning.apps.cnn.html

33 Eric Marrapodi, "Selling Bread for Passover? There's an App for That," CNN, April 19, 2011. http://religion.blogs.cnn.com/2011/04/19/selling-bread-for-passover-theres-an-app-for-that/

34 "Heart Attack? There's an App for That," CNN, January 4, 2011. http://www.cnn.com/video/data/2.0/video/health/2011/01/04/ok.iphone.heart.monitor.koco.html

35 "Need a College? There's an App for That," CNN, October 30, 2010. http://www.cnn.com/video/data/2.0/video/tech/2010/10/30/nr.find.a.college.app.cnn.html

36 "Giving Birth? There's an App for That," CNN, September 21, 2010. http://www.cnn.com/video/data/2.0/video/living/2010/09/21/dnt.ipad.baby.cnn.html

37 "Home Security—There's an App for That," CNN, August 24, 2010. http://www.cnn.com/video/data/2.0/video/us/2010/08/24/dnt.iphone.app.thwarts.burglary.wfaa.html

38 T.J. Holmes, "Want to Save Cash? There's an App for That," CNN, July 31, 2010. http://www.cnn.com/video/data/2.0/video/tech/2010/07/31/nr.money.saving.apps.cnn.html

39 Mario Armstrong, "World Cup? There's an App for That," CNN, June 13, 2010. http://newsroom.blogs.cnn.com/2010/06/13/world-cup-theres-an-app-for-that/

40 Steven Stern, "Cooking Dinner? There's an App for That," CNN, May 10, 2010. http://www.cnn.com/2010/LIVING/home-style/05/10/digital.recipes.cooking/

41 Ami Angelowicz, "Britney Spears, there's an App for That," CNN, November 25, 2009. http://www.cnn.com/2009/SHOWBIZ/11/25/celebrity.iphone.apps/

42 "Web Search interest: App, One Direction, Justin Bieber, God—Worldwide, Jan 2012—Jan 2014," Google Trends, Last accessed August 2014. http://www.google.com/trends/explore?hl=en-US&q=app,+one+direction,+/m/02m-jmr,+justin+bieber&cmpt=q&content=1#q=app%2C%20one%20direction%2C%20justin%20bieber%2C%20God&date=1%2F2012%2025m&cmpt=q

43 "Karl Benz patented the three-wheeled motor car in 1886." Lauren Cox, "Who Invented the Car?," Live Science, June 18, 2013. http://www.livescience.com/37538-who-invented-the-car.html

44 "Cheek to Cheek," Wikipedia, Last accessed August 2014. http://en.wikipedia.org/wiki/Cheek_to_Cheek

45 Matt Carmichael, "Edward Tufte: The AdAgeStat Q&A," Advertising Age, November 9, 2011. http://adage.com/article/adagestat/edward-tufte-adagestat-q-a/230884/

46 "2000 . . . Siemens' Electronics wins a PACE Award for a deceptively simple device. Easily seen as just a replacement for the mechanical key, simply carrying Siemens' Keyless-Go, a credit card-sized transponder, allows the driver to walk up to a locked vehicle, open the door, and press a button to get under way."
"2009 Automotive News PACE Awards," Automotive News, Last accessed August 2014. http://www.autonews.com/Assets/html/09_pace/past_winners.html#2000

Chapter 3
Slap an Interface on It!

1 Rory Reid, "Seagate Barracuda 7200.10: Biggest Hard Drive Ever," CNET, May 10, 2006. http://www.cnet.com/news/seagate-barracuda-7200-10-biggest-hard-drive-ever/

2 "How large is the average movie? A 2 hour SD movie is about 1.5 GB, and a 2 hour HD movie is about 4 GB." "Frequently Asked Questions (FAQ) for purchased movies." Apple, 2014. http://support.apple.com/kb/HT1906

3 Vlad Savov, "Helium-Filled Hard Drives Balloon Storage Space," The Verge, November 4, 2013. http://www.theverge.com/2013/11/4/5063994/hgst-ultrastar-he6-helium-filled-hdd

4 "Access to the Internet via broadband has now spread to 94 percent of Americans, a jump of two percentage points over last year and a huge leap from the 15 percent who had such access just a decade ago."
Allison Terry, "Got broadband? Access now extends to 94 percent of Americans," The Christian Science Monitor, August 24, 2012. http://www.csmonitor.com/USA/Society/2012/0824/Got-broadband-Access-now-extends-to-94-percent-of-Americans

5 2009: 3 seconds, 2012: 1 second.
Chris Gaylord, "4G? LTE? What's the difference?," The Christian Science Monitor, April 30, 2012. http://www.csmonitor.com/Innovation/Tech/2012/0430/4G-LTE-What-s-the-difference

6 Guy Kawasaki, "How to Kick Silicon Valley's Butt," How to Change the World, June 06, 2006. http://blog.guykawasaki.

com/2006/06/how_to_kick_sil.html#comment-18254667

7   Chris Ziegler, "Going the distance: driving the Tesla Model S in the real world," *The Verge,* February 12, 2013. http://www.theverge.com/2013/2/12/3969260/going-the-distance-driving-tesla-model-s-in-the-real-world

8   "Mini Connected, Dashboard Entertainment," MINI Space, August 17, 2012. http://www.minispace.com/en_us/article/mini-connected/456/?eid=456

9   Rafe Needleman, "Beyond the "Evernote Fridge," *Evernote Blog,* January 23, 2013. http://blog.evernote.com/blog/2013/01/23/beyond-the-evernote-fridge/

10 Farhad Manjoo, "Smart appliances: A washer that connects to the Internet and other amazingly dumb 'smart' gadgets," *Slate,* January 11, 2013. http://www.slate.com/articles/technology/technology/2013/01/smart_appliances_a_washer_that_connects_to_the_internet_and_other_amazingly.html

11   "The bins, which have LCD screens with public information and advertising, were first installed in the run-up to the 2012 Olympics. The trash barrels cost 30,000 pounds ($46,500) each to install, according to the Independent."
Rachel Savage, "Snooping Garbage Bins in City of London Ordered to Be Disabled," *Bloomberg,* Aug 12, 2013. http://www.bloomberg.com/news/2013-08-12/snooping-garbage-bins-in-city-of-london-ordered-to-be-disabled.html

12 "Pictures of desserts pop up on the screen midway through the main course, when people start to think about what they will eat next, Ms. Gibson said. Dessert sales increased almost 20% in tests, she said, and coffee sales also rose when featured in a similar way. Chili's is also considering promoting alcoholic beverages during meals, Ms. Gibson said."
Sarah Nassauer, "Chili's to Install Tabletop Computer Screens," *The Wall Street Journal,* September 15, 2013. http://online.wsj.com/news/articles/SB10001424127887323342404579077453886739272?mg=reno64-wsj

13 Bruce Horovitz, "Coke aims for cool with new 146-flavor dispenser," *USA Today,* April 16, 2014. http://www.usatoday.com/story/money/business/2014/04/14/coca-cola-coke-freestyle-soft-drinks-beverages/7478341/

Chapter 4
Jobs

1   "WSJ: What are your top goals for 2014? Ms. Whitman: We've got to continue the innovation engine. There is more work to be done there."
Spencer E. Ante, "H-P CEO Meg Whitman: We Are Doubling Down on Hardware" *Wall Street Journal - Digits,* February 21, 2014. http://blogs.wsj.com/digits/2014/02/21/h-p-ceo-meg-whitman-we-are-doubling-down-on-hardware/

2   "'We innovate by starting with the customer and working backwards,' he says. 'That becomes the touchstone for how we invent.'"
Adam Lashinsky, "Amazon's Jeff Bezos: The Ultimate

Disrupter," *Fortune,* November 16, 2012. http://fortune.com/2012/11/16/amazons-jeff-bezos-the-ultimate-disrupter/

3   "Cook: It's never been stronger. Innovation is so deeply embedded in Apple's culture. The boldness, ambition, belief there aren't limits, a desire to make the very best products in the world. It's the strongest ever. It's in the DNA of the company."
"Live Recap: Apple CEO Tim Cook Speaks at Goldman Conference," *Wall Street Journal - Digits,* February 12, 2013. http://blogs.wsj.com/digits/2013/02/12/live-apple-ceo-tim-cook-speaks-at-goldman-conference/

4   Jesse Solomon, "Google Worth More Than Exxon. Apple Next?" CNN, February 7, 2014. http://money.cnn.com/2014/02/07/investing/google-exxon-market-value/

5   2012 Lobbying (Millions $)
Google, 18.22
Exxon Mobil, 12.97
"Biggest Increases in Lobbying in U.S.," *Bloomberg,* May 28, 2013. http://www.bloomberg.com/visual-data/best-and-worst/biggest-increases-in-lobbying-in-u-dot-s-companies
2014 April–June (Q2) Lobbying (Millions $)
Google, 5.03
Exxon Mobil, 2.80
Pfizer, 1.60
Lauren Hepler, "Google Drops $5M on Q2 2014 Lobbying: Self-Driving Cars, Health, Tax, Immigration," *Silicon Valley Business Journal,* July 28, 2014. http://www.bizjournals.com/sanjose/news/2014/07/28/self-driving-cars-health-tech-immigration-google.html

6   Ashlee Vance, "This Tech Bubble Is Different," *Businessweek,* April 14, 2011. http://www.businessweek.com/magazine/content/11_17/b4225060960537.htm

Chapter 5
Addiction UX

1   "A whopping 96 percent of Google's $37.9 billion 2011 revenue came from advertising . . ."
Meghan Kelly, "96 Percent of Google's Revenue Is Advertising, Who Buys It?," *Venture Beat,* January 29, 2012. http://venturebeat.com/2012/01/29/google-advertising/

2   "$5,089 total revenue in 2012, $4,279 from advertising (figures in millions)"
Ken Yeung, "Facebook's Long Road to 'Mobile Best': HTML5, Native Apps, and Now Home," The Next Web, April 7, 2013. http://thenextweb.com/facebook/2013/04/07/facebooks-long-road-to-mobile-best-html5-native-apps-and-now-home/

3   "The company said that it earned 2 cents per share, excluding some items, for the fourth quarter on revenue of $243 million . . . Advertising revenue for the quarter totaled $220 million."
Natalie Jarvey, "Twitter Reports Ad Revenue Upswing, But Anemic User Growth," *Hollywood Reporter,* February 5, 2014. http://www.hollywoodreporter.com/news/twitter-reports-ad-revenue-upswing-677495

4   "Last year, Yahoo brought in $4.7 billion in revenue, down 6 percent from the previous year, as sales of both display

and search ads, which together made up about four-fifths of Yahoo's revenue, continued to fall."

Vindu Goel, "Yahoo Wants You to Linger (on the Ads, Too)," *New York Times*, June 21, 2014. http://www.nytimes.com/2014/06/22/technology/yahoo-wants-you-to-linger-on-the-ads-too.html?_r=0

5   "Mr. Paternot was the Corey Feldman of the Internet, a leather-pants-wearing prodigy whom a CNN camera crew once captured dancing atop a nightclub table as he declared, 'Got the girl. Got the money. Now I'm ready to live a disgusting, frivolous life.'"

Andres Pinter, "A Star Is Rebooted," *New York Observer*, March 31, 2003. http://observer.com/2003/03/a-star-is-rebooted/

6   Dow Jones News Service, "Another Internet Firm, Theglobe.com, Makes a Spectacular Debut," *Chicago Tribune*, November 13, 1998. http://articles.chicagotribune.com/1998-11-13/news/9811140043_1_theglobe-com-internet-firm-ipo

7   "Two Founders of theglobe.com to Resign as Co-Chief Executives (Jan. 28, 2000) . . . Last week, theglobe.com was taken off the Nasdaq National Market listings because its stock price was too low"

Ianthe Jeanne Dugan And Aaron Lucchetti, "After Becoming Stars of the Dot-Com Boom, Theglobe.com Founders Find Fame Fleeting," *Wall Street Journal*, May 2, 2001. http://online.wsj.com/news/articles/SB988750097459636

8   Ethan Zuckerman, "The Internet's Original Sin," *The Atlantic*, August 14, 2014. http://www.theatlantic.com/technology/archive/2014/08/advertising-is-the-internets-original-sin/376041/

9   Rolfe Winkler, "As Google Builds Out Own Content, Some Advertisers Feel Pushed Aside," *Wall Street Journal*, August 18, 2014. http://online.wsj.com/articles/googles-richer-content-worries-some-advertisers-1408391392

10   Yoree Koh, "Twitter's User Problem: Fastest Gains Are People That Don't See Ads," *Wall Street Journal*, Aug 1, 2014. http://online.wsj.com/articles/twitters-user-problem-fastest-gains-are-people-that-dont-see-ads-1406924973

11   "These themes from my sorting study went directly into the team's decisions about which feeds to make available to people. A 'Photos' feed had been a no-brainer from the start, and the idea of a 'Close Friends' feed had been in the mix and got more traction based on the findings. But the creation of a 'Following' feed was spurred by people's desire for stories related to their interests. The 'All Friends' feed was also born out of my research, which showed people were interested in serendipitous discovery of stories from their full friend lists."

Jane Justice Leibrock, "User Experience Lab: How We Designed a New News Feed Using Your Feedback," Facebook Engineering, March 12, 2013. https://www.facebook.com/note.php?note_id=10151359587673920

12   Robinson Meyer, "Everything We Know About Facebook's Secret Mood Manipulation Experiment," *The Atlantic*, June 28, 2014. http://www.theatlantic.com/technology/archive/2014/06/everything-we-know-about-facebooks-secret-mood-manipulation-experiment/373648/

13   "Facebook has announced a redesigned News Feed that separates streams of content into multiple categories and optimizes the user interface with a 'mobile-inspired' design. Describing the goal of News Feed as providing a 'personalized newspaper,' Mark Zuckerberg says it's being changed to take advantage of more photo and other visual content sharing, as well as the difference between personal stories and posts from public figures."

Adi Robertson, "Facebook Redesigns News Feed with Multiple Feeds and 'Mobile-Inspired' Interface," *The Verge*, March 7, 2013. http://www.theverge.com/2013/3/7/4075548/facebook-redesigns-news-feed-with-multiple-feeds

14   "After an investigation into the problem by Facebook's data team, they discovered that the new News Feed was performing too well. It was performing so well from a design standpoint that users no longer felt the need to browse areas outside of the News Feed as often, so they were spending less time on the site. Unfortunately, this change in user behavior led to fewer advertisement impressions, which led, ultimately, to less revenue."

Dustin Curtis, "Whatever Goes Up, That's What We Do," *Svbtle*, March 27, 2014. http://dcurt.is/facebooks-predicament

15   Julie Zhuo, "Whatever's Best for the People, That's What We Do," *Medium*, March 28, 2014. https://medium.com/@joulee/whatevers-best-for-the-people-thats-what-we-do-ed75a0ee7641

16   "In our view, the most important growth levers for Twitter are growth in market share, users, and time spent."

Rick Summer, "TWTR : Twitter Inc Analyst Report | Analyst Report," *Morningstar*, July 30, 2014. http://analysisreport.morningstar.com/stock/research?t=TWTR&region=usa&culture=en-US&productcode=MLE

17   Mark Gongloff, "Facebook Sucks Up a Ridiculously Huge and Growing Share of Our Time Wasted Online" *Wall Street Journal*, September 26, 2011. http://blogs.wsj.com/marketbeat/2011/09/26/facebook-sucks-up-a-ridiculously-huge-and-growing-share-of-our-time-wasted-online/

18   "Investors and analysts have fixated on Twitter's monthly active users, believing that statistic gauges the service's prospects for becoming a top advertising hub."

Yoree Koh, "Twitter's User Problem: Fastest Gains Are People That Don't See Ads," *Wall Street Journal*, Aug 1, 2014. http://online.wsj.com/articles/twitters-user-problem-fastest-gains-are-people-that-dont-see-ads-1406924973

19   Vlad Savov, "I Am Not Emotionally Prepared for Twitter to Suck," *The Verge*, August 21, 2014. http://www.theverge.com/2014/8/21/6052699/i-am-not-emotionally-prepared-for-twitter-to-suck

20   Maciej Cegłowski, "The Internet with a Human Face - Beyond Tellerrand 2014 Conference Talk," *IdleWords*, May 20, 2014. http://idlewords.com/bt14.htm

21   James Meikle, "Twitter is Harder to Resist Than Cigarettes and Alcohol, Study Finds," *The Guardian*, February 3, 2012. http://www.theguardian.com/technology/2012/feb/03/twitter-resist-cigarettes-alcohol-study

22   Alexandra Sifferlin, "Why Facebook Makes You Feel Bad About Yourself," *Time*, Jan. 24, 2013. http://healthland.time.com/2013/01/24/why-facebook-makes-you-feel-bad-about-yourself/

Chapter 6
Distraction

1 "'When Cliff first published the findings, they were revolutionary and surprising,' Bailenson said. 'Indeed, Bill Gates championed the work as 'amazing.'"
"He was also a professional magician."
"Cliff's brilliance was exceeded only by his generosity and warmth," he said. "I will remember Cliff as a person who made any room a happier place."
Kathleen J. Sullivan, "Professor Clifford I. Nass, Expert on Human/Computer Interactions, Dead at 55," *Stanford Report*, November 4, 2013. http://news.stanford.edu/news/2013/november/cliff-nass-obit-110413.html

2 "Clifford Nass, a Stanford professor whose pioneering research into how humans interact with technology found that the increasingly screen-saturated, multitasking modern world was not nurturing the ability to concentrate, analyze or feel empathy, died on Nov. 2 near Lake Tahoe. He was 55."
William Yardley, "Clifford Nass, Who Warned of a Data Deluge, Dies at 55," *New York Times*, November 6, 2013. http://www.nytimes.com/2013/11/07/business/clifford-nass-researcher-on-multitasking-dies-at-55.html?_r=0

3 ". . . a person's consumption of more than one item or stream of content at the same time"
Eyal Ophir, Clifford Nass, and Anthony D. Wagner, "Cognitive Control in Media Multitaskers," National Academy of Sciences, July 20, 2009. http://www.pnas.org/content/106/37/15583.full

4 Ira Flatow, "The Myth of Multitasking," NPR, May 10, 2013. http://www.npr.org/2013/05/10/182861382/the-myth-of-multitasking

5 "They couldn't help thinking about the task they weren't doing," Ophir said. "The high multitaskers are always drawing from all the information in front of them. They can't keep things separate in their minds."
Adam Gorlick, "Media Multitaskers Pay Mental Price, Stanford Study Shows," *Stanford Report*, August 24, 2009. http://news.stanford.edu/news/2009/august24/multitask-research-study-082409.html

6 Gigaom, "Clifford Nass: Multitasking is Bad for Your Brain," YouTube, May 28, 2013. https://www.youtube.com/watch?v=BEbmUQpwR2E

7 Martha Mendoza, "Oh, the irony: Apple-Samsung Trial Judge Annoyed by Smartphones," *San Jose Mercury News*, April 9, 2014. http://www.mercurynews.com/business/ci_25529665/oh-irony-apple-samsung-trial-judge-annoyed-by

8 Matt Richtel, "Texting Raises Crash Risk 23 Times, Study Finds," *New York Times*, July 27, 2009. http://www.nytimes.com/2009/07/28/technology/28texting.html?pagewanted=all&_r=0

Chapter 7
Screen Insomnia

1 ". . . awarded the Presidential Medal of Freedom by President Barack Obama."

"Oprah Winfrey Fast Facts," CNN, March 21, 2014. http://edition.cnn.com/2013/08/05/us/oprah-winfrey-fast-facts/

2 ". . . easily the most influential celebrity philanthropist in the United States . . ."
Ryan Haggerty, "Giving to Chicago and Beyond" *Chicago Tribune*, May 20, 2011. http://articles.chicagotribune.com/2011-05-20/entertainment/ct-ae-0522-oprah-causes-metro-20110520_1_philanthropy-harpo-janice-peck

3 "Oprah Winfrey, Doctor of Laws"
Katie Koch, "Harvard Awards 9 Honorary Degrees" *Harvard Gazette*, May 30, 2013. http://news.harvard.edu/gazette/story/2013/05/harvard-awards-9-honorary-degrees/

4 Seriously, you're checking the reference on this one? Read it and weep:
Ann Oldenburg, "Oprah Winfrey Signs Off After 25 Years: 'It Is Done,'" *USA Today*, May 21, 2011. http://usatoday30.usatoday.com/life/people/2011-05-20-Oprah-interview_n.htm

5 "Host of 'The Oprah Winfrey Show,' the highest rated talk show in history . . ."
"Oprah Winfrey Fast Facts," CNN, March 21, 2014. http://www.cnn.com/2013/08/05/us/oprah-winfrey-fast-facts/

6 "O, The Oprah Magazine* hit newsstands as a bi-monthly publication for May/June 2000 with unique features such as oversize glossy pages and large print."
Elizabeth Fry, "A Brief History of O The Oprah Magazine" About.com., http://oprah.about.com/od/omagazine/p/OprahMagazine.htm

7 "Oprah Winfrey and Hearst Magazines have won their trademark fight against the publisher of an erotic magazine with nearly the same name."
Jeff Bercovici, "Oprah Puts Lash to German Fetish Title," *Media Life*, July 15, 2002. http://www.medialifemagazine.com:8080/news2002/jul02/jul15/1_mon/news3monday.html

8 "O, The Oprah Magazine 2,417,589"
Neal Lulofs, "The Top 25 U.S. Consumer Magazines for June 2013," Alliance for Audited Media, August 6, 2013. http://www.auditedmedia.com/news/blog/2013/august/the-top-25-us-consumer-magazines-for-june-2013.aspx

9 "Coal generates 44% of our electricity, and is the single biggest air polluter in the U.S.," Union of Concerned Scientists. http://www.ucsusa.org/clean_energy/coalvswind/c01.html

10 "Excessive nitrogen and phosphorus that washes into water bodies and is released into the air are often the direct result of human activities."
"Sources and Solutions | Nutrient Pollution," United States Environmental Protection Agency. http://www2.epa.gov/nutrientpollution/sources-and-solutions

11 Women who live in neighborhoods with large amounts of nighttime illumination are more likely to get breast cancer than those who live in areas where nocturnal darkness prevails, according to an unusual study that overlaid satellite images of Earth onto cancer registries.
The finding adds credence to the hypothesis that exposure to too much light at night can raise the risk of breast cancer by interfering with the brain's production of a tumor-suppressing hormone.
"By no means are we saying that light at night is the only or the major risk factor for breast cancer," said Itai Kloog, of the

University of Haifa in Israel, who led the new work. "But we found a clear and strong correlation that should be taken into consideration."
Rick Weiss, "Lights at Night Are Linked to Breast Cancer," *Washington Post*, February 20, 2008. http://www.washingtonpost.com/wp-dyn/content/article/2008/02/19/AR2008021902398.html

12 "... the most common malignant disease in Israel and the Western world ... One out of every 8 women in Israel may develop breast cancer ..."
"Breast Cancer," Israel Cancer Association, Last accessed August 2014. http://en.cancer.org.il/template_e/default.aspx?PageId=7749

13 "The most common type of cancer on the list is breast cancer, with about 235,000 new cases expected in the United States in 2014. The next most common cancers are prostate cancer and lung cancer."
"Common Cancer Types," National Cancer Institute, Last updated March 31, 2014. http://www.cancer.gov/cancertopics/types/commoncancers

14 "Based on current incidence rates, 12.4 percent of women born in the United States today will develop breast cancer at some time during their lives"
"Breast Cancer Risk in American Women," National Cancer Institute, Last reviewed September 24, 2012. http://www.cancer.gov/cancertopics/factsheet/detection/probability-breast-cancer

15 "Smoking, a main cause of small cell and non-small cell lung cancer, contributes to 80 percent and 90 percent of lung cancer deaths in women and men, respectively."
"Lung Cancer Fact Sheet," American Lung Association, Last accessed August 2014. http://www.lung.org/lung-disease/lung-cancer/resources/facts-figures/lung-cancer-fact-sheet.html

16 Margaret Eby, "Oprah Winfrey Admits She Smoked Marijuana in 1982: 'I Hear It's Gotten Better,'" *NY Daily News*, August 16, 2013. http://www.nydailynews.com/entertainment/gossip/oprah-admits-smoked-marijuana-1982-hear-better-article-1.1428915

17 "We've just learned that the streetlight shining in your bedroom window every night is not only annoying; it may be jacking up your risk of breast cancer. Israeli researchers used satellite photos to gauge the level of nighttime light in 147 communities, then overlaid the photos with a map detailing the whereabouts of breast cancer cases. They discovered that women living in the brightest neighborhoods—with enough light to read a book outside at midnight—were 73 percent more likely to suffer from breast cancer than those residing in areas where most late-night light is celestial."
Catherine Guthrie, "Bright Light May Cause Cancer," *O, The Oprah Magazine*, August 2008. http://www.oprah.com/omagazine/Bright-Light-May-Cause-Cancer-Health-Risks

18 Kloog I., Haim, A. Stevens R.G. and B.A. Portnov ca, The Global Co-Distribution of Light at Night (LAN) and Cancers of Prostate, Colon and Lung in Men, Chronobiology International, 2009, 26: pp. 108 – 125.

19 "Artificial Light At Night: Higher Risk Of Prostate Cancer, Study Suggests." ScienceDaily, February 4, 2009, www.sciencedaily.com/releases/2009/02/090203135015.htm

20 "If light were a drug, the Government would not approve it," said Professor Charles Czeisler of the Harvard Medical School.
Geoffrey Lean, "Burning the Midnight Oil Could Lead to Breast Cancer," *New Zealand Herald*, June 21, 2006. http://m.nzherald.co.nz/technology/news/article.cfm?c_id=5&objectid=10387483

21 "'Once we got fire, and then the electric light bulb was invented, things really started to change,' said Stevens, who published a study last year with colleagues in Israel on the relationship between light at night and breast cancer."
Rob Stein, "Maybe It's Better To Stay in the Dark," *Washington Post*, February 17, 2009. http://www.washingtonpost.com/wp-dyn/content/article/2009/02/13/AR2009021302482_2.html

22 "In January in the journal *PLoS One*, the University of Basel team also compared the effects of incandescent bulbs to fluorescents modified to emit more blue light. Men exposed to the fluorescent lights produced 40 percent less melatonin than when they were exposed to incandescent bulbs, and they reported feeling more awake an hour after the lights went off."
Laura Beil, "In Eyes, a Clock Calibrated by Wavelengths of Light," *New York Times*, July 4, 2011. http://www.nytimes.com/2011/07/05/health/05light.html

23 "Sixteen healthy young men were studied in a balanced cross-over design with light exposure of 3 different light settings (compact fluorescent lamps with light of 40 lux at 6500K and at 2500K and incandescent lamps of 40 lux at 3000K) during 2 h in the evening."
"... with light at 6500K from commercially available compact fluorescent lamps melatonin is suppressed by nearly 40% in comparison to traditional light lamps (3000K)."
Sarah Laxhmi Chellappa, Roland Steiner, et al., "Non-Visual Effects of Light on Melatonin, Alertness and Cognitive Performance: Can Blue-Enriched Light Keep Us Alert?," *PLOS ONE*, January 26, 2011. http://www.plosone.org/article/info%3Adoi%2F10.1371%2Fjournal.pone.0016429

24 Ibid., "Figure 3. Sleepiness and well-being during pre-light, 2-h light (grey bar) at 6500K, 2500K and 3000K, and post-light," http://www.plosone.org/article/fetchObject.action?uri=info:doi/10.1371/journal.pone.0016429.g003&representation=PNG_L

25 "Illuminate D65 represents a phase of daylight with a correlated color temperature of approximately 6500k."
Marc Ebner, *Color Constancy* (Singapore: John Wiley & Sons), p.59.
Available on Google Books (sorry for their awful URL): http://books.google.com/books?id=WVKJST7zE8cC&lpg=PA59&ots=29-rn0Hirs&dq=d65%20%20International%20Commission%20on%20Illumination&pg=PA59#v=onepage&q=d65%20%20International%20Commission%20on%20Illumination&f=false

26 "For the purposes of video and computer imaging, that standard is a color temperature of 6500 kelvins or D65."
Christian Eberle, "Grayscale: Why White Is the Color of Everything - Display Calibration 201: The Science Behind

Tuning Your Monitor," Tom's Hardware, October 13, 2013. http://www.tomshardware.com/reviews/calibrate-your-monitor-theory,3615-4.html

27 "OUR MISSION To prevent business practices that are anticompetitive or deceptive or unfair to consumers; to enhance informed consumer choice and public understanding of the competitive process; and to accomplish this without unduly burdening legitimate business activity."
"About the FTC," Federal Trade Commission, Last accessed August 2014. http://www.ftc.gov/about-ftc

28 "The Lighting Facts label is modeled on the Nutrition Facts label on food packages."
"The FTC 'Lighting Facts' Label: Questions and Answers for Manufacturers | BCP Business Center," Bureau of Consumer Protection, May 2013. http://www.business.ftc.gov/documents/bus26-lighting-facts-questions-and-answers-manufacturers

29 "Laboratory studies have also found that human breast and prostate cancer cells grow more slowly when exposed to melatonin in petri dishes, and human breast and prostate tumors implanted in rats grow faster when the animals' melatonin is suppressed by light exposure."
Rob Stein, "Maybe It's Better To Stay in the Dark," Washington Post, February 17, 2009. http://www.washingtonpost.com/wp-dyn/content/article/2009/02/13/AR2009021302482.html

30 "'We can't say yet, but the evidence is accumulating that light at night, and the consequent decrease in melatonin, may be a major driver of breast cancer,' he said."
Judy Foreman, "Melatonin, Sleep Aid That May Fight Cancer," New York Times, October 6, 2005. http://www.nytimes.com/2005/10/05/health/05iht-snmel.html

31 "They discovered that when brightness settings were lowered and the devices were held just over a foot from a user's face, it reduced the risk that the light would be bright enough to suppress melatonin secretion and disrupt sleep."
"Are Smartphones Disrupting Your Sleep? Mayo Clinic Study Examines the Question," Mayo Clinic News Network, Jun 3, 2013. http://newsnetwork.mayoclinic.org/discussion/are-smartphones-disrupting-your-sleep-mayo-clinic-study-examines-the-question-238cef/

Chapter 8
The Screenless Office

1 If you enjoy corporate bullshit:
Emma Green, "The Origins of Office Speak," The Atlantic, April 24, 2014. http://www.theatlantic.com/features/archive/2014/04/business-speak/361135/

2 Office-type papers in thousands of tons:
1960, 1,520 tons
1970, 2,650 tons
1980, 4,000 tons
U.S. Environmental Protection Agency Office of Resource Conservation and Recovery, "Table 15. Products Generated in the Municipal Waste Stream, 1960 To 2012," Municipal Solid Waste Generation, Recycling, and Disposal in the United States Tables and Figures for 2012, February 2014. http://www.epa.gov/epawaste/nonhaz/municipal/pubs/2012_msw_dat_tbls.pdf

3 Anna Quindlen, "About New York," New York Times, May 5, 1982. http://www.nytimes.com/1982/05/05/nyregion/about-new-york.html

4 "Paperback Best Sellers; Mass Market," New York Times, January 25, 1981. http://www.nytimes.com/1981/01/25/books/paperback-best-sellers-mass-market.html

5 "The Office of the Future," Businessweek, June 30, 1975. http://www.businessweek.com/stories/1975-06-30/the-office-of-the-futurebusinessweek-business-news-stock-market-and-financial-advice

6 "Founded in 2003 and headquartered in Luxembourg, Skype is a division of Microsoft Corp."
"About Skype - What is Skype," Microsoft, Last accessed August 2014. http://www.skype.com/en/about/

7 "Business Brief," The Economist, December 27, 1980: p.3.

8 "This is CRYPTOLOG—a new vehicle for the interchange of ideas on technical subjects in Operations."
Herbert E. Wolff, "A letter of introduction," Cryptolog, August 1974. https://www.nsa.gov/public_info/_files/cryptologs/cryptolog_01.pdf

9 ". . . everyone knows that traffic analysts are clear-eyed, clean-limbed people who draw meticulously neat—if arcane—squares and circles on paper, and that cryppies are two-headed people who tend to twitch. The machine people are those pale ones who inhabit, like troglodytes, the bowels of the basement. Collectors are—uh—aren't they the can-clangers who come around three times a week with a truck?" (Classified), "What Is a Collector?," Cryptolog, August 1974. https://www.nsa.gov/public_info/_files/cryptologs/cryptolog_01.pdf

10 "'You can never go wrong by betting that change will go slower than everyone expects,' says a sage Saffo. 'We're still lurching into the paperless office future. That's a little bit of a surprise to me, but I didn't expect paper to disappear completely.'"
Matt Bradley, "What Ever Happened to the Paperless Office?," Christian Science Monitor, December 12, 2005. http://www.csmonitor.com/2005/1212/p13s01-wmgn.html

11 "America's white-collar workers have been generating less paper since 2001, and that trend is likely to continue, according to InfoTrends, a consultancy."
"Paper Usage: A Greener Office," The Economist, Oct 10, 2008. http://www.economist.com/node/12405651

12 Department of Agriculture, "Paper and Paper-Based Packaging Promotion, Research and Information Order," Federal Register: The Daily Journal of the United States Government, September 16, 2013. https://www.federalregister.gov/articles/2013/09/16/2013-22330/paper-and-paper-based-packaging-promotion-research-and-information-order

13 "Most American children spend about 3 hours a day watching TV. Added together, all types of screen time can total 5 to 7 hours a day."
"Zero to Eight: Children's Media Use in America 2013," Common Sense Media, October 28, 2013.

https://www.commonsensemedia.org/research/
zero-to-eight-childrens-media-use-in-america-2013

14 "According to the Kaiser Family Foundation, kids ages 8–18 now
spend, on average, a whopping 7.5 hours in front of a screen for
entertainment each day, 4.5 of which are spent watching TV."
CDC Division of Community Health, "Screen Time vs. Lean
Time," makinghealtheasier.org, Last accessed August 2014.
http://makinghealtheasier.org/getmoving

15 "In fact, adults are exposed to screens—TVs, cellphones,
even GPS. devices—for about 8.5 hours on any given day,
according to a study released by the Council for Research
Excellence on Thursday."
Brian Stelter, "8 Hours a Day Spent on Screens, Study Finds,"
New York Times, March 26, 2009. http://www.nytimes.com/
2009/03/27/business/media/27adco.html?_r=1&

16 Aric Sigman, "Well Connected? The Biological Implications
of 'Social Networking'," *Biologist*, February 2009. http://
www.aricsigman.com/IMAGES/Sigman_lo.pdf

Chapter 9
Back Pocket Apps

1 "It's called Phantom Vibration Syndrome, and it's actually
something that happened to me . . . It was quite annoying
. . . and I wanted to know if other people were experiencing
it as well, and so I said, let's do a survey . . . We actually got
quite a good response, about three-quarters of the people we
surveyed gave us an answer, which is unusual . . . I personally
found it very troubling . . . We didn't discover it, but we're the
first ones to describe it . . . there are actually three Facebook
groups for sufferers of Phantom Vibration Syndrome . . . It's
not technically a phantom, it's technically a hallucination . . ."
The BMJ, "Phantom Vibrations," YouTube, Dec 17, 2010.
https://www.youtube.com/watch?v=WlEfdsxOteM

2 "In all, 115/169 (68%, 95% confidence interval 61% to 75%)
reported having experienced phantom vibrations."
Michael B. Rothberg, Ashish Arora, Jodie Hermann, Reva
Kleppel, Peter St Marie, Paul Visintainer, et al., "Phantom
Vibration Syndrome Among Medical Staff: A Cross Sectional
Survey," *BMJ*, November 24, 2010. http://www.bmj.com/
content/341/bmj.c6914

3 "Most (89%) of the 290 undergraduates in our sample had
experienced phantom vibrations, and they experienced
them about once every two weeks, on average."
Michelle Drouin, Daren H. Kaiser, Daniel A. Miller, "Phantom
Vibrations Among Undergraduates: Prevalence and
Associated Psychological Characteristics," *Science Direct*,
April 14, 2012. http://www.sciencedirect.com/science/article/
pii/S0747563212000799

4 "Nearly 90 percent of college undergrads in a 2012 study
said they felt phantom vibrations."
Elise Hu, "Phantom Phone Vibrations: So Common
They've Changed Our Brains?: All Tech Considered,"
NPR, September 27, 2013. http://www.npr.org/blogs/
alltechconsidered/2013/09/30/226820044/phantom-phone-
vibrations-so-common-they-ve-changed-our-brains

5 This audio illusion—called phantom phone rings or, more

whimsically, ringxiety or fauxcellarm—has emerged recently
as an Internet discussion topic and has become a new
reason for people to either bemoan the techno-saturation of
modern life or question their sanity.
Brenda Goodman, "I Hear Ringing and There's No One
There. I Wonder Why," *New York Times*, May 4, 2006.
http://www.nytimes.com/2006/05/04/fashion/thursday
styles/04phan.html

6 "'The Tell-Tale Heart' is a famous short story by American
author Edgar Allan Poe. It was first published in January
1843 in the short-lived *Pioneer* magazine."
"The Tell-Tale Heart," Shmoop, Last accessed September
2014. http://www.shmoop.com/tell-tale-heart/

7 Edgar Allan Poe, "The Works of Edgar Allan Poe—Volume
2," Project Gutenberg, May 19, 2008. http://www.gutenberg.
org/files/2148/2148-h/2148-h.htm

8 ". . . a collection he began in the house of Piero di Braccio
Martelli in Florence, in 1508."
"Digitised Manuscripts," British Library, Last accessed
September 2014. http://www.bl.uk/manuscripts/FullDisplay.
aspx?ref=Arundel_MS_263

9 "Leonardo da Vinci's notebooks are the living record of
a universal mind. They encompass all the interests and
experiments of this self-taught polymath, from mathematics
to flying machines."
Jonathan Jones, "Leonardo da Vinci's Notebooks Are
Beautiful Works of Art in Themselves," *The Guardian*,
February 12, 2013. http://www.theguardian.com/
artanddesign/jonathanjonesblog/2013/feb/12/
leonardo-da-vinci-notebooks-art

10 Martin Gayford, Karen Wright, *The Grove Book of Art Writing*
(New York: Grove Press), p.447.
Available on Google Books (sorry for their awful URL):
http://books.google.com/books?id=vI02ncIOLiYC&lpg=
PA447&pg=PA447#v=onepage&f=false

11 "Pareidolia, as this experience is known, is by no means a
recent phenomenon. Leonardo da Vinci described seeing
characters in natural markings on stone walls, which he
believed could help inspire his artworks."
David Robson, "Neuroscience: Why Do We See Faces in
Everyday Objects?," BBC, July 30, 2014. http://www.bbc.
com/future/story/20140730-why-do-we-see-faces-in-objects

12 "Apophenia is an error of perception: The tendency to
interpret random patterns as meaningful . . . Pareidolia is
visual apophenia . . . For our hominid ancestors, pattern
recognition was essential for recognizing both food and
predators."
John W. Hoopes, "11-11-11, Apophenia, and the Meaning of
Life," *Psychology Today*, November 11, 2011. http://www.
psychologytoday.com/blog/reality-check/201111/11-11-11-
apophenia-and-the-meaning-life

13 "The murder is carefully calculated, and the murderer hides
the body by cutting it into pieces and hiding it under the
floorboards. Ultimately the narrator's guilt manifests itself in
the hallucination that the man's heart is still beating under
the floorboards."
"The Tell-Tale Heart—Overview," Barnes & Noble, Last
accessed September 2014. http://www.barnesandnoble.

com/w/the-tell-tale-heart-edgar-allen-poe-edgar-allan-poe/11 10565661?ean=2940014490115

14 "300–500 a day on average."

Xu Beixi, "Top Writers on Quora: How Many Notifications Do Top Writers on Quora Receive Every Day?" Quora, February 12, 2014. http://www.quora.com/Top-Writers-on-Quora/How-many-notifications-do-Top-Writers-on-Quora-receive-every-day

15 "Users swipe their screens to unlock their phones an average of 110 times a day, according to data from the app company Locket."

Elise Hu, "New Numbers Back Up Our Obsession with Phones : All Tech Considered," NPR, October 10, 2013. http://www.npr.org/blogs/alltechconsidered/2013/10/09/230867952/new-numbers-back-up-our-obsession-with-phones

16 "Kleiner Perkins Caufield Byers - Companies," KPCB, Last accessed September 2014. http://www.kpcb.com/companies

17 "In fact, people check their phones 150 times a day, according to Kleiner Perkins Caufield & Byers's annual Internet Trends report."

Joanna Stern, "Cellphone Users Check Phones 150x/Day and Other Internet Fun Facts," ABC News, May 29, 2013. http://abcnews.go.com/blogs/technology/2013/05/cellphone-users-check-phones-150xday-and-other-internet-fun-facts/

18 "To better understand attitudes about mass mobility, Time, in cooperation with Qualcomm, launched the Time Mobility Poll, a survey of close to 5,000 people of all age groups and income levels in eight countries: the U.S., the U.K., China, India, South Korea, South Africa, Indonesia, and Brazil"

Nancy Gibbs, "Your Life Is Fully Mobile," Time, Aug. 16, 2012. http://techland.time.com/2012/08/16/your-life-is-fully-mobile/

19 "Meanwhile, some young people say a cracked screen gives you a sort of street cred, like you've been through some real-life stuff, even if it happened on the mean streets of Bethesda."

"They whip out their phones and dial up Web sites selling the latest 'cracked screen wallpaper' and "pre-cracked screen savers." . . . 'I mean, they're going to crack it at some point, so why not just get it out of the way?' one slogan reads."

Emily Wax, "Beat-Up Cellphones with Cracked Screens Are Point of Pride for Some Young People," Washington Post, May 17, 2013. http://www.washingtonpost.com/lifestyle/style/beat-up-cellphones-with-cracked-screens-are-point-of-pride-for-some-young-people/2013/05/17/0334ebe0-be36-11e2-89c9-3be8095fe767_story.html

20 "Sweaty workouts killing iPhones? One NBC television affiliate in Houston is reporting on consumer complaints that sweat from working out while wearing or handling an iPhone is killing the devices."

David Martin, "Sweaty Workouts Killing iPhones?," CNET, April 8, 2009. http://www.cnet.com/news/sweaty-workouts-killing-iphones/

21 "iPhone and iPod: Liquid Damage Is Not Covered By Warranty," Apple, Last accessed September 2014. http://support.apple.com/kb/ht3302

22 Rich Trenholm, "Quarter of iPhones Have a Broken Screen, says new poll," CNET, February 7, 2013. http://www.cnet.com/news/

quarter-of-iphones-have-a-broken-screen-says-new-poll/

23 Victor H., "Americans Replace Their Cell Phones Every Two Years, Finns—Every Six, a Study Claims," Phone Arena, July 11, 2011. http://www.phonearena.com/news/Americans-replace-their-cell-phones-every-2-years-Finns-every-six-a-study-claims_id20255

24 Brad Molen, "iPhone 6 and 6 Plus Review: Bigger and Better, but With Stiffer Competition," Engadget, September 16, 2014. http://www.engadget.com/2014/09/16/iphone-6-and-6-plus-review/

25 "Protective phone cases have become practically a necessity since the introduction of smartphones. After all, why pay hundreds of dollars for a phone and not spend a little bit more to protect it?"

Gregory Schmidt, "Cellphone Cases to Prepare You for Anything, Even a Flat Tire," New York Times, April 23, 2014. http://www.nytimes.com/2014/04/24/technology/personaltech/cellphone-cases-to-prepare-you-for-anything-even-a-flat-tire.html

26 "The NPD Group, which gathers analytics on retail behavior, surveyed more than 3,200 smartphone owners over age 13."

Marshall Honorof, "One-Quarter of Smartphone Owners Spurn Cases," Tom's Guide, December 26, 2013. http://www.tomsguide.com/us/smartphone-owners-spurn-cases,news-18024.html

27 "I Hate 'Battery Low!'" Facebook, Last accessed September 2014. https://www.facebook.com/pages/I-hate-battery-low/147670411993839

28 Hilary Lewis, "Here's a Hard-Charging App," New York Post, October 21, 2012. http://nypost.com/2012/10/21/heres-a-hard-charging-app/

29 Caitlin McGarry, "iPhone 6 Pocket Problems: Some Buyers Report That Sitting Down Bends Phones," Macworld, September 23, 2014. http://www.macworld.com/article/2687107/iphone-6-pocket-problems-some-buyers-report-that-sitting-down-bends-phones.html

30 "Over 200+ grown-up campers will go off-the-grid and take over Camp Navarro (a historic and nostalgic scouts camp) in the redwoods to celebrate what it means to be alive. Trade in your computer, cell phone, Instagrams, clocks, hashtags, business cards, schedules, and work-jargon for an off-the-grid weekend of pure unadulterated fun. Together we create a community where money is worth little . . . and individuality, self expression, friendship, freedom, and memories are valued most."

"Camp Grounded: Summer Camp for Adults" Digital Detox & Camp Grounded Blog, Last accessed September 2014. http://blog.thedigitaldetox.org/camp-grounded/

31 "The app's precision and power consumption need work, but I'm convinced its simplicity represents the future of self-tracking."

Rachel Metz, "Every Step You Take, Tracked Automatically," MIT Technology Review, February 12, 2013. http://www.technologyreview.com/news/510491/every-step-you-take-tracked-automatically/

32 Sumathi Reddy, "Why We Keep Losing Our Keys," Wall Street Journal, April 14, 2014. http://online.wsj.com/news/articles/SB10001424052702304117904579501410168111866

33 Esure, "We're a Bunch of 'Losers,'" esure.com, March 21, 2012. http://www.esure.com/media_centre/archive/wcmcap_100800.html

34 "Y Combinator-backed Lockitron aims to replace physical keys entirely by letting you control your door lock with your phone . . ."
Alexia Tsotsis, "Lockitron Lets You Unlock Your Door with Your Phone," TechCrunch, May 13, 2011. http://techcrunch.com/2011/05/13/lockitron-lets-you-unlock-your-door-with-your-phone/

35 "It works like this. You replace either part or all of your door lock with Lockitron's parts (depending on the kind of lock you have). Then, when you get home you fire up the app on your phone and hit the 'unlock' button."
Charlie Sorrel, "Lockitron: Unlock Your Home with Your Cellphone," *Wired*, May 8, 2011. http://www.wired.com/2011/05/lockitron-unlock-your-home-with-your-cellphone/

36 Natasha Lomas, "Lockitron Still Hasn't Shipped to Most Backers Over a Year After Its $2.2M Crowdfunding Effort," TechCrunch, Jan 16, 2014. http://techcrunch.com/2014/01/16/lockitrons-long-march/

37 "Self checkouts in North America will increase by up to 10% in the next few years, says research and advisory firm IHL Group. The biggest growth is expected at convenience, hardware, and drug stores. Self-checkout lanes can reduce labor costs and improve customer service, especially for quick shopping trips. But they can backfire if shoppers have problems scanning their items, says Kurt Jetta of consumer analytics company TABS."
Jayne O'Donnell and Sarah Meehan, "More Stores Moving to Self Checkouts Despite Higher Rates of Theft," *USA Today*, April 9, 2012. http://usatoday30.usatoday.com/money/industries/retail/story/2012-04-06/self-scanning-checkout/54117384/1

38 "The thefts allegedly occurred at self-checkout lanes as the thieves scanned cheap items and bagged the more expensive ones, despite the presence of attendants."
"While some grocery chains like Big Y and Kroger have done away with self-checkout lanes, other retailers have welcomed them in . . ."
Enjoli Francis, "Self-Checkout Gets Extra Set of Eyes with Video Software," ABC News, Apr 10, 2012. http://abcnews.go.com/blogs/technology/2012/04/self-checkout-gets-extra-set-of-eyes-with-video-software/

39 Chris Matyszczyk, "Major Grocery Chain Gets Rid of Self-Checkout," CNET, July 9, 2011. http://www.cnet.com/news/major-grocery-chain-gets-rid-of-self-checkout/

40 "Unexpected item in the bagging area? Totally expected feeling of rage pumping through your body? You're not alone. New research suggests 48% of Britons think self-service checkouts are a nightmare, neither quick nor convenient. Quite the opposite in fact, and their complaints are all too familiar."
"Tesco, the UK's biggest supermarket, also leads the do-it-yourself checkout league, with self-service counters in 256 stores. The tills process 25% of all transactions in those shops. Sainsbury's has them in 220 stores and is planning more."

Denise Winterman, "The problem with self-service check-outs," BBC News Magazine, December 9, 2009. http://news.bbc.co.uk/2/hi/8399963.stm

41 Claire Carter, "Shoppers steal billions through self service tills," Telegraph, 29 Jan 2014. http://www.telegraph.co.uk/finance/personalfinance/household-bills/10603984/Shoppers-steal-billions-through-self-service-tills.html

42 Shelly Banjo, "Returning to Wal-Mart: Human Cashiers," The Wall Street Journal, Aug. 15, 2014. http://online.wsj.com/articles/wal-mart-pledges-to-staff-checkout-lanes-during-holidays-1408112765

43 Claire Carter, "Shoppers Steal Billions Through Self Service Tills," *Telegraph*, January 29, 2014. http://www.telegraph.co.uk/finance/personalfinance/household-bills/10603984/Shoppers-steal-billions-through-self-service-tills.html

44 Jessica Wohl, "McDonald's slump offers no easy fix," *Chicago Tribune*, September 18, 2014. http://www.chicagotribune.com/business/ct-mcdonalds-fix-0918-biz-20140917-story.html

45 Leslie Patton, "McDonald's expanding build-your-burger test in search of growth," *Chicago Tribune*, September 18, 2014. http://www.chicagotribune.com/business/breaking/sns-wp-blm-news-bc-mcdonalds20-20140920-story.html

46 Techonomy Media, "Jack Dorsey Explains Square's Pay-by-Voice Technology," YouTube, Jul 20, 2012. https://www.youtube.com/watch?v=2zoeiNBdPdo

47 "MasterCard International, which first tested the PayPass in 2003"
Sewell Chan, "A Test at 25 Stations: Subway Riding Without the Swiping," *The New York Times*, January 31, 2006. http://www.nytimes.com/2006/01/31/nyregion/31fare.html

48 Marc Perton, "Chase to Issue RFID Credit Cards," Engadget, May 20, 2005. http://www.engadget.com/2005/05/20/chase-to-issue-rfid-credit-cards/

49 Marc Perton, "Amex to Include RFID in All New Blue Cards," Engadget, June 7, 2005. http://www.engadget.com/2005/06/07/amex-to-include-rfid-in-all-new-blue-cards/

50 Sarah Perez, "Visa to Launch Contactless Mobile Payments for iPhone," ReadWrite, May 6, 2010. http://readwrite.com/2010/05/06/visa_to_launch_contactless_mobile_payments_for_iphone

51 "Launching Google Wallet on Sprint and Working with Visa, American Express, and Discover," Official Google Blog, September 19, 2011. http://googleblog.blogspot.com/2011/09/launching-google-wallet-on-sprint-and.html

52 "Albertsons LLC, which operates 217 stores in seven Western and Southern states, will eliminate all self-checkout lanes in the 100 stores that have them and will replace them with standard or express lanes, a spokeswoman said. 'We just want the opportunity to talk to customers more,' Albertsons spokeswoman Christine Wilcox said. 'That's the driving motivation.'"
Anika Anand, "Major Grocer Getting Rid of Self-Checkout Lanes," NBC News, July 10, 2011. http://www.nbcnews.com/id/43687085/ns/business-retail/t/major-grocer-getting-rid-self-checkout-lanes/#.VCZfumSwltv

53 Marcus Wohlsen, "Square Wallet Had Everything Going for It. And Now It's Dead," *Wired*, May 12, 2014. http://www.wired.com/2014/05/square-wallet-folds/

54 "This is only the latest sign that the partnership between the mobile payments company and the coffee titan has run its course. As we previously reported, the deal is costing Square millions (at least $20 million in 2013 alone), and Starbucks is content with how well its doing on its own." Tricia Duryee, "Square Bails on Wallet App in Latest Fallout from Troubled Starbucks Partnership," GeekWire, May 12, 2014. http://www.geekwire.com/2014/square-bails-wallet-app-starbucks-fails-promote/

55 "The promise of Square's partnership with Starbucks is that it will yield a seamless payment experience for customers. But that's not the case. Rather, what we found—even at locations where Square worked—is that Starbucks employees have received little if any training with Square, and more often than not only learned of the partnership and digital payment method from customers themselves." Austin Carr, "Starbucks's Shoddy Square Rollout Baffles Baristas, Confuses Customers," *Fast Company*, March 20, 2013. http://www.fastcompany.com/3005410/industries-watch/starbuckss-shoddy-square-rollout-baffles-baristas-confuses-customers

Chapter 10
Lazy Rectangles

1 Louis Columbus, "Using Customer Analytics to Improve Corporate Performance," *Forbes*, July 13, 2014. http://www.forbes.com/sites/louiscolumbus/2014/07/13/using-customer-analytics-to-improve-corporate-performance/

2 Alan Cooper, *The Inmates Are Running the Asylum: Why High Tech Products Drive Us Crazy and How to Restore the Sanity* (Indianapolis, IN: Sams Publishing), p.123.

3 William D. Smith, "Show Pledges Electronics for Every Taste," *New York Times*, June 27, 1967. http://timesmachine.nytimes.com/timesmachine/1967/06/27/83127329.html

4 Laura June, "Incredible Photos from the CES Vault: 1967 to 2013," The Verge, January 4, 2013. http://www.theverge.com/2013/1/4/3828848/ces-photo-history

5 "Viper SmartStart from Directed Electronics Awarded Best of Innovations Honors at 2010 Consumer Electronics Show," Directed, November 10, 2009. http://www.directed.com/Company/Press/2009/20091110.aspx

6 James R. Healey, "Hands-Free Tailgate Coming on Next Ford Escape," *USA Today*, October 31, 2011. http://usatoday30.usatoday.com/money/autos/story/2011-10-31/ford-tailgate-gestures/51020918/1

7 Dale Buss, "Ford Debuts Escape Advertising with Liftgate Sleight of Foot," *Forbes*, July 2, 2012. http://www.forbes.com/sites/dalebuss/2012/07/02/ford-debuts-escape-advertising-with-liftgate-sleight-of-foot/

8 Steve Tengler, "Tesla's Groundbreaking UX: An interview with User Interface Manager Brennan Boblett," *UX Magazine*, November 4, 2013. http://uxmag.com/articles/tesla%E2%80%99s-groundbreaking-ux-an-interview-with-user-interface-manager-brennan-boblett

9 "Children and Cars: A Potentially Lethal Combination DOT HS 810 636," NHTSA, Last accessed September 2014. http://www.nhtsa.gov/people/injury/enforce/childrenandcars/pages/unattend-hotcars.htm

10 "CARWINGS | Nissan Innovation Labs," Nissan USA, Last accessed September 2014. http://www.nissanusa.com/innovations/carwings.article.html

11 Derek Thompson, "Why Do All Movie Tickets Cost the Same?," *The Atlantic*, January 3, 2012. http://www.theatlantic.com/business/archive/2012/01/why-do-all-movie-tickets-cost-the-same/250762/

12 Doug Gross, "The 10 Most Annoying Smartphone Habits," CNN, October 22, 2010. http://www.cnn.com/2010/TECH/mobile/10/22/annoying.smartphone.habits/

13 Jakob Nielsen, "100 Million Websites," Nielsen Norman Group, November 6, 2006. http://www.nngroup.com/articles/100-million-websites/

14 "In the August 2014 survey we received responses from 992,177,228 sites . . ." Netcraft, "August 2014 Web Server Survey," Netcraft, August 27, 2014. http://news.netcraft.com/archives/2014/08/27/august-2014-web-server-survey.html

15 Peter Passell, "Economic Scene; End of the Game for Motor City?," *New York Times*, October 23, 1991. http://www.nytimes.com/1991/10/23/business/economic-scene-end-of-the-game-for-motor-city.html

16 Doron P. Levin, "Mazda Reportedly Planning to Make Luxury Car in U.S.," *New York Times*, August 17, 1991. http://www.nytimes.com/1991/08/17/business/mazda-reportedly-planning-to-make-luxury-car-in-us.html

17 Jim Mateja, "Hottest Offering From Mazda: Solar-powered Cooling," *Chicago Tribune*, September 24, 1991. http://articles.chicagotribune.com/1991-09-24/business/9103120605_1_solar-power-premium-motor-car-solar-ventilation

18 "The Solar Powered Ventilation System uses an electric fan to draw outside air into, through, and out of the cabin once the inside temperature reaches 86 degrees Fahrenheit. It will lower the cabin temperature to near the outside ambient temperature to help make the cabin more comfortable when reentering the vehicle. It must be turned on prior to leaving the vehicle and cannot perform cooling such as with an air conditioner." (See disclosures) "Hybrid Cars | Toyota Prius 2015," Toyota, Last accessed September 2014. http://www.toyota.com/prius/#!/Welcome

19 "But the company got caught off-guard in another way, too: The solar moonroof option has been far more popular than Toyota expected, and buyers have ordered it at rates much higher than the company had imagined." John Voelcker, "2010 Toyota Prius: Solar Sunroof Smash Success, Hard To Get," Green Car Reports, August 12, 2009. http://www.greencarreports.com/news/1034110_2010-toyota-prius-solar-sunroof-smash-success-hard-to-get

Chapter 11
Computer Tantrums

1 Ryan Lytle, "Computer Science Continues Growth on College Campuses," *US News & World Report*, July 12, 2012. http://www.usnews.com/education/best-colleges/articles/2012/07/12/computer-science-continues-growth-on-college-campuses?page=2

2 Robinson Meyer, "Stanford's Top Major Is Now Computer Science," *The Atlantic*, Jun 29, 2012. http://www.theatlantic.com/technology/archive/2012/06/stanfords-top-major-is-now-computer-science/259199/

3 Jonathan Swartz, "Stanford's Newest Majors Marry Computer Science and the Humanities," *USA Today*, March 14, 2014. http://college.usatoday.com/2014/03/14/stanfords-newest-majors-marry-computer-science-and-the-humanities/

4 "From the age of 12, the chess genius from Azerbaijan Garry Kasparov was setting new standards. After becoming the youngest player to win the USSR Junior Championship he went on to win the World Junior Championship at age 16. His style was aggressive and dynamic. On his seventeenth birthday he achieved the grandmaster title."
"Kasparov World Championship Match (1984)," Chess Games, Last accessed October 2014. http://www.chess-games.com/perl/chess.pl?page=2&tid=55015&eresult=

5 "In 1984 aged 21, Garry Kasparov was the youngest player in chess history to compete in a World Championship final match."
"Garry Kasparov," Harry Walker Agency, Last accessed October 2014, http://sbm.sa/sites/default/files/dc/Kasparov_Garry.pdf

6 "Sounding almost as exhausted as Karpov, who lost 8kg during the match . . ."
Matthew Weaver, "Karpov v Kasparov: The Guardian's Coverage of an Epic World Chess Championship Match," *The Guardian*, September 22, 2009. http://www.theguardian.com/news/blog/2009/sep/21/kasparov-karpov-chess-rematch

7 "The World Chess Championship 1984 was a match between challenger Garry Kasparov and defending champion Anatoly Karpov for the World Chess Championship title. After 5 months and 48 games, the match was abandoned in controversial circumstances with Karpov leading five wins to three (with 40 draws), and replayed in the World Chess Championship 1985."
"Announcing his decision at a press conference, Campomanes cited the health of the players, which had been strained by the length of the match (5 months: September 10, 1984 to February 8, 1985).
. . . The match became the first, and so far only, world championship match to be abandoned without result. The restarted match (the World Chess Championship 1985) was best of 24, with the champion (Karpov) to retain his title if the match was tied 12–12. Because Karpov's two-point lead from the 1984 match was wiped out, Karpov was granted the right of a return match (the World Chess Championship 1986) if he lost."
"World Chess Championship 1984," Wikipedia, Last accessed October 2014. http://en.wikipedia.org/wiki/World_Chess_Championship_1984

8 15:37 (Talk show interview)
21:00 "How do you make a computer blink?"
1:04:08 (Head in hands)
(Viewable online at https://www.youtube.com/watch?v=EtMdMmrfipY)
Game Over: Kasparov and the Machine. Directed by Vikram Jayanti. Ontario: Alliance Atlantis Communications, 2003.

9 "The 1997 match took place not on a standard stage, but rather in a small television studio. The audience watched the match on television screens in a basement theater in the building, several floors below where the match was actually held. The theater seated about 500 people, and was sold out for each of the six games."
"Icons of Progress: Deep Blue," IBM100, Last accessed October 2014. http://www-03.ibm.com/ibm/history/ibm100/us/en/icons/deepblue/

10 "On May 11, 1997, Deep Blue came out on top with a surprising sixth game win—and the $700,000 match prize."
"Kasparov loses chess game to computer—This Day in History," History.com, Last accessed October 2014. http://www.history.com/this-day-in-history/kasparov-loses-chess-game-to-computer

11 Murray Campbell, PhD, IBM TJ Watson Research Center, email message to book fact-checker, November 16, 2014.

12 Klint Finley, "Did a Computer Bug Help Deep Blue Beat Kasparov?" *Wired*, September 28, 2012. http://www.wired.com/2012/09/deep-blue-computer-bug/

13 Murray Campbell, PhD, IBM TJ Watson Research Center, email message to book fact-checker, November 16, 2014.
Larry Evans, "Chess," *Sun Sentinel*, November 2, 2003. http://articles.sun-sentinel.com/keyword/deep-blue

14 "Ultimately, Deep Blue was retired to the Smithsonian Museum in Washington, DC"
"Icons of Progress: Deep Blue," IBM100, Last accessed October 2014. http://www-03.ibm.com/ibm/history/ibm100/us/en/icons/deepblue/

15 Deep Blue, 11.38 GFLOPS
Intel Core i7, 107.55 GFLOPS
"Parallel Processing—Have Today's Desktop PCs Surpassed IBM's Deep Blue of 1997?," SuperUser, Last accessed October 2014. http://superuser.com/questions/250070/have-todays-desktop-pcs-surpassed-ibms-deep-blue-of-1997

16 "Error Message: Your Password Must Be at Least 18770 Characters and Cannot Repeat Any of Your Previous 30689 Passwords," Microsoft Support, Last accessed December 2014. http://support.microsoft.com/kb/276304

Chapter 12
Machine Input

1 Jay Schadler, "Virtual Reality," ABC Primetime Live, September 19, 1991.

2 "The Active Badge. This harbinger of inch-scale computers contains a small microprocessor and an infrared transmitter. The badge broadcasts the identity of its wearer and so can trigger automatic doors, automatic telephone forwarding, and computer displays customized to each person reading them."

Marc Weiser, "The Computer for the 21st Century," *Scientific American*, September 1991, http://web.media.mit.edu/~anjchang/ti01/weiser-sciam91-ubicomp.pdf

3   Roy Want, Andy Hopper, Veronica Falcão, and Jonathan Gibbons, "The Active Badge Location System," ACM Transactions on Information Systems (TOIS), January 1992, http://alumni.media.mit.edu/~dmerrill/badge/Want92_ActiveBadge.pdf

4   Tennessee, West Virginia, Alabama, Florida, Wyoming, Kentucky, Virginia, Georgia, South Dakota, Texas, Arkansas, Missouri, Vermont
    Connecticut, Arizona, California, Indiana, Utah, Florida, Hawaii, New York, Colorado, New Mexico, Missouri, Washington
    "2013 Caving Accident and Incident Reports," National Speleological Society, Last accessed October 2014. https://caves.org/pub/aca/13index.html

5   Stephen Regenold, "'Best in Show' Awards: Latest, Greatest Gear for 2012!," Gear Junkie, January 23, 2012. http://gearjunkie.com/outdoor-retailer-best-in-show-winter-2012

6   "Seau was the fifth overall pick in the 1990 NFL draft—a freakish combination of height (6'3"), weight (248 lbs.), and speed (4.61)."
    Ty Schalter, "Junior Seau's All-Around Dominance Will Never Be Seen from an NFL LB Again," Bleacher Report, May 3, 2012. http://bleacherreport.com/articles/1170420-junior-seaus-all-around-dominance-will-never-be-seen-from-an-nfl-lb-again

7   ABC 10, "The Life and Death of Junior Seau," YouTube, May 3, 2012. https://www.youtube.com/watch?v=gTu8bR0tglY

8   Christopher L. Gasper, "Seau shakes off late hit," *Boston Globe*, December 22, 2008. http://www.boston.com/sports/football/patriots/articles/2008/12/22/seau_shakes_off_late_hit/

9   Dom Cosentino, "The Night Junior Seau Picked Up A Marine Captain's Tab And Serenaded Bar Patrons With A Ukulele," *Deadspin*, September 3, 2012. http://deadspin.com/5907297/the-night-junior-seau-picked-up-a-marine-captains-tab-and-serenaded-bar-patrons-with-a-ukulele

10 Greg Bishop, Rob Davis, "Junior Seau, Famed N.F.L. Linebacker, Dies at 43—Suicide Is Suspected," *New York Times*, May 2, 2012. http://www.nytimes.com/2012/05/03/sports/junior-seau-famed-nfl-linebacker-dies-at-43-in-apparent-suicide.html

11 Mary Pilon, Ken Belson, "Junior Seau Had Brain Disease," *New York Times*, January 10, 2013. http://www.nytimes.com/2013/01/11/sports/football/junior-seau-suffered-from-brain-disease.html

12 Jake Flanagin, "Boycott the N.F.L.?," *New York Times*, September 18, 2014. http://op-talk.blogs.nytimes.com/2014/09/18/boycott-the-n-f-l/?_php=true&_type=blogs&_r=0

13 Ken Belson, "Brain Trauma to Affect One in Three Players, N.F.L. Agrees," *The New York Times*, September 12, 2014. http://www.nytimes.com/2014/09/13/sports/football/actuarial-reports-in-nfl-concussion-deal-are-released.html

14 Tom Farrey, "Study: 1 in 27 Head Injuries Reported," ESPN, October 3, 2014. http://espn.go.com/espn/otl/story/_/id/11631357/study-says-26-27-potential-concussions-unreported-college-football

15 Shane Dingman, "Reebok's Checklight Measures Hits to the Head. But Is It Useful in Predicting Concussion?," *The Globe and Mail*, March 1, 2014. http://www.theglobeandmail.com/life/health-and-fitness/health/is-reeboks-skull-impact-monitor-useful-in-predicting-concussion/article17498255/

Chapter 13
Analog and Digital Chores

1   68% of all women say they do not have enough time to do what they want.
    "Are You Too Busy For Your Friends?," LifeStyle, Last accessed October 2014. http://www.lifestyle.com.au/health/are-you-too-busy-for-your-friends.aspx

2   Alex Goldmark, "Young Adults: We're Just Too Busy to Get Driver's Licenses, Says Survey," WNYC, August 6, 2013. http://www.wnyc.org/story/310971-young-adults-were-too-busy-get-drivers-license/

3   "They report being too busy as a primary barrier preventing them from better managing their stress . . ."
    Norman B. Anderson et al., "Stress in American Findings," American Psychological Association, November 9, 2010. https://www.apa.org/news/press/releases/stress/2010/national-report.pdf

4   Deborah Andrews, "We Really ARE the Great Unwashed! Brits 'Too Busy' to Wash Hands After Using Loo While 58% of Men Skip Daily Shower," *Daily Mail Online*, June 18, 2012. http://www.dailymail.co.uk/femail/article-2161019/Brits-busy-wash-hands-using-loo-58-men-skip-daily-shower.html

5   "Christians worldwide are simply becoming too busy for God, a newly released five-year study revealed. In data collected from over 20,000 Christians with ages ranging from 15 to 88 across 139 countries, The Obstacles to Growth Survey found that on average, more than 4 in 10 Christians around the world say they "often" or "always" rush from task to task. Busyness proved to be the greatest challenges in Japan, the Philippines, South Africa, the United Kingdom, Mexico, and Indonesia. Christians in Uganda, Nigeria, Malaysia, and Kenya were least likely to rush from task to task. But even in the less-hurried cultures, about one in three Christians report that they rush from task to task. In Japan, 57 percent agreed."
    Audrey Barrick, "Survey: Christians Worldwide Too Busy for God," *Christian Post*, July 30, 2007. http://www.christianpost.com/news/survey-christians-worldwide-too-busy-for-god-28677/

6   Dave Gilson, "Overworked America: 12 Charts That Will Make Your Blood Boil," *Mother Jones*, July/August 2011. http://www.motherjones.com/politics/2011/06/speedup-americans-working-harder-charts

7   "NY Times Non-Fiction Best Sellers 2014," Good Reads, Last accessed October 2014. http://www.goodreads.com/list/show/72828.NY_Times_Non_Fiction_Best_Sellers_2014

8   "Volunteering in the United States, 2013," Bureau of Labor

Statistics, February 25, 2014. http://www.bls.gov/news.
release/volun.nr0.htm

9 Rush Limbaugh, "Obama Solves Energy Crisis: Inflate
Your Tires," *The Rush Limbaugh Show*, July 31, 2008.
http://www.rushlimbaugh.com/daily/2008/07/31/
obama_solves_energy_crisis_inflate_your_tires

10 "The Department of Transportation estimates that 5 million
gallons of fuel per day are wasted due to low tire pressure.
That's more than 2 billion gallons per year, just because
people don't take the time to inflate their tires properly."
Philip Reed, "How to Check Your Car's Tire Pressure
and Inflate Tires," Edmunds.com, June 12, 2014. http://www.
edmunds.com/how-to/how-to-check-tire-pressure-and-
inflate-tires.html

11 "According to the Society of Automotive Engineers, some
260,000 accidents occur each year that involve improper
tire pressure, and more than 10,000 people are injured in
these incidents."
"The National Highway Traffic Safety Administration studied
crash data from between and 2005 and 2007, and determined
that vehicles with low tire pressure were three times likelier to
be involved in accidents where tire-related problems were a
factor than vehicles with properly-inflated tires."
Jason Parks, "How's the Air in Your Tires? Here's Why
You Should Know" Safe Auto Insurance Company, May 31,
2012. http://blog.safeauto.com/hows-the-air-in-your-
tires-heres-why-you-should-know/

12 Page 4, Table One
National Center for Statistics and Analysis
Research and Development, "Air Pumps at U.S. Gas
Stations: An Investigation into Factors Associated with
Gauge Accuracy," National Highway Traffic Safety
Administration, June 2002. www-nrd.nhtsa.dot.gov/
Pubs/809-454.PDF

13 Goodyear, "KnowHow for iPhone on the App Store
on iTunes," iTunes, Last accessed September 2014.
https://itunes.apple.com/us/app/knowhow-for-iphone/
id596134704?mt=8

14 (2:56)
Corporate Valley, "Inspiring Google Story—Larry Page,"
YouTube, April 22, 2013. https://www.youtube.com/
watch?v=f_eiMKp4QW8

15 "Whirlpool Duet Washer & Dryer: Teen Jeans," YouTube, May
13, 2013. https://www.youtube.com/watch?v=FO_3vraRd50

16 "The home appliance industry is a multi-billion dollar
industry with 583 million appliances being shipped worldwide in 2013 alone."
"Home Appliance Industry—Statistics & Facts," Statista,
Last accessed October 2014. http://www.statista.com/
topics/1068/home-appliances/

17 "The average American family does about eight loads of
laundry a week (400-plus per year)."
"LG WT5101HV Washing Machine - Top Loading Washer,"
Good Housekeeping, Last accessed October 2014. http://
www.goodhousekeeping.com/product-reviews/appliances/
washer-reviews/lg-wt5101hv-washing-machine#slide-5

18 "How many people have allergies? Over 50 million Americans

suffer from allergies, and approximately 55 percent of all U.S.
citizens test positive to one or more allergens."
Allergy Frequently Asked Questions (FAQ)," AchooAllergy,
Last accessed October 2014. http://www.achooallergy.com/
allergy-faqs.asp

19 (Yes, I cited *The Daily Mail*, but please don't consider them
a bulletproof source . . . do your homework!)
Deni Kirkova, "Half of Men Can't Use a Washing Machine
Properly and a Quarter Can't Even Figure Out How to
Switch It On," *Daily Mail Online*, June 12, 2013. http://www.
dailymail.co.uk/femail/article-2340216/Half-men-use-washing-
machine-properly-quarter-figure-switch-on.html#ixzz2eyGy9Kr

20 Frederick Muench, PhD, "The Burden of Choice,"
Psychology Today, November 1, 2010. http://www.
psychologytoday.com/blog/more-tech-support/201011/
the-burden-choice

21 TED, "Barry Schwartz: The Paradox of Choice," YouTube,
January 16, 2007. https://www.youtube.com/watch?v=
VO6XEQIsCoM#t=552

22 "Adaptive Wash technology automatically senses the size
of each load and uses the right amount of water to keep
colors vibrant wash after wash."
"Whirlpool Washer," RCWilley, Last accessed September 2014
http://www.rcwilley.com/Appliances/Laundry/Washers/Top-
Load/WTW8500BW/3809722/Whirlpool-Washer-View.jsp

23 "Whirlpool's Advanced Moisture Sensing System has
three built-in sensors to read incoming and outgoing air
temperatures while monitoring moisture levels inside the
dryer so that the drying cycle ends when everything is
perfectly dry. An inlet thermister in the heater box reads the
temperature of incoming air. Moisture sensor strips inside
the drum communicate damp signals of tumbling items. And
an outlet thermister in the exhaust reads the temperature of
the outgoing air . . ."
"Whirlpool Dryers—Advanced Moisture Sensing," YouTube,
October 25, 2010. https://www.youtube.com/watch?v=
yP4Cyc3kp5g

24 "Whirlpool Dishwasher Sensor Cycle," YouTube, January 22,
2013. https://www.youtube.com/watch?v=-ONoToFSR00

25 "About Us," TripIt, Last accessed October 2014. http://
www.tripit.com/press/about

26 Kevin Purdy, "TripIt Adds Automatic Itinerary Importing
from Your Gmail Inbox," Lifehacker, August 11, 2010. http://
lifehacker.com/5610002/tripit-adds-automatic-itinerary-
importing-from-your-gmail-inbox

27 "What Is Background Uploading?" Dropbox, Last accessed
October 2014. https://www.dropbox.com/en/help/500

28 Aldrin Calimlim, "Automatic Photo and Video Uploading
Comes to Dropbox for iOS," AppAdvice, June 14, 2012.
http://appadvice.com/appnn/2012/06/automatic-photo-
and-video-uploading-comes-to-dropbox-for-ios

29 "About IFTTT," IFTTT, Last accessed October 2014.
https://ifttt.com/wtf

30 mach3maelstrom, "If I miss a call from my mom/wife/gf, text
her that I'll call her back. by mach3maelstrom," IFTTT, April
25, 2014. https://ifttt.com/recipes/166322-if-i-miss-a-call-
from-my-mom-wife-gf-text-her-that-i-ll-call-her-back

Chapter 14
Computing for One

1 Morley Safer, "The Age Of The Millenials," CBS News, May 25, 2008. http://www.cbsnews.com/videos/the-age-of-the-millenials/ (5:52)

2 Alan Fram, "One in Four Read No Books Last Year," *Washington Post*, August 21, 2007. http://www.washingtonpost.com/wp-dyn/content/article/2007/08/21/AR2007082101045_pf.html

3 Joshua Topolsky, "Inside TED: The Smartest Bubble in the World," The Verge, March 5, 2013. http://www.theverge.com/2013/3/5/4061684/inside-ted-the-smartest-bubble-in-the-world (4:39)

4 "Since the top 500 titles account for more than 80 percent of downloads, zombie apps are being left on the shelves." "Apps ignored by the thousands at Apple, Google sites," *San Francisco Chronicle*, June 2, 2014. http://www.sfgate.com/business/article/Apps-ignored-by-the-thousands-at-Apple-Google-5523662.php

5 Dan Frommer, "Most Smartphone Users Download Zero Apps Per Month," Quartz, August 22, 2014. http://qz.com/253618/most-smartphone-users-download-zero-apps-per-month/

6 (Also available via Google Books: http://books.google.com/books?id=ZqMQOT9SMhAC&pg=PA193&lpg=PA193) Richard G. Bias and Deborah J. Mayhew, *Cost-justifying Usability: An Update for an Internet Age* (San Francisco: Morgan Kaufmann), p.193

7 Ker Than, "World's Oldest Cave Art Found—Made by Neanderthals?," *National Geographic*, June 14, 2012. http://news.nationalgeographic.com/news/2012/06/120614-neanderthal-cave-paintings-spain-science-pike/

8 Gil Press, "A Very Short History of Big Data," *Forbes*, May 9, 2013. http://www.forbes.com/sites/gilpress/2013/05/09/a-very-short-history-of-big-data/

9 Peter J. Denning, "Saving All the Bits," RIACS Technical Report, October 15, 1990. http://ntrs.nasa.gov/archive/nasa/casi.ntrs.nasa.gov/19910023503.pdf

10 "Ten years later, in 1990, a normal hard drive held about 40 MB, with more expensive options able to store more than 100 MB." "Amazing Facts and Figures about the Evolution of Hard Disk Drives," Royal Pingdom, February 18, 2010. http://royal.pingdom.com/2010/02/18/amazing-facts-and-figures-about-the-evolution-of-hard-disk-drives/

11 "MyLifeBits," Microsoft Research, Last accessed October 2014. http://research.microsoft.com/en-us/projects/mylifebits/

12 Andrew Ng, "Lecture 1 | Machine Learning (Stanford)," YouTube, http://youtu.be/UzxYlbK2c7E?t=53s

13 ". . . received his M.S. in statistics from the University of Chicago, his Ph.D. in statistics at McGill University and joined Google as a statistician . . . In the Ads Team we work on a variety of flavours of statistical problems, . . ." Jeff Leek, "Interview with Nick Chamandy, Statistician at Google," *Simply Statistics*, February 2, 2015. http://simplystatistics.org/2013/02/15/interview-with-nick-chamandy-statistician-at-google/

14 "Gokul Rajaram: Executive Profile & Biography," *Businessweek*, October 26, 2014. http://investing.businessweek.com/research/stocks/private/person.asp?personId=40480108&privcapId=61767588

15 Ashlee Vance, "This Tech Bubble Is Different," *Businessweek*, April 14, 2011. http://www.businessweek.com/magazine/content/11_17/b4225060960537.htm#p2

16 Michael S. Rosenwald, "For Tablet Computer Visionary Roger Fidler, a Lot of What-Ifs," *Washington Post*, March 10, 2012. http://www.washingtonpost.com/business/for-tablet-computer-visionary-roger-fidler-a-lot-of-what-ifs/2012/02/28/gIQAM0kN1R_story.html

17 "Some colleagues were openly dismissive of Goldman's ideas. Why would users need LinkedIn to figure out their networks for them?" Thomas H. Davenport and D.J. Patil, "Data Scientist: The Sexiest Job of the 21st Century," *Harvard Business Review*, October 2012. http://hbr.org/2012/10/data-scientist-the-sexiest-job-of-the-21st-century/ar/1

Chapter 15
Proactive Computing

1 "During the second World War, the robot was stored in the basement of the Weeks's family home in Ohio, where he became 8-year-old Jack's playmate." Noel Sharkey, "Sign In To Read: The Return of Elektro, the First Celebrity Robot," *New Scientist*, December 25, 2008. http://www.newscientist.com/article/mg20026873.000-the-return-of-elektro-the-first-celebrity-robot.html?full=true

2 Standing over 7 feet tall and weighing in at 300 pounds Jack Weeks, "Hey . . . Where's My Legs??," Internet Archive, September 7, 2004. http://web.archive.org/web/20041011003402/http://www.maser.org/k8rt/

3 "But when Westinghouse cleared its warehouses for World War II production, Elektro ended up in the basement of an engineer who had worked on the robot's wiring." "'He showed us . . . and we managed to put the head on the torso and played with it as children, wheeling it around in games of cowboys and cops and robbers." "Elektro went back on the road for Westinghouse after the war, visiting county fairs and opening department stores. Weeks went along as an assistant." Emma Jacobs, "America's First Celebrity Robot Is Staging a Comeback," NPR, April 2, 2012. http://www.npr.org/2012/04/02/149850779/americas-first-celebrity-robot-is-staging-a-comeback

4 "Elektro in 1939 shows off his early brushed-aluminum skin . . . The 7-foot-tall creation took voice commands via a telephone handset." Amanda Kooser, "Elektro: 1939 Smoking Robot Saved from Oblivion," CNET, April 5, 2012. http://www.cnet.com/news/elektro-1939-smoking-robot-saved-from-oblivion/

5 RedLightBulbs, "Elektro the Robot Breaks a Balloon," YouTube, Last accessed October 2014. https://www.youtube.

com/watch?v=sdLEQNmsXag

6 Stuart Sikes, "And Now for the Rest of the Siri Story," Parks Associates, March 28, 2012. http://www.parksassociates.com/blog/article/and-now-for-the-rest-of-the-siri-story

7 Ryan W. Neal, "Apple iOS 7: 85 Percent of People Haven't Used Siri, 46 Percent Think Apple Oversold Its Release," International Business Times, October 23 2013. http://www.ibtimes.com/apple-ios-7-85-percent-people-havent-used-siri-46-percent-think-apple-oversold-its-release-1437900

8 Rolfe Winkler, "What Google Gains from Nest Labs," The Wall Street Journal, January 14, 2014. http://online.wsj.com/articles/SB10001424052702303819704579321043556056678

9 "Simultaneous poems—poems in which multiple languages are read at once rendering each unintelligible—offered an alternative approach to abstract poetry. By destroying everyday language, sound poems offered both a metaphor for the destruction caused by war and a commentary on the deceitfulness of language."
"DADA - Techniques - Sound," National Gallery of Art, Washington, DC, Last accessed October 2014. http://www.nga.gov/exhibitions/2006/dada/techniques/sound.shtm

10 "The flood of messages—up to 150 a day—adds to their already heavy clinical workloads, leaves them with very little time for the task of alert management, and frustrates the process of providing timely follow-up care."
Nicole Lewis, "Healthcare Providers Frustrated by Excessive EHR Alerts," InformationWeek, April 19, 2011. http://www.informationweek.com/healthcare/electronic-health-records/healthcare-providers-frustrated-by-excessive-ehr-alerts/d/d-id/1097265?

11 Liz Kowalczyk, "Patient Alarms Often Unheard, Unheeded," Boston Globe, February 13, 2011. http://www.boston.com/lifestyle/health/articles/2011/02/13/patient_alarms_often_unheard_unheeded/

12 "Early Detection," EarlySense, Last accessed October 2014. http://www.earlysense.com/early-detection/

13 "Reducing Alarm Fatigue," EarlySense, Last accessed October 2014. http://www.earlysense.com/reducing-alarm-fatigue/

14 Lakers Nation, "Lakers Injuries with Dr. Klapper: Kobe Bryant's Torn Achilles with Dr. Klapper," YouTube, April 16, 2013. https://www.youtube.com/watch?v=SIAASV3t5wc

15 "Standing on crutches in front of his locker with his sweaty game uniform on his back and tears in his eyes, Kobe Bryant confirmed the worst news to hit the Los Angeles Lakers in a season already full of heartbreaking disappointments."
Dave McMenamin, "MRI Scheduled to Confirm Kobe Injury" ESPN, April 13, 2013. http://espn.go.com/los-angeles/nba/story/_/id/9166874/kobe-bryant-los-angeles-lakers-probably-tore-achilles-team-says

16 Dr. David Geier, "Is It Fair to Blame Mike D'Antoni for Kobe Bryant's Injury?," Sports Medicine Simplified, April 19, 2013. http://www.drdavidgeier.com/blame-mike-dantoni-kobe-bryant-achilles-injury/

17 "NBA teams lost $358 million last season; $44 million alone by the injury-ridden Los Angeles Lakers."

Brian Kamenetzky, "The Next Big Thing in Sports Data: Predicting (And Avoiding) Injuries," Fast Company, August 25, 2014. http://www.fastcompany.com/3034655/healthware/the-next-big-thing-in-sports-data-predicting-and-avoiding-injuries

18 Howard Beck, "Sophisticated Cameras to Begin Tracking Every N.B.A. Play," New York Times, September 5, 2013. http://www.nytimes.com/2013/09/06/sports/basketball/sophisticated-cameras-to-begin-tracking-every-nba-play.html

19 "NBA Stats—Player Tracking," NBA.com, Last accessed October 2014. http://stats.nba.com/playerTracking.html

20 Zach McCann, "Player Tracking Transforming NBA Analytics," ESPN, May 5, 2012. http://espn.go.com/blog/playbook/tech/post/_/id/492/492

21 Tom Haberstroh, "NBA Innovating Injury Prevention," ESPN, April 3, 2014. http://insider.espn.go.com/nba/story/_/id/10721396/nba-how-catapult-technology-changing-nba-injury-prevention-training-methods

Chapter 17
Privacy

1 Scott Schaut, Director of The Mansfield Memorial Museum, email message to author, December 15, 2014.

2 Umika Pidaparthy, "What You Should Know about iTunes' 56-page Legal Terms," CNN, May 6, 2011. http://www.cnn.com/2011/TECH/web/05/06/itunes.terms/

3 Eric Slivka, "Apple's 500 Million iTunes Store Accounts Offer Significant Potential for Growth in Services," Mac Rumors, June 4, 2013. http://www.macrumors.com/2013/06/04/apples-500-million-itunes-store-accounts-offer-significant-potential-for-growth-in-services/

4 "Understand the Causes: False Confessions / Admissions," The Innocence Project, Last accessed November 2014. http://www.innocenceproject.org/understand/False-Confessions.php

5 "Microsoft by the Numbers," Microsoft, Last accessed November 2014. http://news.microsoft.com/bythenumbers/index.html

6 "Microsoft Software License Agreement," Microsoft, Last accessed November 2014. http://products.office.com/en-US/microsoft-software-license-agreement

7 Aleecia M. Mcdonald & Lorrie Faith Cranor, "The Cost of Reading Privacy Policies," I/S: A Journal of Law and Policy for the Information Society. August 2008. http://moritzlaw.osu.edu/students/groups/is/files/2012/02/Cranor_Formatted_Final.pdf

8 That's actually 54,000,000,000/24

9 "Facebook has finally responded to frustration over its privacy policies, by recruiting a small blue dinosaur to offer advice to users."
"Facebook sends in blue dinosaur to dispel privacy fears," The Week UK, May 23, 2014. http://www.theweek.co.uk/technology/58661/facebook-sends-in-blue-dinosaur-to-dispel-privacy-fears

10 It's for these reasons that we disagree with the ruling. That said, we obviously respect the court's authority and are doing our very best to comply quickly and responsibly. It's a huge task, as we've had over 70,000 take-down requests covering

250,000 web pages since May. So we now have a team of people reviewing each application individually, in most cases with limited information and almost no context.

David Drummond, "We Need to Talk about the Right To Be Forgotten," *The Guardian*, July 10, 2014. http://www.theguardian.com/commentisfree/2014/jul/10/right-to-be-forgotten-european-ruling-google-debate

11 "Some 68% of internet users believe current laws are not good enough in protecting people's privacy online . . ."
Ee Rainie, Sara Kiesler, Ruogu Kang, and Mary Madden, "Anonymity, Privacy, and Security Online," Pew Research Center's Internet & American Life Project, September 5, 2013. http://www.pewinternet.org/2013/09/05/anonymity-privacy-and-security-online/

12 "Presley has already appeared six times on national television, but it is his appearance on *The Milton Berle Show* on June 5, 1956, that triggers the first controversy of his career. Presley sings his latest single, 'Hound Dog,' with all the pelvis-shaking intensity his fans scream for. Television critics across the country slam the performance for its 'appalling lack of musicality,' for its 'vulgarity' and 'animalism.' The Catholic Church takes up the criticism in its weekly organ in a piece headlined 'Beware Elvis Presley.' Concerns about juvenile delinquency and the changing moral values of the young find a new target in the popular singer."
"Culture Shock: Flashpoints: Music and Dance: Elvis Presley," PBS, Last accessed November 2014. http://www.pbs.org/wgbh/cultureshock/flashpoints/music/elvis.html

13 Emily Nussbaum, "Kids, the Internet, and the End of Privacy: The Greatest Generation Gap Since Rock and Roll," *New York Magazine*, February 12, 2007. http://nymag.com/news/features/27341/

14 Michelle Dennedy, chief privacy officer at security software firm McAfee.
Marco della Cava, "Privacy Integral to Future of the Internet of Things," *USA Today*, July 11, 2014. http://www.usatoday.com/story/tech/2014/07/10/internet-of-things-privacy-summit/12496613/

15 Molly Wood, "Facebook Generation Rekindles Expectation of Privacy Online," *New York Times*, September 7, 2014. http://bits.blogs.nytimes.com/2014/09/07/rethinking-privacy-on-the-internet/

16 Mary Madden, Amanda Lenhart, Sandra Cortesi, and Urs Gasser, "Teens and Mobile Apps Privacy," Pew Research Center's Internet & American Life Project, August 22, 2013. http://www.pewinternet.org/2013/08/22/TEENS-AND-MOBILE-APPS-PRIVACY/

17 "Teens, Social Media, and Privacy: New Findings from Pew and the Berkman Center," Berkman Center, May 21, 2013. http://cyber.law.harvard.edu/node/8325

18 "But recent papers from Harvard, Berkeley, and University of Pennsylvania researchers show that kids and young adults do want to keep information private."
Jennifer Valentino-Devries, "Do Young People Care About Privacy Online?," *Wall Street Journal*, Apr 19, 2010. http://blogs.wsj.com/digits/2010/04/19/do-young-people-care-about-privacy-online/

19 Chris Jay Hoofnagle, Jennifer King, Su Li, and Joseph Turow, "How Different Are Young Adults from Older Adults When it Comes to Information Privacy Attitudes and Policies?" April 14, 2010. http://papers.ssrn.com/sol3/papers.cfm?abstract_id=1589864

20 Chris Matyszczyk, "Online Game Shoppers Duped into Selling Souls," CNET, April 16, 2010. http://www.cnet.com/news/online-game-shoppers-duped-into-selling-souls/

21 Computerphile, "Blindly Accepting Terms and Conditions?," YouTube, February 5, 2014. https://www.youtube.com/watch?v=9Hb2oMIRI0I (0:33)

22 "About Me," Professor Tom Rodden, Last accessed November 2014. http://rodden.info/

23 Executive Office of the President, "The Big Data and Privacy Review," White House, May 1, 2014. http://www.whitehouse.gov/issues/technology/big-data-review

24 Dave Morin, "We Are Sorry," Path Blog, February 8, 2012. http://blog.path.com/post/17274932484/we-are-sorry

25 "Path Social Networking App Settles FTC Charges it Deceived Consumers and Improperly Collected Personal Information from Users' Mobile Address Books," Federal Trade Commission, February 1, 2013. http://www.ftc.gov/news-events/press-releases/2013/02/path-social-networking-app-settles-ftc-charges-it-deceived

26 Jon Pareles, "Jay-Z Is Watching, and He Knows Your Friends," *The New York Times*, July 5, 2013. http://www.nytimes.com/2013/07/05/arts/music/jay-z-is-watching-and-he-knows-your-friends.html

27 Jay-Z, "Mr. Carter on Twitter," Twitter, July 8, 2013. https://twitter.com/S_C_/statuses/354337385468805122

28 "Only Glympse puts you in control—you set who sees you and for how long. Safe for families, friends, colleagues, and one-time meetings."
"What Is Glympse?," Glympse, Last accessed November 2014. https://www.glympse.com/what-is-glympse

Chapter 18
Automatic

1 Peter J. James, Nick Thorpe, *Ancient Inventions* (New York: Ballantine Books), p.130.

2 "Ownership," Horton Automatics, Last accessed November 2014. http://www.hortondoors.com/about-us/Pages/Ownership.aspx

3 "A Short History of the Airbag," Consumer Affairs, September 25, 2006. http://www.consumeraffairs.com/news04/2006/airbags/airbags_invented.html

4 Associated Press, "Around 15,000 saved by air bags in last 20 years," NBC News, July 10, 2004. http://www.nbcnews.com/id/5410761/ns/us_news/t/around-saved-air-bags-last-years/#.VFqXNot4pkk

5 "Oldsmobile Presents Motoring's Magic Carpet: Hydra-Matic," Prelinger Archives, https://archive.org/details/1809_Oldsmobile_Presents_Motorings_Magic_Carpet_Hydra-Matic_B-44_194_07_30_39_00

6 "1940 Cars Offer Added Comfort," *New York Times*, October 15, 1939.

Index

Let's keep chatting.

Well, thanks for reading my book. I really appreciate it. The conversation continues through the hashtag #NoUI, and at www.nointerface.com.

And don't hesitate to reach out to me at golden.krishna@gmail.com or through Twitter via @goldenkrishna.

You can also check out other great books by Peachpit at www.peachpit.com.